# In Search of the New England
# COYOTE

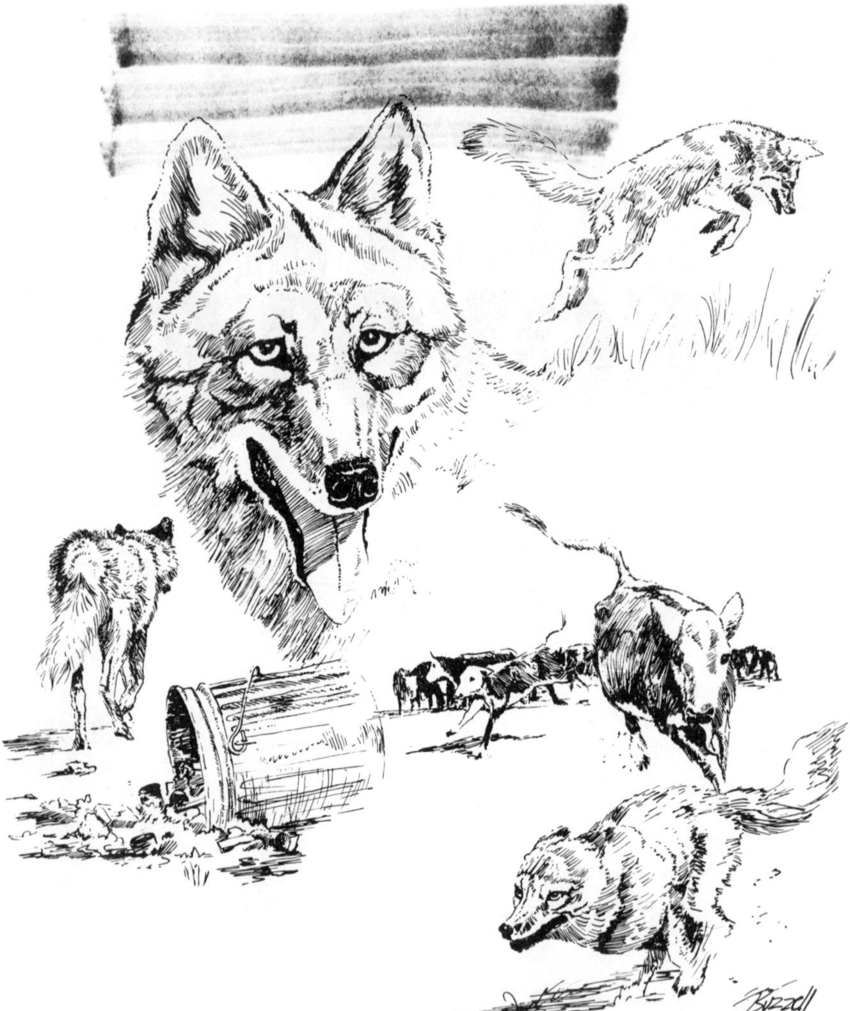

# In Search of the New England COYOTE

PETER ANDERSON

Illustrations by
Robert Shetterly and Russell Buzzell

The Globe Pequot Press

Chester, CT 06412

Copyright © 1982 by Peter Anderson
Illustrations on pages 25, 43, 65, 87, 101, 161, and 209 copyright © 1982
by The Globe Pequot Press

All rights reserved in all countries.
No part of this book may be reproduced
in any form or by any electronic or mechanical means
including information storage and retrieval systems
without permission in writing from the publisher,
except by a reviewer who may quote brief passages in a review.

Library of Congress Catalog Card Number 81-82607
ISBN:0-87106-959-8
Printed in the United States of America

Illustrations appearing on page ii, 11, and 145 by Russell Buzzell
are published with permission from the Massachusetts Division of Fisheries & Wildlife.

Cover and book design by Barbara Marks
Cover photograph by Bill Byrne

# Contents

| | | |
|---|---|---|
| 1 | A Small Town in Massachusetts | 1 |
| 2 | Mystery on Magic Mountain | 19 |
| 3 | On Silent Feet | 39 |
| 4 | "Oh, They're Very Human" | 59 |
| 5 | On the Hunt | 71 |
| 6 | Sign of the Lion | 93 |
| 7 | Bears Do Not Hibernate | 113 |
| 8 | The Hounds of Sebec | 135 |
| 9 | The Trapper | 149 |
| 10 | The Fur Dealer | 167 |
| 11 | Rusty and Sawyer | 183 |
| 12 | The Coyote and the Wolf (Cousins or Brothers?) | 201 |
| | Bibliography | 219 |

# – 1 –
# A Small Town in Massachusetts

Michael Babiak lives on an old farm in Chesterfield, a small town in western Massachusetts where steep hills form narrow valleys. The gentler slopes were pasture and field in the 1800s before farmers moved west to Ohio and the good land there. The farmers who remained in western Massachusetts lost their sons to the mills and grew old, and when the old farmers died, the farms were sold, to summer people mostly, many of them New Yorkers, and the summer people grew good lawns but little else. Cedar grew in the abandoned fields, then hardwoods; by the middle of this century, the forest had returned to central and western Massachusetts. Coyotes live in this new forest not far from the edge of the cleared land of Michael Babiak's farm.

Michael Babiak bought his farm in 1936, did not see coyotes in his hillside pastures for the first thirty years. "The first one I saw, oh, fifteen years ago [about 1966], I was in bed, and the coyote he'd be out there at six in the morning chasing rabbits. She [Mrs. Babiak] said to me it was not a fox, which we had plenty of, and I said, 'Then it must be a wolf.' she had those glasses up there [pointing to a shelf] to look at them. They'd howl at ten o'clock, twelve o'clock. We never got no sleep. Then I butchered a cow one day and dumped it [the entrails] in the manure pile. I saw 'em, got a good look at them. I called them coydogs." He and others in New England thought the new creature was a cross between coyotes and dogs. Scientists would learn how to tell coydogs from coyotes and while they learned from scientific study, Babiak could watch coyote in an outdoor laboratory, his farm. His first thought, that the strange animal was a wolf, may have been close to the truth.

Coyotes are low-energy predators, do not spend much energy chasing a healthy animal. They conserve their strength, prefer to chase an old or sick or young animal, an animal they can catch and kill quickly. Coyotes are smart enough to know what animals are vulnerable. They are also playful. Babiak saw them chasing his black Angus calves in the pasture, though the calves were too big and too well protected by their mothers to be good prey for a coyote. However, it was not all play, for this den of Chesterfield coyotes would eat one of Babiak's calves and be responsible for killing a second calf. The carcass of this second calf would be good bait to trap a coyote, and Babiak used it that way.

A coyote of the western plains or the southwestern desert weighs about twenty-five pounds. The New England coyote is considerably bigger; a big male may weigh forty-five pounds, an unusually large male sixty pounds, though that top figure is disputed. However, the coyotes of the colder states, Minnesota, Michigan, are bigger than twenty-five pounds, an indication that coyotes need to be bigger, need more body fat in order to survive the colder climates. There is this theory: The new coyote bred with the small Canadian wolf of Ontario on its trek east, and this wolf gene produced a bigger coyote. The new animal is not the product of a coyote and a wild dog, though there is some breeding of dog with coyote, and there are some coydogs.

Biologists have a test to tell coydog from coyote, a test they perform on animals found dead on the road or on carcasses turned in by trappers. The animal's skull is cleaned of flesh and measured fifteen ways, the measurements fed into a computer to produce a number. This number is placed on a graph. A coyote's number fits in a certain section of the graph. A dog's number will fit in another place on the graph, a wolf's number in a third place on the graph. No skulls yet found in New England fit the wolf figure because the timber wolf has been extirpated here. There are a lot of woods for a wolf to hide in, though, and no one can say with certainty that no timber wolf exists in New England, only that no one can produce evidence of him.

The animal farmer Babiak's wife saw through the kitchen window was not a timber wolf but a meat-eating predator of the same family. The animals he saw were bigger than a fox, smaller than a large dog, and colored somewhat like a German shepherd, with gray and black fur atop their backs, buff and gray underneath. I once reported for my paper, *The Boston Globe*, that nearly a thousand coyotes were trapped in Maine in 1979. This story drew angry letters from antitrapping readers of the *Globe*, one of whom wrote that I was gullible for reporting such a figure, a thousand coyotes, because most of the trapped animals were pet German shepherds sold as coyote fur. There is wide variation of color in New England coyotes, and it is possible, I suppose, that a fur buyer might confuse a German shepherd pelt with that of a coyote, but he would not confuse a thousand pelts. I have seen several coyote pelts, a few stuffed coyotes and many coyote pictures, and when I see my first live coyote, I will know it is not a German shepherd.

Some dairy farmers appreciate coyotes because they eat the groundhogs that make holes into which valuable milkers step and break their legs. Farmer Babiak raises black Angus beef cattle and does not appreciate coyotes. "These Angus are awful good mothers, but when they have a calf they leave it under a bush and go out and feed with the others. Every little while they go back to see the calf. They go up and feed it a couple times a day. They're damn good mothers just the same."

Since about 1965 he had been hearing the coyote howling at night ("they sound like kids hollering") and seeing them during the day. He started putting his cattle in a pasture protected by electric fencing, but that required a lot of moving of the cattle, and Babiak relaxed his guard. "So I heard a cow bellowing up there, and I went up to her and sure enough her calf was half eaten from the back end. I went back up later and it was gone." The coyotes had eaten what they could and later dragged the carcass into the woods. This was the spring of 1972, a confirmed instance of coyote predation in Massachusetts, though Massachusetts wildlife officials are uncertain if the coyote killed the calf or if the calf was stillborn. They do not dispute Babiak's idea that coyotes ate the calf, for Babiak would offer proof, the coyote.

The progeny of the coyotes who ate the calf in 1972 may still live in the woods beyond Babiak's pasture. Some of the original coyotes who fed on the calf may still live there, for coyotes live to be ten or twelve years old in the wild, longer in captivity. In New England, they have only two enemies, dog and man. They can protect themselves against dogs, Babiak found out. And in Massachusetts they are now protected against trapping. The leg-hold trap was banned in Massachusetts in July 1975, though trapping is still allowed in water sets, traps put in water where, once caught, the animal drowns. Coyotes are shy around water, usually, and hard to trap there. They are hard to trap on land, also, but Babiak did not know that then. In the spring of 1972, before the leg-hold trap was banned, Babiak decided he would trap the coyote that ate his Angus calf.

Babiak's dead calf was half eaten from the rear. Coyotes usually tear open the ribs, then eat forward inside the animal.

Dogs usully eat the hind quarters, tear open the rear of the prey, eat around the anus, making almost a circle around the tail. Although Babiak had seen the coyotes often, the animal that killed his calf might have been a dog. Wildlife officers might have been skeptical if Babiak had not been able to trap the coyote. Some time after Babiak found the first calf half eaten, he lost a second calf.

The second calf had foundered, Babiak said. I asked him what that meant and he raised his voice, "Foundered. Don't you know what that is?" I didn't. We were sitting in the kitchen. I was facing the window out of which his wife had seen the first coyotes back about 1966. I have sat in many country kitchens talking to farmers and farmers' wives, getting material for newspaper stories, but all of this experience could not make up for my having been raised in the city where there were no animals except dogs and cats and the ragman's horse. The ragman disappeared when I was a boy and then there was no animal in my neighborhood bigger or wilder than a large dog. I had found my way to Babiak's farm on a winter's day after getting directions from Guy Thrasher at his store in the next town, South Worthington. When I had parked my car in Babiak's farmyard, I could see him atop his tractor a hundred yards up a rise in front of his barn. He had watched me as I walked up that rise toward him, watched me the way country people watch strangers. I had introduced myself, explained my purpose was to learn of the black Angus lost to a New England coyote eight years previously, and then, when he dismounted from his tractor and we were walking back to his farmhouse I had said, motioning toward the black hulks in the snow: "Those are black Angus, I guess." He said: "I guess they are." His tone was full of meaning. Only a city boy would have to guess about Angus, and only a city boy would have to ask the meaning of a foundered calf.

I had stopped in Guy Thrasher's store in South Worthington for the directions to Babiak's place only a mile or so from the store because it is in the last mile that I lose my way. Thrasher's store is a tumbledown building close to the road that runs in the narrow valley formed by the Little River. It is not a general store but a specific store. He raises flowers in summer and sells them in his store; in spring he makes and sells maple sugar. The winter day I stopped, his store was stocked with candy, cigarettes, soda, a bushel or two of apples and nothing else that I could see. He was a trapper more than a storekeeper, I think, and this day he invited me to sit by the wood stove. He was waiting for a delivery of Pepsi Cola from Brattleboro, Vermont. Then he planned to set some beaver traps. He bade me sit, and so indeed I did.

Guy Thrasher sat on one side of the stove, I on the other. There was no room to turn our chairs towards one another. Thrasher is a native of South Worthington and is eighty years old, his mind bright. I asked him about the coyotes in South Worthington, and he said: "It's too bad they won't let us trap them. They're driving out all the game. I hunted deer with a girl who works for me, and the woods were dead of game. Years ago, trailing deer, you heard chipmunks, gray squirrels. Now they're dead. I lay it to coyotes. Three or four years ago I was going into the big country, that's what I call it because you have to walk in for miles, to trap beaver and found coyote tracks all over the beaver dams. The dam was a regular path of coyote tracks. The coyote learnt to stay quiet and when beaver come out of the lodge, the coyote grab them."

If all things are relative, then the relativity of big country is even more relative than most things. The country around Chesterfield and South Worthington is big country for Massachusetts, big enough for beaver, for bear and for coyotes. A Bostonian set off the wrong way from a road here could wander a while, but by northern New England standards this is pretty country rather than big country.

The Pepsi truck from Brattelboro arrived, almost precisely on time, delivering two cases of pint bottles, a two-week supply for Thrasher's store. He finished his story. "There are several coyote dens around here. They live up in the ledges where the bobcats used to live. Rabbits are cleaned out, squirrels, chipmunks. How coyotes live I don't see. They've cleaned out the game. Up here the do-gooders want no trapping which just hurts the animals." Thrasher says the ban on leg-hold traps set on land allows the coyote to proliferate and kill small game and allows the fox to proliferate to the point that the foxes themselves are suffering, from mange. He can still trap beaver and other water-dwelling furbearers and he used to get a lot of muskrat in the area he calls the big country, but the last time he set traps there he got no 'rats because, he says, coyotes have sat silently upon the beaver dams waiting for beaver and muskrat to come within reach of their jaws. He did get a mink up in the big country. He says, "Mink are probably too quick for the coyote."

House cats should be too quick for coyotes, also, but they may not be, not all the time. Domestication slows down an animal, if only by a moment. No one feeds the coyote, and hunger makes him faster. Thrasher taps about one thousand sugar maples each spring. He remembers when flying squirrels were quite common and used to fall into sap buckets (before his buckets were fitted with covers). He doesn't see them any more. "The coyotes eat all the flying squirrels."

Thrasher gave me directions to Michael Babiak's house, to go across the bridge over the Little River, and in a few minutes I had found farmer Babiak upon his tractor and had made the faux pas, having to guess that his animals were black Angus. A half hour later in his kitchen I had committed a faux pas by implication because I did not know the meaning of foundered. He told me: "A calf gets foundered by a lot of running." It was an accurate, incomplete definition. The dictionary says founder means "to cause to become disabled or lame." In the case of this second calf, a coyote had chased the calf unto lameness and death. The carcass of this foundered calf would bring death to one coyote of the group that ran in Babiak's pastures.

Babiak had some small traps, nothing big enough for a coyote though, and he went to Guy Thrasher to borrow bigger traps. By chance, a wildlife officer was talking to Thrasher that day, and was interested in proof of the new coyote and said to Babiak: "If you catch anything, tell me. You'll probably won't know what it is." Babiak says he hollered at the wildlife officer: "Who the hell are you?" Babiak was nearly seventy years old then, a man who had been observing coyotes in his fields for some time. He would know a coyote when he saw it. Thrasher's traps were ready to use; that is, they were not shiny new but had been steeped in bark broth to take sheen off the metal and kill the scent of man. Babiak put out several traps, "big, Number 2 traps with long jaws" around the carcass of his foundered calf. He pulled up some ferns, tossed them over the traps to disguise them. Afterwards he read how it is nearly impossible for an amateur to catch a coyote. If he had known that, he might have gone to greater lengths.

"The first morning, nothing. The next morning I caught one, just by the tips of his claws." Babiak may have been lucky, or the coyote may have been unwary. Coyotes often tear free of the trap, leaving hair in the trap, so great is their will to escape and their ability to bear pain. These coyotes are unlikely to be trapped again, so well do they learn from one encounter. In contrast, raccoons may be trapped, escape and be trapped again. Babiak was wearing his farm gloves and boots the day he set the traps, and the gloves and boots were full of the smell of the barn and its animals. "I didn't have no scent." He had used a ten-foot length of chain to attach the trap to a tree. Babiak thinks this length of chain enabled the coyote to walk about; if the chain had been shorter, the animal might have pulled his paw free of the trap.

Hampshire College in Amherst, Massachusetts, wanted a live coyote to study, and Babiak had that thought in mind when he approached the trap. It was a big coyote. Guy Thrasher says it weighed forty or fifty pounds. Babiak said, "I didn't gamble. I shot him." Later a student from Hampshire College came to the Babiak farm to try to catch other coyotes of the group that lived near Babiak's fields. "For two seasons he tried. He caught crows, 'coons, you name it, but no coyotes."

Babiak still hears the coyotes but has not been bothered by them lately, though there was one calf that disappeared. "The cow had a calf and was hollering for it. I hunted for it several days and it was wedged in some rocks, head first. Something had chased it terribly." He thinks it was coyotes. When his herd was bigger he used to see coyotes chasing calves, but a calf was safe if its mother was in the field. The big Angus mothers chase the coyotes. "They just run away, circling like a dog. They remind you of a good dog. They're pretty damn fast, too."

Coyotes were bold enough to approach within two hundred feet of his house to chase the calves, and then Babiak would go to the big rock at the top of his hillside pasture and sit there waiting with his rifle in midmorning, though coyotes are not supposed to be active that time of day because coyotes are crepuscular: They feed early in the day and late in the day and are not often seen at other times. "I'd sit up there looking down into the ravine. So I'd see them and so I pick up the rifle—if I held it in my hand I would get them, but the coyote see me pick it up and sneak back into the woods."

Coyotes are shot in New England, but it is easier to trap them than to get a shot at them, because of their crepuscular habits, I suppose, and because the coyote is reputedly smart enough to know when a man is carrying a rifle. Some people believe they are smart enough to know the effective range. Babiak: "I had one awful good shot. He was chasing a calf, and I went up there and the wind was blowing toward me [away from the coyote so he could not smell Babiak]. He came so close I should have had him, and he was a big one." Babiak blames his missing the shot on his failing eyesight. Coyotes have good eyesight and sense of smell, but they are not wraiths, cannot dodge bullets, although some of the coyote literature makes them out as super canines. There is a considerable body of lore about the western coyote but nearly none for the New England coyote. The animal has not been here long enough to become the subject of lore.

I believe the western lore because there is too much of it to be made up. Western coyotes have been seen jumping in the snow, coming down with all four paws bunched, punching into the snow to plug tunnels of mice. When coyotes have blocked the tunnels, they dig out the mice, eat them. They have been seen beside bull elk in winter. The bull paws away snow to get at grass, coincidentally exposing mice for the coyote, though the coyote's presence is not coincidental but based on intelligence and knowledge only partially understood by man.

Coyotes are less wary of a man on a machine than of a man afoot, a trait they share with deer. A man roaring on his snowmobile past a wintering deer herd may excite the deer less than a man on cross country skis moving by in silence. I have never come upon deer in their winter yard; but I have seen them in summer from an auto, stopped the vehicle and watched them, and been surprised when, sometimes, they stood and watched me watch them. Deer are more apt to bolt from a man afoot. Babiak says: "Nothing is afraid of you on a tractor. I was spreading manure early in spring. Over there [he pointed to the next farmhouse] they had a big German shepherd hit by a car and he walked funny. I thought it was that dog. I saw him following me seventy-five yards behind me. I talked to him by name before I figured it was a coyote. He followed me all day and might get within two hundred feet." Babiak doesn't think the coyote was finding any rodents stirred up by his tractor. He thinks the coyote was just curious, and he may be right, for the coyote is a curious creature, the male more than the female. Trappers who have failed to get a particularly smart coyote sometimes prey upon the predator's curiosity. One western

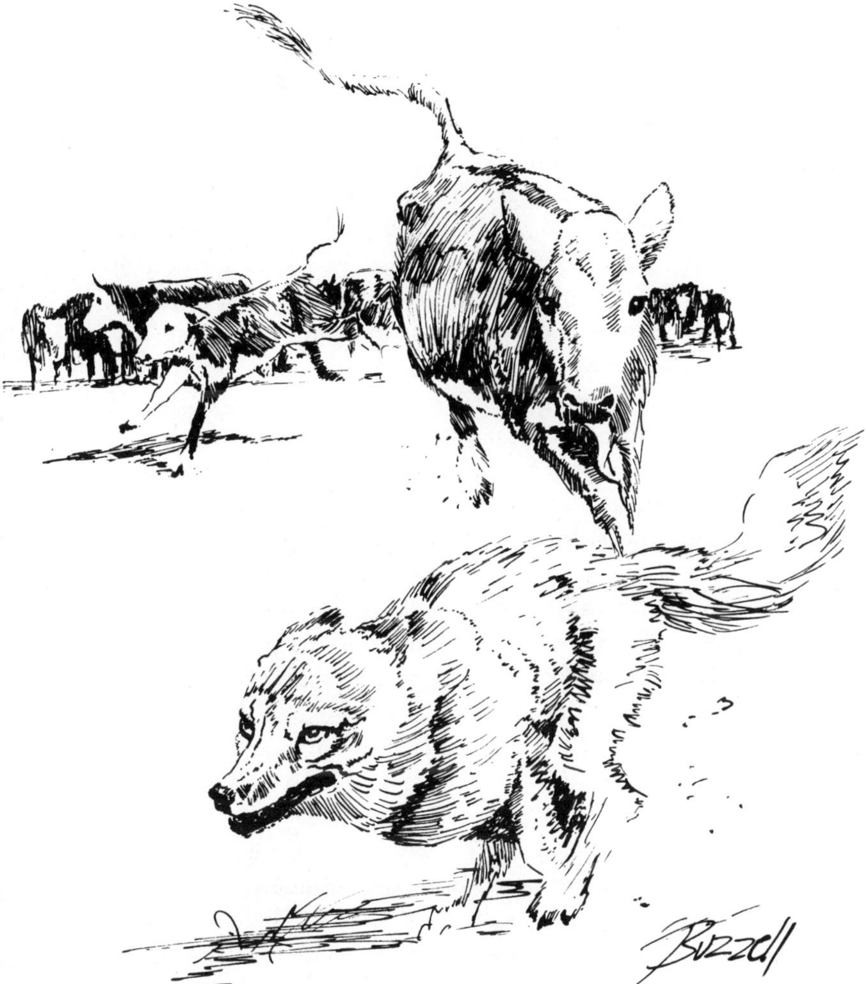

trapper buried an alarm clock on a coyote run, and this coyote, too wary to be attracted by bait, could not resist approaching the ticking sound in the ground and stepped into the trap.

I talked to Babiak in December 1980, and by then he had let his herd decline from about seventy-five cattle to eight, but because of his age, not because of coyotes. He still hears coyotes but sees them less, is bothered by them less. His healthy Angus are too big for a coyote to kill (though a large animal weakened by hunger or sickness can be brought down by coyotes). The calves of these Angus are vulnerable only when very young. Babiak is not a hunter, he is a producer, and he has not waged war on the coyotes of Chesterfield. Men grow more tolerant of some important things as they age. I think he appreciates the coyote's will to live, though he did not say that to me. I talked to a wildlife officer some years before my interview with Babiak, and this officer was in charge of a game preserve where deer were as numerous as cows in a green field. He told me he used to work in the wilderness, looked forward to deer season and the chance to hunt, but that after a few years of protecting deer, he had no desire to shoot them.

Farmer Babiak did not try to burn out the den of coyote pups or poison the adults. (Both methods have been used by government agents in the western United States.) He did not want to kill the coyotes; he wanted compensation for the eaten calf and for the calf foundered by coyotes. Massachusetts farmers are paid compensation for livestock lost to dogs. There is no compensation paid for losses to coyote, and some coyote kills are blamed on dogs, probably. Babiak's farm lies in Hampshire County which paid $5,326.30 in dog damage claims in 1979. Dogs do considerably more damage to sheep than coyotes do in Massachusetts because there are many more dogs in the state. In 1970 the state's coyote population was estimated to be five hundred. In 1980 the population may have been one thousand, though there is no precise way to know; nor is there even an approximate way to know except through the number of complaints by sheep farmers or beef cattle farmers such as Babiak, or by the number killed accidentally on the roads. It is not always possible to tell whether dogs or coyotes have killed a piece of livestock, though dogs are more likely to kill for the canine pleasure of killing while coyotes normally kill only for the pleasure of eating. Coyotes are not being considerate in this tendency, only saving their energy. Dogs and coyotes are not enemies under all circumstances; sometimes they mate. Babiak's German shepherd, however, was chewed up by a creature near the farm. Babiak is certain the victor was a coyote. It was a good dog, the German shepherd, Babiak says. "We were walking up back. Apparently he came across a coyote. I didn't see it, but it wasn't another dog." Babiak would have been able to tell from the sounds if it were two dogs fighting. Babiak's dog was bleeding when he reached it. The coyote had torn the German shepherd's testicles.

The Chesterfield coyote has no natural enemies here. It is at the top of the predator chain in Massachusetts, except for the black bear, and bear are not considered predators by biologists except when a biologist is being chased by one. The habitat is good here in Chesterfield, forest running up to old fields. Wildlife biologists call it the edge effect. Many of the farms have grown over into forest, but there are farms like Babiak's left, and even the nonfarmers, people who drive some distance to work, to Pittsfield, for instance, have food for coyotes: chickens, corn in the garden, melons in season (coyotes out west reputedly can pick out ripe watermelon). On other days coyotes may feed on garbage, offal or house cats grown fat.

Babiak gave the body of the trapped coyote to Hampshire College for study. Later, Jay Lorenz, a student, came to Babiak's farm in hopes of trapping more coyotes. Lorenz was studying the New England coyote for his master's thesis in zoology. Lorenz was the young man of whom Babiak says; "He caught crows, 'coons, you name it, but no coyotes." Lorenz was inexperienced then, was just learning how to trap a coyote. Lorenz says:

"Sometimes you get lucky. A lot of times coyotes will be attracted to carcasses and return to it, and every once in a while you get one to step into the trap." Lorenz moved his research project to Vermont when the leg-hold trap was outlawed in Massachusettts. "Up there, sometimes I would put out a carcass and the coyote would just drag the carcass over the traps. They are very wary. Part of [a trapper's] success depends on the previous experience of a coyote. A good trapper will go through maneuvers to make the trap. All canids are very sensitive to different scents. Their sense of smell is more developed than their sight. I've had domestic dogs, taken them inside and had them navigate a stairs just by their nose. I've heard of blind sled dogs that could perform well. If you have a lot of human scent, the coyote will avoid it." He thinks Babiak is right, that Babiak's scent was masked by his work gloves and boots. There is another possibility, that the coyote trapped by Babiak had never seen another coyote caught in a trap, had himself never been trapped and thus was unwary. The coyote for all his instinctive intelligence must learn to avoid a trap himself and cannot inherit that ability. At least, that is the current theory.

No one knows the extent of a coyote's intelligence. Hampshire College biologist Lorenz tells this story: "I was trying to track coyotes in the snow north of Montpelier. Wardens let me put out a deer carcass, and I checked it every day for a week, but there would be a day I couldn't get out to the carcass because of some personal business, and I would go out there the next day and the carcass would be gone, and it would have snowed by then and I would find no tracks. Somehow they seem to have a sixth sense and knew I wouldn't be there. It could have been they knew I was there each day or they could have been on a travel circuit, and they just happened to come onto the carcass the day I wasn't there.

"Another time, in the Hawley Forest [in Massachusetts],

we were tracking coyotes, I don't know how many, maybe three were traveling together that day. We never saw them but after four hours of tracking them in the snow we saw human footprints and realized they were our own where we had stopped for lunch. They had just led us around in a circle. They were not more than a quarter of a mile in front of us, but we never saw them. They could hear us or smell us. I know there are good reports about wolves being able to detect a moose half a mile away and head directly for the moose. It seems logical it was scent [that alerted the coyote to Lorenz] because coyotes couldn't see through the hills and trees. I can't see how they could have seen us. We couldn't see them. The whole idea is, coyotes have been around New England for fifty years, and, look, there are a lot of coyotes out there and we never seem to see them. I spent five years looking for them, and I think I saw six in the wild. It was three years before I ever saw my first live coyote, and I was out in the woods looking for them. The ones I did see, I was driving down the road at six in the morning and saw dogs crossing a field. Then I realized by their gait that I was seeing coyotes. It was just a matter of luck."

Lorenz was interested in plants, got interested in coyotes by chance. "At that time [early 1970s] very little was known about the eastern coyote." There is much to discover about the animal yet. Lorenz does not accept all current, majority opinion. "There is the old myth that a coyote will feed only on the old and the weak and young [and then only when it needs something to eat], and I wouldn't say that's true. It's not true all the time. My own feeling is I don't believe in that myth, not based on what I saw in New England, but I spent a summer in Colorado. Coyotes kill lambs out west and sometimes they just kill them and leave them."

Wolves kill only to eat, most of the time, but wolves kill for other purposes, sometimes. The wolf and the coyote are similar animals but separate species of the wild canid family. It is uncertain how separate. When Babiak told his wife she was seeing a wolf out her kitchen window, he may have hit upon the truth. Biologist Lorenz says:

"The wolf and the coyote have the same chromosome number and can interbreed. The assumption is that the two populations are distinct species if the gene pools are isolated [but] there is some question how isolated the gene pool of the coyote is from that of the wolf. Coyotes seem to live in a different habitat than wolves. Wolves are known to kill coyotes in Minnesota. But, on the other hand, in Ontario they call fifty-five-pound animals wolves. Over the border [into New England] they find a thirty-five-pound animal and call it a coyote. In between they find a forty-five-pound animal, and there is no way, not by skull analysis or any other kind of analysis, you can tell a cross coyote or a wolf or a big coyote.

"We studied the sweat glands of wolves and coyotes. Western coyotes sweat through the feet; the wolves we tested included several from Alaska, and they do not sweat through the feet. The eastern coyotes do not sweat through their feet. So if we try to classify the eastern coyote on the basis of sweat glands, it would be a wolf. It is mostly on the basis of size that we set up the eastern coyote as a coyote rather than a wolf. So I go along with that because it is easier to communicate with people that way, but I'm not convinced it's true. We'll never know where the coyote came from. No one saw it happen, no one saw breeding taking place."

The coyote has been called the prairie wolf, the brush wolf, the bush wolf, the barking wolf, and in New England it has a new name, "the new wolf." The new wolf got another new name at the Northeast Wildlife Conference in New Haven in February 1975. People at the meeting agreed to call it the eastern coyote. Helenette Silver, a retired New Hampshire biologist, wrote of that meeting: "No animal of such apparent economic unimportance has so captured popular interest. Participants and attendees gathered from as far away as Alaska, Canada and Kansas. They set up impromptu meetings before and after the official session, with the final one breaking up at 3:30 A.M. on the third day. At last the coyote was among friends." When the eastern coyote began eating calves and sheep and deer it was also among enemies.

# – 2 –
# Mystery on Magic Mountain

The couple from New Jersey liked their new vacation home in Vermont, liked being able to see beaver swimming in the pond on their property. Beaver are busy by reputation and in fact, and if they stay in one place long enough that place will become wet. The New Jersey couple came to know beaver are a nuisance and asked a local trapper to solve the problem. The trapper came to their house, told them how he would rid their land of the beaver; the couple agreed and headed home to New Jersey. Somewhere along the interstate highway they stopped, found a phone and called the trapper. They told him to take out the traps, please. They could not bear the thought of a beaver suffering death by drowning in a trap.

Walt Cottrell, a Vermont wildlife biologist, told me that story one night as we drove from North Springfield, Vermont, to Grafton. Another Vermont state biologist, Charles Willey, told me a similar story in his office in St. Johnsbury. A woman from Connecticut had bought a pretty house with a pretty pond up in the Northeast Kingdom of Vermont and was delighted to find beaver living in this pond until the level of the pond began to rise. Willey advised her to have some of the beaver trapped each year, but that idea was abhorrent to her. The pond rose beyond its spring flood mark up into her lawn, and, reluctantly, she allowed a local man to trap some of the beaver. The next year the problem remained, and the woman was reluctant to have more beaver trapped but changed her mind the morning she saw her lawn trees, balm of Gileads, down. The beaver had gone too far, were no longer attractive creatures from a children's book, and they were extinguished.

Newcomers appreciate the beauty of the Vermont landscape but do not always understand how things work in the woods. Newcomers have helped keep Vermont beautiful, and when the time comes they will try to protect the coyote because it is a wild creature and beautiful in its way. Later, the newcomers might raise a few sheep for the pleasure of it and find one day the half-eaten carcass of a lamb on their side lawn.

A traveler can spot many houses of the newcomers, especially the summer people, on any road in any pretty part of Vermont. This traveler's game is easier to play in winter because the well-kept house upon the hill almost surely belongs to a summer person if the driveway is not plowed. This January morning I was traveling north on Route 103 to Cuttingsville and an appointment with a sheepbreeder who had lost animals to predators. He gave me good directions, thirteen miles north of Ludlow to the railroad overpass. His house was the seventh on the left past the overpass. I was so busy watching the countryside, I did not see the railroad overpass and would have missed the house except for the sheep. Daniel Korngiebel's house is close by the side of the road, his sheep shelter next to the house. Korngiebel was in the back of a covered truck working on sheep, placing an electronic instrument against the belly of the ewes, using sound waves to test them for pregnancy. The testing method is quite accurate.

Korngiebel has about two hundred sheep, Corriedales, Dorsets, Shropshires, Oxfords; he raises them for meat, for wool and for sale to other breeders. For many years he did not lose any sheep to coyotes. "The first coyotes we heard of was twenty-five years ago on a big farm on the Vermont side of Lake Champlain. They had a hundred sheep and kept talking about fast dogs. They couldn't hit them with bullets, though they were good shots, and it put 'em out of [the sheep] business." Coyotes are fast, can run thirty miles an hour, perhaps faster. Korngiebel's problem started about 1971 when he began grazing his sheep in summer on Magic Mountain, a ski area in Londonderry. Sheep are both grazers and browsers. A browser walks about eating a tuft of grass here, a bit of a tree limb there; a grazer puts its head down in a field and eats all the grass in its path. Deer are browsers; cows are grazers. Browsing sheep keep back the underbrush; grazing sheep eat grass. Between grazing and browsing, sheep help keep a ski slope clear.

Korngiebel lost one or two sheep the first summer he put his flock on Magic Mountain. The second year he lost about 15. The carcasses were unmarked, Korngiebel said, except for a gash on the windpipe. Korngiebel and others thought some disgruntled former employee of the ski slope was shooting the sheep. The third year Korngiebel lost 130 out of 300 sheep. These dead sheep were apparently unmarked until the wool was spread on their throats to reveal a gash. A state policeman tried to solve the mystery by staking out the area, using two sheep for bait, but he was unsuccessful. One morning 33 carcasses were found and other sheep were missing besides the 33. Korngiebel says: "I skun out two myself. One had a crease on the hind quarter. The other one had a pinch on the throat."

A veterinarian autopsied a few of the carcasses, ruled the animals had been killed by coyotes. Some people did not believe it. Coyotes were new to Cuttingsville and Londonderry then, unknown and unseen, and people do not always believe what they do not see.

I believe much of what I read, especially if it is written by scientists rather than romanticists, and the coyote literature suggests that coyotes are predators in the way man is a predator, killing for food and not often for wanton pleasure. Yet what happened at Magic Mountain was slaughter for its own sake. Nor was it done by a young coyote just learning how to kill. An inexperienced coyote might nip at the rear legs of a sheep, tear at its haunches and belly the way a dog does, but the mature coyote likes to approach a sheep from the front, eyes it the way a sheepdog does, stares at it, makes the sheep back up or transfixes it with his eyes. Then the coyote grabs the sheep by the throat, some atavistic knowledge telling it just where, and tears the throat or just hangs suspended by its jaws from the throat, pinching the sheep's windpipe shut, suffocating it. After the kill, a coyote often tears open the sheep's belly, eats a fetus if present, then moves forward to the heart and liver and intestines. An experiment recounted in *Rangeman's Journal* tells of a coyote eating five pounds from the rump of a live seventy-pound sheep. Later a sheepbreeder would tell me how some of his sheep died after their bellies had been ripped by coyotes and the sheep, trying to run, got their legs tangled in their own intestines.

Few of the sheep lost by Korngiebel were eaten. "At no time did it appear they went in because they needed a meal," he said. The literature says a coyote kills a sheep, feeds upon it, tries to drag it away if he can. He will not kill again until he is hungry. What happened to Korngiebel's sheep was not supposed to happen, a mystery on Magic Mountain.

Most of the sheep killed on Magic Mountain were lambs, weighing 50 to 70 pounds, but Korngiebel said coyotes have no trouble killing his ewes weighing 125 pounds. Sheep are so easy for coyotes to kill that they take their time doing it, about thirteen minutes from the beginning of attack until the death, and yet if a sheep shows a little fight, the coyote is likely to break off and find an easier sheep to kill. If sheep were less tame, they would be more safe. One scientist suggests some defensive instincts be bred back into sheep made too tame by eight thousand years of domestication.

Coyotes have taken to eating sheep only in modern times.

The coyote was a creature of the western plains, ate what was left of buffalo after wolves had killed it. When the buffalo was slaughtered almost unto extinction, the coyotes could exist on prairie dogs, but when prairie dog habitat was despoiled by herds of livestock, the coyote learned to eat sheep. Yet not all coyotes kill sheep. Even sheepraisers say this, and many of them would also agree that coyotes do not normally kill for the pleasure of it. Perhaps a rogue coyote killed 130 of Korngiebel's sheep on the mountain that summer. There are rogue elephants, man-eating tigers. I could start a story about the rogue coyote that lives on Magic Mountain. It would be plausible, because no one knows for certain what coyotes do, especially the eastern coyote, though 33 sheep in one night is many sheep for one rogue coyote, however wanton.

Korngiebel no longer puts his sheep on Magic Mountain in the summer; he puts them instead in meadows near the road and has lost far fewer sheep to coyotes than before. The domestic dog is killing his sheep now. He lost thirty-four sheep to dogs in 1980, thirty-one of the thirty-four with their left hind legs torn. He lost some sheep to coyotes in roadside pastures before, but even these losses have subsided, and he does not know why. All the sheep-killing coyotes could not have been shot or trapped or run over on Route 103. Korngiebel says: "People still see 'em. Maybe they're not hungry. There are rabbits to be eaten and wild turkey, too." Korngiebel does not hear coyotes howling, though townspeople living not far from him do. Other sheep owners near Cuttingsville have seen as many as five or six coyotes at a time.

Korngiebel, for all the sheep he has lost, has seen only one live coyote. A neighbor had killed a deer up on a mountain that rises behind the river that runs behind Korngiebel's house, and the neighbor dragged the deer down the mountain and across Korngiebel's field in the morning. That afternoon, Korngiebel saw a coyote, nose to the ground, walk across this field beside his house, following the scent left by the dead deer. Coyotes are supposed to be shy creatures in full daylight, but as with so many other things written about coyotes, it is not always so.

There is something puzzling about all the dead sheep on Magic Mountain. If a disgruntled former employee of the ski slope shot the sheep, what creature was pinching the throat of the sheep? The finest rifleman in Vermont could not kill sheep by creasing their throats. I spoke by phone with Stuart Archimbault, district game warden in Londonderry. He thought some carcasses had been taken to veterinarian Dr. Frank K. Krohn in Springfield and other carcasses to veterinarian Dr. Gerald Scanlan in Brattleboro. Dr. Krohn told me on the phone he would have remembered the incident if he had worked on the carcasses. Warden Archimbault has no doubts as to what happened. "There is no question in my mind the sheep were shot due to wounds in the neck and head area. No arrest was made. This was speculation as to the killer. We do know it was a high caliber rifle. We found some spent cartridges up on the ski trails." Dr. Scanlan told me he had not examined the Magic Mountain sheep carcasses, was sure he would remember if he had. Sheepraiser Korngiebel cannot remember how he learned coyotes were responsible for the slaughter, but that word came to him second or third hand.

There is a possible explanation to all this: Some sheep were shot by a disgruntled ski area employee; some were killed by dogs; and some were killed by coyotes, perhaps the ones whose carcasses disappeared. There is a more bizarre possibility: Throats of sheep were cut by members of a sect performing a sacrifice. Precisely what happened is a mystery, the mystery of Magic Mountain.

Sheep do well enough on Vermont's steep land and thin soil. There were nearly two million sheep in Vermont in 1840 when New England was an agricultural land and before the Erie Canal and the railroads opened up better land in the west.

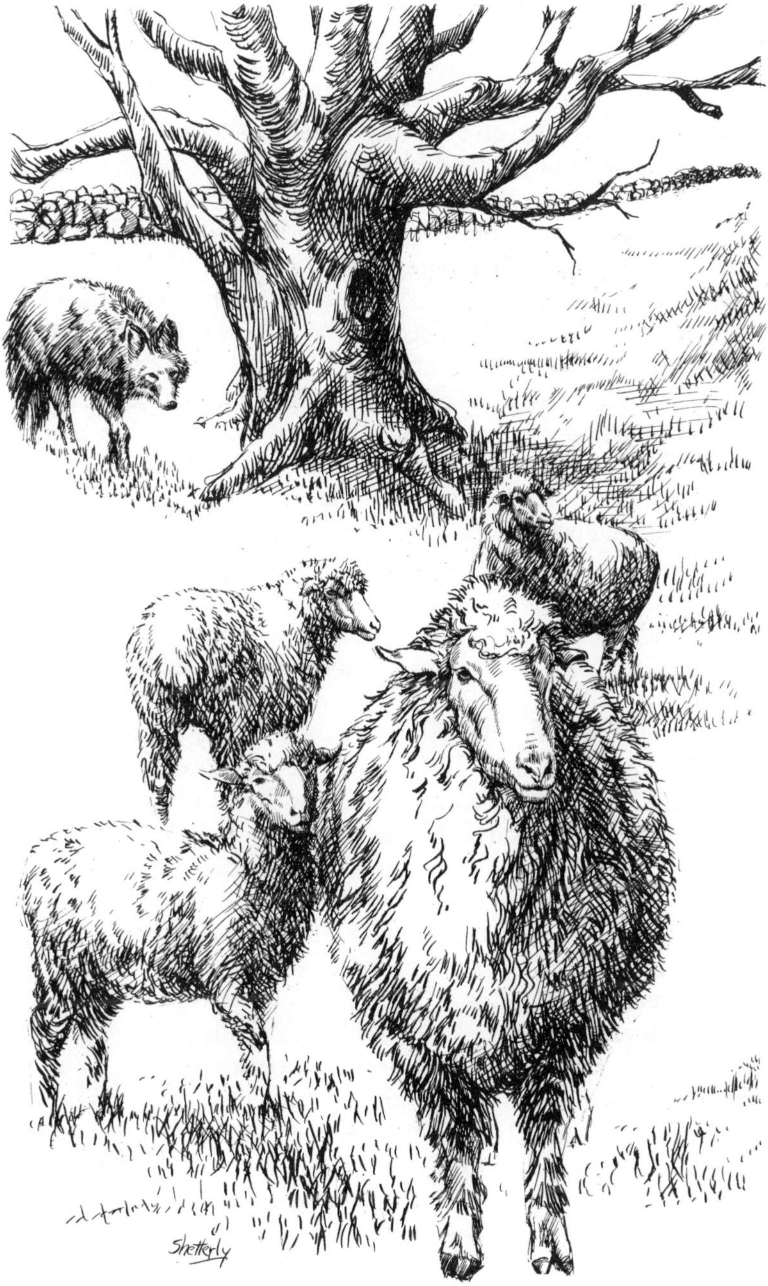
Shetterly

America's sheep population was moved west where great flocks could be shepherded on open land. Sheepraising is returning to Vermont because people such as William Yates and his wife Hilda want to make their land productive. They raise about 150 ewes on their land in Brownsville beside Route 44 at the foot of Mt. Ascutney. I arrived there at 3:00 P.M. when William Yates would be home from Windsor where he teaches high school biology. Yates is like many people who live on Vermont farms: He works out, meaning he has a job in town.

Brownsville is a small place, had 5,000 sheep 130 years ago. Yates totaled up figures from old town records to get that number. Cattle became more profitable than sheep, he says, and sheep declined. Refrigeration and the railroad and later the interstate highways made dairy farming possible. By 1970 there were only about 3,700 sheep in Vermont; but by 1980 the number had grown to 12,000. Sheep require less capital than cows and somewhat less care, do not have to be milked twice a day. There were no coyotes in Vermont when two million sheep grazed here. That is, there were no coyotes that people knew about, no skulls for scientists to measure. There was an occasional mountain lion and a few cousins of the coyotes, wolves. Evidence suggests the eastern timber wolf was exterminated, the last bountied wolf in Maine was taken in 1908. The last mountain lion killed in Vermont, November 24, 1881 in Barnard, stands stuffed in a museum near the State House in Montpelier. Now the sheep have a predator again, the coyote, but no one knows how many coyotes there are in the state. Ben Day, chief of Vermont's Wildlife Division, will make a guess, two thousand, and add: "That would be a family unit per town or a couple units per town." Yates, however, does not think there are any active coyotes in Brownsville. "I have seen a coydog. The animal I saw had a dog's head and hind quartes and midsection of a wolf." Yates might see evidence of coyotes if he did not keep his sheep behind electric fences.

Yates protects his sheep with a five-strand fence electrified with a New Zealand device. Animals can sense an electric fence without touching it, he says. Also: "I've seen horses rub their whiskers on a fence to test it, and farmers will touch a fence with a piece of grass to test whether a fence is on or off and take a small shock." Coyotes and other wild animals, the fisher for instance, probably know there is something dangerous in an electric fence they approach. Another sheepraiser told me of seeing fisher tracks leading up to a fence, then veering to a parallel course along the fence. Perhaps fisher and coyotes can smell ozone produced by the electric current.

Western coyotes climb over regular fences to get at sheep; presumably, eastern coyotes would do the same if the fences were not charged with electricity. A coyote could leap the thirty-nine-inch electric fence if it were placed close enough to a stone wall, for instance, or walk over the fence when heavy snow drifted against it. They could dig under the fence if hungry enough, determined enough, but coyotes prefer to husband their energy. At any rate, Yate's purpose in electric fencing is protection from dogs, not coyotes.

Yates has sheep pasture across Route 44 on the slope of Mt. Ascutney. Tourists walk near his pasture in summer, and one day a man from New York was walking there with his small poodle. The poodle got into the sheep, and the New Yorker, making a joke out of ignorance, said he hoped his tiny dog would not bother those big sheep. The ewe picked out by the poodle stood her ground as best she could, but later Yates found where the small dog had torn at the ewe's behind. "That dog was only a 'yipper,' one you could break in two with your hands."

Dogs do not know precisely what to do with sheep and tend to mangle them rather than kill them. Very young dogs are more unsure of what to do, but young wolves, for instance, know instinctively what the idea is: to grab prey by the throat, kill it and eat it. Many types of dogs have been bred over centuries for an ability to retrieve game without damaging it, and that may account for the uncertain, sloppy killing technique of some dogs and explain why they do not eat what they kill. House cats, domesticated but untrained, have no trouble knowing how to kill chipmunks and know how to eat them. My cat begins by eating the chipmunk's head.

A sheep farmer can legally shoot a dog worrying his sheep, though the New Yorker who owned the small poodle would have been flabbergasted if Yates had done so. The dog owner did not know his poodle was "worrying" sheep. Yates says: "Dogs can kill a lamb without touching it. Sheep run from dogs or become frightened and the calcium in their system is depleted. They can become paralyzed and die. Just the presence of a predator is enough to kill a lamb."

Korngiebel, the breeder who lost 130 sheep in one summer on Magic Mountain and a lesser number in roadside pastures in Cuttingsville, thought of trying to trap coyotes, but a trapper told him it would be unwise. Korngiebel's fields were too close to the road; dogs of his neighbors would be trapped. Yates says there will be a lot more trapping of coyotes if Vermont establishes a statewide leash law. Then, any dogs caught in leg-hold traps would be dogs not on a leash, and sheepbreeders would be exempt from legal problems and from some part of the animosity of neighbors whose dogs might be harmed. New Hampshire enacted a ten-dollar coyote bounty law in 1961, but the law was repealed in 1964 partly because dogs were being shot, not all of them accidentally.

Yates led me from the kitchen table of his farmhouse to the barn to show me his Suffolk and Hampshire sheep. He is uncertain why there should be less coyote activity in his town of Brownsville than in Cuttingsville, Korngiebel's town. Cuttingsville is in the Champlain Valley where coyotes first appeared in Vermont in the 1940s. Coyotes came from the west, from the Adirondacks around the south end of the big lake and from Ontario by way of Quebec around the north end of the lake. Yates thinks the coyotes might be migrating still from west to east across Vermont and that the mountains between Cuttingsville and Brownsville might have slowed their advance. His theory is plausible enough, but state biologists say the coyote is now in parts of Massachusetts, Connecticut and Rhode Island, everywhere in Vermont and most everywhere in New Hampshire and Maine, and has migrated as far east as Nova Scotia. One biologist says if coyotes learn how to board ships, they will keep moving east, to Europe. After leaving Yates I was going north from Brownsville, going to Tunbridge, Vermont, where there is an abundance of coyotes.

Tunbridge looks the way a Vermont town is supposed to look, very pretty, a road along the river, some fields beside the river and then steep hills and hillside farms. All about the farms is hardwood forest and softwood forest, a good place for deer and for coyote, because both animals like living in the forest, eating in the fields.

I followed directions, went left on the road by the cemetery and up the hill to the first crossroad, turning left there. It is easy enough driving *u*phill on snow-packed roads. The sun was on the snow, houses on the hillside pretty. I thought I could spot houses of the summer people, unplowed driveways, and then I was at the farmhouse of Cornelia and Henry Swayze. Cornelia is an officer of the Vermont Sheepbreeders Association. She and her husband raise 350 sheep. He says: "Every single sheep producer on both sides of the first branch of the White River, that's the valley from Tunbridge to Chelsea, about ten producers, has had sheep attacked by coyotes." Cornelia says:

"We had coyotes before we had losses, when there was just one little family of coyotes ten years ago. They didn't multiply, and we didn't lose sheep. Then I guess as the coyote population increased, they went under the woven wire fence and in winter when snow had drifted over the fences, coyotes would cross. That is usually in February or March when the snow is deepest. Our coyote damage is always to the most lively, best sheep, never to the weaselly ones about to die. Foxes will take those."

Their sheep are protected by electric fence now, their losses fewer, but in the summer of 1980 coyotes denned in a pasture before it was fenced. "We have lost lambs to them and we will have to do something," Cornelia Swayze says. The Swayze farm is away from town, away from the main roads; they can trap coyotes without worrying about neighbors' dogs, and one fall, eight coyotes were trapped on their farm and adjoining property.

Tunbridge coyotes are not easy to trap. Henry Swayze has sheep carcasses to use for bait, but the coyotes are suspicious and reluctant to return to feed on a previous kill, an indication that the eastern coyote is learning what the plains coyote knows, the coyotes which eat from a carcass a second time may be trapped or poisoned. Plains coyotes saw their kind die from poisoned carcasses, and the survivors became fussy eaters. Coyotes in the west would eat what they could from a lamb they had killed, then leave it and kill another lamb when again they were hungry instead of feeding several days on the original carcass. Coyotes had to kill more to eat the same amount of food; ranchers trying to control the coyote were making them bigger killers than before, an irony. Such cleverness keeps the coyote alive, and biologist Ben Day says: "He is going to outlive all the sheepherders in the west." By implication, he also meant all the sheepherders in the east as well.

Cornelia: "I see them. My kids see them. They don't go killing the way dogs do. It's not as if you hear them. Sometimes they kill on successive nights then not show up for a while." Her husband Henry: "Coyotes take lambs away, animals fifteen and sixteen pounds. They tend to vanish at night."

Though eight coyotes were trapped in one season on and near his farm, Henry says they have had poor success trapping overall. "In the long run you have to keep the coyote out of the pasture [with electric fencing or guarding dogs]. You do get certain coyotes that are more trouble than others. If there is plenty of easy feed, rabbits, coyotes will take the rabbits and leave the sheep alone. . . . I've never been able to see coyotes when I had my rifle. Of course, I'm not out there hunting them, either." He says that shepherds are used out west and can keep the sheep together, but at night coyotes can walk into the edge of the flock, kill one, eat from it or drag the carcass away.

In Vermont the coyotes are increasing, he says. "If there is no natural or biological check, then people will lose pets and some people may be attacked." I had heard that coyotes will eat house cats but did not know they would attack people, and at the time I thought his statement dramatic and inaccurate. I was to learn differently.

It was Henry Swayze who told me coyotes sometimes would kill a sheep by ripping open the belly rather than pinching the windpipe shut and that the stricken sheep would run until tripped by its own entrails. Two renegade sheep were able to return to the fold from the woods. One had a slight wound on the belly, the other had a hunk of meat the size of a man's fist taken out of a rear leg. That sheep was still alive when I was there but was not as "thrifty" as the others, meaning that sheep did not keep himself as healthy as the others. Their Border collie will not always go into the woods to turn around renegade sheep. Laddie is well trained and brave enough but stands at the edge of the woods, his hair standing on end, aware of the coyote scent in the woods.

Robert O'Brien lives near the Swayze farm but on the other side of the Tunbridge mountain, a steeper side, on a dirt road off the mountain road. O'Brien's sheep-guarding dog, a Great Pyrenees, met my car at the beginning of a long driveway leading up to O'Brien's house, a driveway with old sugar maples on each side. The Great Pyrenees was beside me when I got out of the car. He was big, his head the size of a polar bear's, and he put this great head against my thigh, his toothed mouth against my gloved fingers, and walked with me step by step to the farmhouse door. This was a dog bred to stand up to the coyote and would not, presumably, stand on the road, afraid to enter the woods where the sheep had strayed and where there was scent of the coyote.

Hilda Yates in Brownsville had told me of O'Brien the day before, suggested I should hear his coyote story. It was only coincidence that the O'Brien farm and the Swayze farm were in the same town. I assumed he was a typical Vermont farmer despite his Boston Irish name, but I was wrong. He raises seventy-five sheep, sometimes as many as a hundred on his old and pretty hillside farm, but he has worked out, as a college English teacher, Vermont state senator and candidate for governor. He is an articulate man, educated at Dartmouth, and gave me my first eyewitness account of the eastern coyote attacking a sheep. He also told me how he happened to come to this farm on the hill.

Chance meetings divert careers. An invitation turned O'Brien towards Vermont; a day he spent with a friend at Putney, Vermont, and that day was perfect, stuck in his mind. He was graduated from Dartmouth in 1940, had a scholarship to Harvard Graduate School in the fall and decided he would hitchhike through Vermont, beginning in White River Junction, not far from Dartmouth. A man in a truck picked him up, and O'Brien asked him if any farmer would hire a man who did not know how to hold a rake.

"He lived in Tunbridge and took me to the front yard of a farmer there who was not feeling too well, and the farmer came out, looked at me and said, 'I'll hire you. Dollar a day and room and board.' I was delighted and stayed with him.

"About July fourth I heard a dog bark and saw a fellow coming up the road on a bicycle, a Dartmouth friend. I had written to him, and he decided to come up. Three other Dartmouth friends heard I was on a farm, and one of them had a car. They came out with golf clubs and such, but we went right out back to hay. I gave each one a pitchfolk. At the end of the afternoon they said, 'Do you suppose your boss can find us a job?' Six of us from Dartmouth stayed that summer."

The Dartmouth six and others, recent graduates from Harvard, formed a group. They wanted to rehabilitate rural areas such as Tunbridge, places of abandoned farms and encroaching forest.

"We formed the Camp William James Association after the man who wrote 'The Moral Equivalent of War.' That was our Bible then." Writer Dorothy Thompson spent summers in Vermont, heard of this group and became interested in their idea, spoke of them to President Franklin Roosevelt who listened to her, presumably, because of her influence as a syndicated columnist for the *New York Herald Tribune*. President Roosevelt even met with some of the Tunbridge group.

"He [FDR] offered us an abandoned CCC camp in Sharon [a town near Tunbridge]. We left Tunbridge, took over the camp. That lasted a brief time because people who ran the CCC group, members of a machinist union from New Jersey, were given CCC jobs by FDR and worried about their jobs. The machinists said we were Nazis, a Hitler Youth group. At the time, the lend-lease bill was before Congress, and we thought our efforts should not jeopardize that, so we withdrew from the CCC camp and came back to Tunbridge. Then I had a chance to talk to Lincoln Filene [of the Boston department store], and through a fund we bought a farm just down the road and moved in. We went out to work on farms, about thirty of us. When we left the CCC camp we were able to invite women to join, and women worked out on the farms with us. I was hired to log up here [on his present farm] one winter, and when I saw this abandoned, beautiful farm, the avenue of maple trees, I was taken with the place.

"I came back in 1941, bought the farm and returned here after the war, still interested in rural rehabilitation. All this area in back [and he pointed to the forest above his house] had been farmed, and was productive and now is abandoned. Obviously this land would not support a dairy farm. It is hilly and the soil thin. It looked ideal for sheep, and I started a sheep operation."

The woods had grown up around the old farmhouse by 1941, the avenue of maple trees on the driveway was cluttered by brush. Sheep helped O'Brien clear the land by browsing on the brush and brambles. He has thirty acres of cleared pasture beside the woods; he and his sheep have produced the edge effect, good habitat for coyotes.

O'Brien has lost three sheep to predators, dogs he thought, but he is not so sure of that after what happened one Sunday in the summer of 1980.

"I was out for an afternoon walk and went down the road and then into the woods behind the house. I had a dog with me [but not the Great Pyrenees] and was startled to see my ram down in the pasture up against a fence. An animal was trying to get behind the ram. I watched for a few seconds before realizing what it was, a coyote. I ran and the coyote ran toward the house away from me. I got a good look at it. Its head looked like a fox. The animal was larger than I expected, stood as high as a German shepherd. It did not have a nice coat and wasn't an attractive animal. I'd say it was over fifty pounds, and it moved with enormous speed."

O'Brien's ram weighed 175 pounds, three times more than the coyote, but the difference in size would not have been enough to save the ram if he had not defended himself well. The coyote kept fronting the ram, perhaps trying to eye it, to stare it down. Each time the coyote went left or right, the ram would turn to face the coyote. The ram was keeping his vulnerable behind up against the fence where the coyote could not reach.

The rest of his observations that day come from this account he wrote for the Vermont *Sheepbreeders Newsletter*:

"My ram appeared to have suffered no injury and followed me up to a shed where there were three other rams. Evidently, the coyote had somehow been able to separate the intended victim from his companions, for all the animals appeared nervous.

"The attacked ram had already been sold at the time . . .

and the new owner came a few days later to pick him up. Soon after, she had him sheared, and it was then discovered that there were two incisions on a rear thigh, revealing how close the coyote had come to a kill. Apparently the ram's heavy fleece (wool ten inches long) as well as his courage helped him to survive until I accidentally came to his rescue. . . . It represents such an ominous change in the conditions under which I have raised sheep in Vermont for over twenty years, and because it threatens my operation in such an obvious way . . . [long before the coyote incident] I fenced in more than half the land and divided it into a half-dozen more or less heavily-wooded lots. The sheep were rotated from lot to lot, sometimes staying day and night for a month on land that was a half-mile from my house. These pasture routines continued for more than fifteen years with no predator losses.

"During this time I cut hundreds of cords of pulpwood from these lots while the sheep worked on the choke cherries, brush and brambles. Gradually and almost imperceptibly openings developed and grass reappeared on land that had been in the process of returning to dense woodland. Over the years we have raised nearly seven hundred lambs on what had once been wild terrain and impoverished soil.

"Coyotes now threaten to put an end to these efforts. If my sheep cannot be safely pastured in *daytime*, on open land one hundred yards from my house, I certainly cannot put them in more remote semi-wooded pastures. There is too much other work for me to do to stand guard over my flock all the time. . . . Electric fences offer no economically feasible solution [because his fields would require so much fencing] . . . and the use of guard dogs is just beginning to be explored and cannot be expected to offer immediate relief. . . ."

O'Brien got the Great Pyrenees after he wrote that letter. He doesn't know if the dog scares off coyotes, but he hears him barking sometimes, and he has lost no sheep since acquiring the dog. O'Brien puts his sheep into the barn at night since the coyote attack. We walked up to that barn so that O'Brien could point out the distinctions of his Romney sheep, handsome creatures, their faces pictures of peace. Inside, while O'Brien talked, the Great Pyrenees lay at my feet and pawed my leg. If he had been a small dog and no threat, I might have been concerned lest he tear my L. L. Bean flannel-lined khaki winter traveling pants, but in his case I was pleased to bend over to scratch his proffered chest as he wished me to do. I left O'Brien in the barn, said goodbye to him there, a 1940 liberal who retains his enthusiasm, a man who realized part of his youthful goal. He has rehabilitated one part of the rural countryside.

The Great Pyrenees walked behind me to the car. When I had arrived, his polar bear face looked formidable; now that I knew him better, he just looked baleful. I drove down the mountain road to Tunbridge Village to the store there. O'Brien had told me storeowner Bruce Bellemeur had shot a coyote, and so indeed he had, in the fall of 1980, though coyotes are not easy to shoot because they are not often seen on open ground in daylight. Bellemeur spoke from behind his grocery counter:

"I shot one the first day of deer season. Deer hunters must have jumped a coyote lying in the woods, and he came over a knoll and right out in the open out of the hardwood. He was going fast. I led him five feet and shot him." The coyote was about eighteen inches high at the shoulder and weighed forty pounds, Bellemeur says.

Bellemeur has seen several coyotes in Tunbridge, perhaps as many as ten at different times. A friend of Bellemeur while fishing in the river that runs through town saw a coyote in the meadow chasing mice and watched him for some time. "Right today I could take you up to the two main ridges [pointing outside his store] and show you more coyote tracks than deer tracks on those two ridges (not that there are more coyotes than deer). There's softwood cover on those ridges for coyote and they hunt rabbits there." He also shot a coyote in the 1979 deer season, at seven in the morning. "That one was mangy. I shot it right through the middle with a thirty-oh-six, and it crawled thirty feet to show you how strong they are. I shot it again to put it out of its misery."

A Tunbridge trapper told Bellemeur this story: A coyote stepped into his trap and was caught. The trap was anchored to the ground with a stake, and the coyote pulled this stake free. A chain attached to the trap had a three-pronged hook on it, and these steel prongs were pulled straight by the coyote when the prongs became entangled in a tree. The trapper followed the hobbled coyote in the snow until he came upon it again entangled by the chain and prongs in a tree. The trapper shot the coyote and on the way back out of the woods saw an unusual thing written in the snow. A second coyote had followed the trapper, using a parallel route. The trapped coyote's mate had watched over his death. The trapper felt badly about that coyote, Bellemeur said, because of its courage and strength and because of the second set of tracks. Bellemeur himself does not want to see the coyote annihilated. "The reason I shoot them is because there are so many. I wouldn't want them all gone." Bellemeur has hunted out west where the coyotes are smaller and not as strong and does not think of the Tunbridge animal as a coyote. "I call 'em the eastern wolf."

# – 3 –
# On Silent Feet

Dolly was born premature, cared for by a doctor who took him into his house and put him in an incubator. When a neighbor saw the little baby, she said, "Oh, what a pretty dolly," and that is how Dolly got his name. He runs a store in Jackman, Maine, Dolly's Supermarket, and has several animals mounted above food cases in his store, one of them a coyote. I had seen carcasses of skinned coyotes in dry riverbeds in Arizona where they had been dumped by fur hunters, but the first full-bodied coyote I saw was at Dolly's.

A few years later, in Coos County, New Hampshire, a game warden patrolling a woods road got out of his car to check deer sign and also pointed out coyote tracks to me. He said he could not always tell coyote tracks from those of dogs, but a coyote print is narrower than a dog's print. A coyote will generally walk straight up a hill whereas a dog walks up a hill on an angle. Also, a coyote will often go straight across a clearing in the woods, anxious to reach cover on the other side, whereas a dog will wander about the clearing before reaching the other side. Dogs have lost their stealth through domistication. The best indication of coyote tracks is the way a coyote places one print almost in front of the other so the track looks as if it had been made by a two-legged animal. Coyotes can place their feet in this single file fashion because their chests are narrow. It is easy enough to find coyotes' tracks in New England but difficult to see one.

A coyote crossing Route 128 near Lexington, Massachusetts, was hit and killed by a car, its body taken to state game officials for study. The month and day was December 15, the year uncertain, either 1976 or 1977. The year is not as important as the fact the coyote was killed only twelve miles from Boston. March 4, 1979, another coyote was killed by a car, on Route 95, 1.3 miles north of Exit 10 on the Canton-Sharon line in Massachusetts. Coyotes had come a long way from the American west to the suburbs of Boston. No one is certain how long this migration of a species took because no one saw them, and coyotes move on silent feet.

A coyote was trapped in Amherst, Massachusetts, in 1936 and was believed to be a western coyote released in the area, but in 1957 a coyote was shot in Otis, Massachusetts, and other coyotes were trapped the next year at the Quabbin reservoir reservation in west-central Massachusetts, not far from Amherst. The 1936 coyote might have been part of the early migratory wave into New England and might have taken the natural route down the Connecticut River Valley from Vermont into Massachusetts. It is reasonable to think coyotes existed in New England at least as far back as 1936 because the animal is so elusive, so trap-wary that it could have been here without anyone knowing of its existence.

When coyotes become numerous, they may take a range closer to towns, and once accustomed to the sight and smell of man they become less wary of man, fear him less. Once emboldened, the coyote shows itself occasionally, if only for a moment or two, crossing a turnpike in daylight or a street in a New England town. In the 1970s a family of coyotes lived in Concord, the capital of New Hampshire. Concord is not a big city; it has wooded neighborhoods and fields within its city limits. Nevertheless, coyotes had moved into the capital city of the state. Joseph E. Wiley, a New Hampshire wildlife biologist, said the family of mother and father and pups was sighted several times one summer and that a woman who lived in the city, awakened at three in the morning by howling, called the state biologists for advice on what to do. Wiley says he did not know what to tell the woman except that she might go out and bang some pans, quiet the coyotes that way. "Finally," says Wiley, "they left [Concord] but were around for a whole season and into the fall. I know of a couple still around."

I wonder how close coyotes are getting to Boston, New England's major city. I know of no evidence that they have gotten closer than did the coyote killed twelve miles from the city on Route 128 in Lexington, but Boston is a dog-ridden city, and coyotes could skulk the city at night without being recognized and retreat before daybreak to cover on the outskirts of the city. Coyotes could get fat off garbage because city garbage is highly nutritious; it has nurtured the herring gull to historic proliferation. If recognized in the city, a coyote would cause more skepticism than interest. Bostonians would assume the coyote had escaped from a zoo. At any rate, a foraging coyote would not be the meanest animal in town.

The coyote lived on the plains of the American west when big game, elk and buffalo, lived there, eating carrion left by bigger predators or perhaps killing the big animals themselves by hunting in packs. No one knows for sure because wildlife biologists were not there to watch, though biologists since have studied coyotes in Jackson Hole, Wyoming, and learned they become less solitary there in order to feed on elk.

The coyote had moved even before the big game was shot out, moving south to Central America. The coyote also moved north to Alaska and was first seen there in 1915, perhaps following the gold miners to eat their pack animals as they died.

By 1950 coyotes had reached Point Barrow, an unlikely climate for an animal associated in the public mind with the dry and hot American west.

Coyotes remaining on the American plains took to killing sheep, and ranchers took to killing coyotes, and the poisoning campaign may have pressured some coyotes to move east beginning in the late 1800s. Coyotes had an established population in Michigan by 1920, moving into areas where logging operations had cleared the forest. This Great Lakes coyote continued the trek east.

Maine wildlife biologist Henry Hilton uses these dates for the first recorded incidence of the eastern coyote: Vermont 1942; New Hampshire 1944; Connecticut 1955; Massachusetts 1957; Maine 1961. Though wildlife people knew the coyotes were there, many citizens did not. Hilton used to address Maine groups in the 1970s and people would say to him, "You mean we have coyotes in Maine!" Rhode Island wildlife officials received the body of a coyote killed on the road in December 1978, froze the carcass and in 1979 identified it as a coyote by computer measurement. Though the dates are good guides, they are not precise.

Moose are easier to count than coyotes. Moose are bigger, less shy and probably less intelligent than the coyote. Henry Laramie, a wildlife biologist for the New Hampshire Fish and Game Department, says: "I could account for 222 moose four years ago [in 1976]. I called each C.O. [New Hampshire wardens are called conservation officers] and asked him where he know there were moose, 'the ones you're sure about.' I plotted the reports on a map, and if two wardens from adjoining areas each reported four moose, I'd subtract four from the total." Laramie knew the conservation officers could not know the locations of all the moose in the state so he took the reported figure of 222, doubled it, rounded it off and estimated, arbitrarily, that there were 500 moose in the state.

Coyotes are difficult to count, but wildlife biologists can

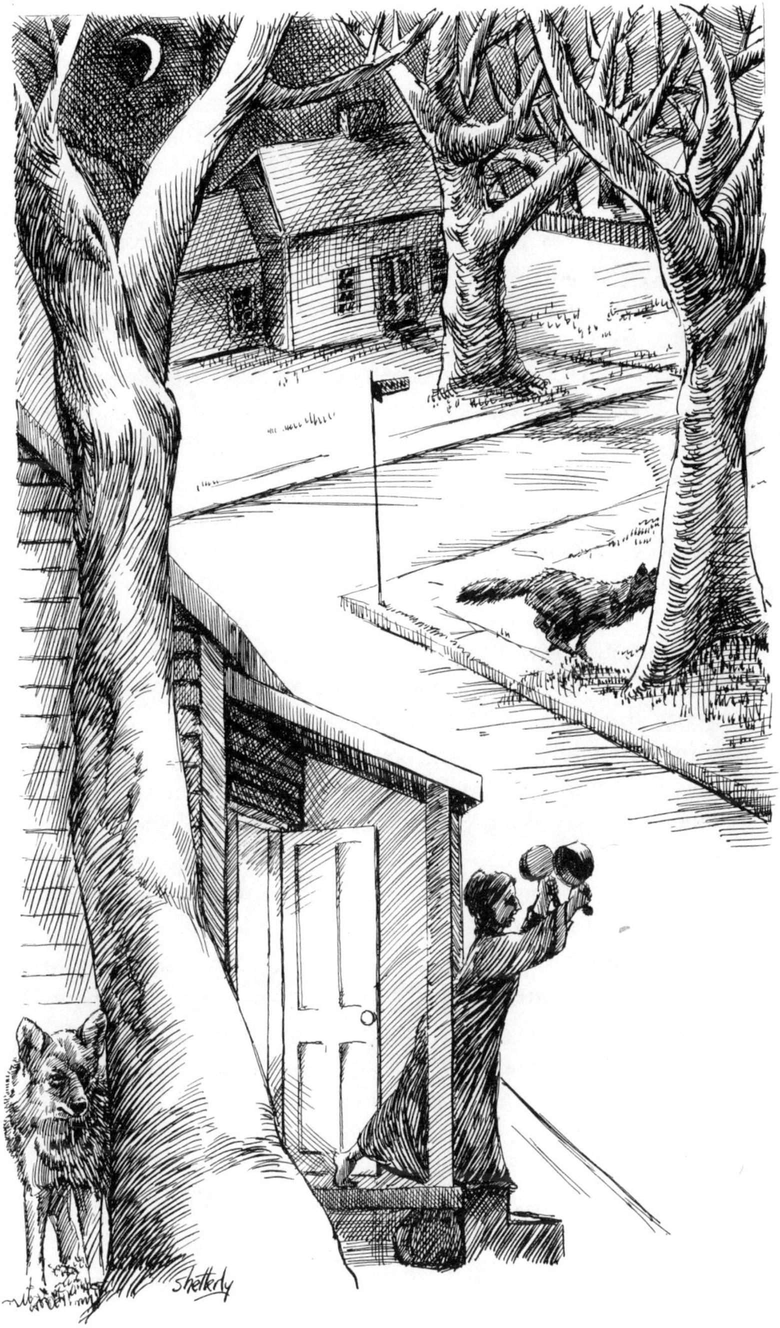
shetterly

estimate a population by the number of animals trapped and sighted and killed on the roads and by tracks in the snow. State biologist Chet McCord estimates there are one thousand coyotes in Massachusetts; Ben Day of Vermont estimates two thousand in his state; Joe Wiley of New Hampshire said, "People get excited at figures of predators," and was reluctant to give a number but estimated there are two to three thousand coyotes in New Hampshire. Maine is as big as the other five New England states put together. (This is only a small exaggeration: Maine is 33,215 square miles; the total of the other five states is 33,393 square miles.) Henry Hilton, Maine's coyote authority, estimates the state's coyote population at seven to ten thousand, though he says that is only a guess.

I met a man who hunts, traps and does some flying in central Maine, and he told me he can spot coyote and moose tracks while flying low over clearings in the forest. He sees a lot more coyote tracks than moose tracks and takes that as proof there are more coyotes than moose. Maine has an estimated twenty thousand moose, and he figures the state must have more than twenty thousand coyotes. I thought his idea reasonable at the time until later I realized that the coyote is active 65 percent of its waking hours, that it must travel for its food, crisscrossing areas in search of prey, and cannot browse on brush in a clearing as a moose might do. One coyote makes more tracks than one moose.

This same fellow in central Maine told me coyotes in his town hunted an area until it was denuded of game, then moved on, not returning to the original area for some time. Male coyotes without mates do roam great distances, and there is documentation of a coyote moving 70 miles from Vermont into New York and other documentation of a coyote moving 100 air miles (many more miles than that by land) from Quebec into Aroostook County, Maine. However, families of coyotes, mother, father and pups, generally stay within a particular hunting range week after week. This fellow in central Maine who was wrong about the coyote tracks was wrong about their hunting range, too.

The word coyote comes through the Spanish from Aztec *coyotl*. The Aztecs and other Indian tribes admired the coyote. It is a member of the dog family as are wolves, jackals and foxes, all animals that depend on speed for running down prey, as opposed to cats which wait and pounce upon prey as well as chase them. The coyote has been called prairie wolf, brush wolf, barking wolf, American jackal. Biologists call it *Canis latrans*, meaning barking dog, and the eastern coyote is called *Canis latrans var.* (*var.* for variant). The eastern coyote looks something like a German shepherd, has gray hair tipped with black on its back, lighter hair on its belly and legs; but there are so many color variations in the eastern coyote that no one color description is totally accurate. Some are blond, some reddish. A hunter I met in Maine said he shot a coyote in a trap, then was alarmed lest he had shot a dog because the coyote was red, as red as a red fox.

Alfred J. Godin describes the eastern coyote this way in his book, *Wild Mammals of New England*.

"The coyote resembles a small collie dog but is more slender, with erect pointed ears and a bushy, drooping tail. It is recognized by its long, narrow, pointed muzzle, small rounded nose, round pupil and yellow iris of the eye, large ears which are directed forward but are movable, slender legs and small feet. There are five toes on the forefoot, . . . and the hind foot has four toes. . . . The fur is dense, long, and coarse. The sexes are colored alike and show slight seasonal color variation, but coloration varies greatly among individuals, though it is usually gray to cinnamon gray. . . ."

The eastern coyote should have a more foxlike look to its face than a German shepherd, and it walks more with the caution of the wild, less with the arrogance of the biggest dog on the street.

They were called coydogs in the 1950s and 1960s, and some of the animals were. There were not enough mates for the first big wave of coyotes coming into New England, and coyotes mated with domestic dogs to produce the coydog. This hybrid could look like a dog or more like a coyote. It had the outward characteristics of both dogs and coyotes and was capable of reproducing. Coydogs, however, can only breed back towards a dog and not towards a coyote. Coydogs have died out in New England to an extent, especially in northern New England. Coydogs are born in February when they are apt to die of cold. Coydog pups born in Caledonia County, Vermont, or Sagadahoc County, Maine, are likely to die, although coydogs born in Connecticut may survive the lesser cold of February there. Also, male coydogs, like male dogs, do not stay with the mother to feed and protect the pups as male coyotes do. Nevertheless, the name coydog persists, and some country people prefer to describe a coyote that way even though there are thousands of coyotes now and few coydogs. It is easier somehow for people to believe there are coydogs behind their house than to believe the creatures howling in the night are coyotes, creatures of the American west.

There is a great difference in size between the smallest coyote of the western desert and the larger coyotes of colder, forested regions such as New England, and the New England coyote is big enough to prey on deer. The largest coyote on record, taken in Wyoming in 1937, weighed 74.8 pounds, an animal large enough to be suspicious. Could it have been a wolf, a German shepherd? Dr. James Sherburne, a U.S. wildlife biologist working at the University of Maine in Orono, says the adult coyotes he and his students work with weigh from 29 to 35 pounds. Sherburne has a five-year-old male coyote who is well fed, lives in a cage on campus and weighs 45 pounds. "That's the biggest I've seen."

Henry Laramie, a New Hampshire state biologist, says he gets reports of large animals taken in New Hampshire, one in Startford described as a 100-pound wolf. "It shrunk a lot on the way down to Concord. It was 60 pounds, a big coyote." There were reports of an 80-pound coyote, but it weighed only 48 pounds without its skin, which might have weighed five pounds, bringing the live weight to 53 pounds. "We got one killed in Croydon in 1976 that weighed 63 pounds close as we can figure. We had to go to Massachusetts to a taxidermist to get the carcass. By the time we got there the head had been taken off and some of the legs, but reconstructing the thing it weighed 63 pounds. . . . The record weight, a male form Cornish, weighed 74 pounds, their weight, so it's not official. We didn't weigh it. We have enough trouble believing ourselves," said Laramie.

I had been traveling for more than three months in search of coyote lore, inquiring in places such as Northfield and Tunbridge, Vermont; Chesterfield, Massachusetts; Concord, New Hampshire; Carthage, Maine. Some days I worked by phone, as when I talked to a biologist at the University of Connecticut who told me of a student, Jim Agostine, who was working on coyotes in Boston, only five miles or so from my desk at the *Boston Globe*; and one day in February I found a parking space behind the Museum of Fine Arts, walked through a winter's wind across Huntington Avenue and into once-forgotten streets of Roxbury where Agostine does his graduate study on coyotes in the laboratory of Northeastern University. There are more cars, more pedestrians in the streets around Northeastern University than in all of Northfield and Tunbridge and Carthage put together, times ten. There is no cover in Roxbury, only asphalt, yet it is here where the coyotes are.

Agostine has performed necropsies on more than four hundred coyotes in two years, coyotes from New Hampshire (plus a few from Connecticut and one from Vermont). Necropsy is the correct word for an animal autopsy, one of only a few words I needed to learn in talking to coyote researchers, not because my vocabulary is large but because our conversations were not technical, only specific. One word I learned was crepuscular, the word describing an animal that feeds in early morning and in the evening. Coyotes are supposed to be crepuscular but will hunt at noon when they feel like it.

Agostine is trying to determine through skull measurements and other data if the eastern coyote extended its range from Michigan to New England without picking up wolf genes or dog genes along the way, genes that would explain the larger size of the new animal. There are many things he can learn through necropsy: the animal's age (by slicing a tooth and counting cementum layers, like rings on a tree); food habits (stomach contents); size; sex (studies often find more males than females, probably because male coyotes are more curious than females and thus easier to catch, but Agostine did not find more males among four hundred coyotes); reproduction rate (by examining scars on the uterus). He sections testes of males. This is one way to test if a questionable carcass is that of a dog or coyote because a dog always has spermatogenesis. (Another new word for me. It means sperm is flowing.) I mentioned my attendance at a coyote necropsy to colleagues at the *Globe* at lunch, sparing them clinical details but mentioning the fact that male coyotes have a bone in their penis called a bacula. My friends thought I was joking, but I told them I had seen a boxful of baculae that morning, and I had.

Agostine hunts deer in Connecticut, in Litchfield County, a heavily wooded part of a suburbanized state. He heard his first coyote there in 1974 or 1975. "There had been a lot of talk of coydogs, but I was not sure what I was hearing. Last fall [1980] I was hunting there and while dragging out a buck that a friend shot, I heard a coyote pretty plainly." He has heard them out west, at Yellowstone. "Oh, it's beautiful. They howl on one side of the lake, then on another, for fifteen minutes, then stop." A dairy farmer in East Conway, New Hampshire, told me that coyote howl was eerie; Babiak, the farmer in Chesterfield, the small town in Massachusetts, said the howling sounded like children fighting. But to biology student Agostine the howls are beautiful. Agostine has not seen an eastern coyote, not for certain, not in the wild, only the four hundred coyotes on his laboratory table.

Agostine studies carcasses of coyotes provided by New Hampshire. That state and all the New England states want coyote knowledge. Knowledge is a weapon to counter arguments of those who would try to exterminate the predator. Wildlife officials would like to make deer hunters understand that much of what hunters believe about the coyote is not true or is only partly true, especially the idea that coyotes go through the woods eating every calorie, leaving the forest bare of deer and raccoon and the bogs empty of beaver. Agostine had done twenty-two necropsies the previous day but had saved one for me.

The coyote on the table was gray and brown, a male taken June 9, 1980 in the area of Moultonboro, New Hampshire, its body frozen since then. Agostine lit a cigarette, took two or three puffs, put the cigarette out and put on gloves. He described for me what he observed. It was a rather typical coyote except its pelt was thin. If the pelt had been good fur, the animal would have arrived without it. Agostine suspected parasites because of the condition of the animal's fur, but he found none while I watched. Some coyotes suffer from tapeworms and roundworms. Some coyotes have heartworms, a parasite that can kill the animal by clogging its heart and lungs. He could find no mark of a trap on its foot and did not know how it had died. This animal had a full bladder; some trappers take the urine to lure other coyotes. Agostine does not like dealing with full bladders, but went ahead with his job and sliced the bladder, the urine spilling out. I had been watching from the distance of a step or two from the carcass. I wanted to be able to disguise my squeamishness and, if necessary, make an escape, but squeamishness abates with age and I am becoming abated.

Agostine knows no anatomical reason for a coyote's great strength. No one I talked to did know, and I suspect the coyote is no stronger than a dog, only wilder, and for that reason will try to bend steel traps and sometimes succeed and escape, whereas a domestic dog will lie by the trap waiting for some human to extricate him. Most of the four hundred animals Agostine has necropsied weighed from thirty to thirty-five pounds, though two or three were much larger, the largest being a female weighing sixty pounds and taken near Maidstone, Vermont, a female supposed to have been raiding a captive herd of deer. Agostine had the paws of this animal in a jar. Weight studies may be misleading because animals weighed in the laboratory are apt to have been trapped, and young animals are more susceptible to trapping than are adults. More than half of Agostine's animals were young coyotes.

The animal he was cutting on the table weighed thirty-nine pounds. Its stomach was full, showing signs of two different mammals. He has found coyotes with whole chickens in their stomachs, but his food study is complicated because food he finds may have been bait in the trap. I told Agostine a beaver trapper in a small town in western Maine had told me that coyote trappers liked to use house cats for bait. Agostine smiled. He gets some orange and red and calico hairs in his stomach samples and suspects the hair might be from house cats. When that beaver trapper told me the story I pictured men shooting house cats for coyote bait, not realizing the obvious, that trappers were more likely to pick up dead cats off the highway.

We talked as he worked. Four hundred coyotes were a lot of coyotes to cut open. He said the necropsies could become repetitious, but the real bother was disposal of the carcasses after all measurements were taken. He had to carry the carcasses across campus to an incinerator and wondered if that explained why many biologists preferred to study small animals.

He found the wound on the coyote on the table. His skull had been smashed. Probably he had been trapped, had lain there until the trapper came upon him and clubbed him. Strangely, a trap strong enough to hold a coyote does not always scar the paw, though often a coyote that pulls his numbed paw out of a trap has left a bit of toe in the trap. It is not so hard to trap a coyote, a man in Pittsfield, Maine, told me. The trick is to hold him.

Coyotes go hungry, for all their daring and resourcefulness. Agostine finds as much as twenty-five millimeters of fat just inside the skin on the backbone of coyotes trapped in late October or November. Coyotes trapped in spring have almost no fat. There was some fat on this June coyote on Agostine's table. The smell from the cadaver was not noxious, not even strong. I advanced to within one pace of it as Agostine worked.

He did not go through all the steps of his necropsy while I was there. It would take weeks to study all the organs for parasites; it would also take some time for the carrion beetles to eat the flesh off the coyote's skull. Carrion beetles, Dermestidae beetles, are common enough. Agostine and his fellow students catch the beetles under rocks and breed them in the laboratory. After beetles eat the flesh of the coyote skulls, the skulls are cleaned with warm water and then with ammonia, and then accurate measurements of skull parts can be taken from the bare bones.

The measurements of four hundred New Hampshire coyote skulls when compared to skulls from Ontario and the Great Lakes region should tell Agostine something, certainly should provide him with documentation for his master's thesis, might even lead to a discovery that would put Agostine's name in the eastern coyote literature along with the names of Hilton of Maine, Silver of New Hampshire, Lawrence and Bossert of

Harvard. Four hundred necropsies is a laborious way to prove a point, but it is the scientific way. If he could prove, for instance, that the New England coyote is just a coyote-coyote that has no gene of the Ontario Algonquin wolf, Agostine would make a mark in his field. Few nonbiologists would know of his work or of its importance, but within the biology business, Agostine would be somebody. A collection of coyote skulls were piled near his laboratory table, skulls of the coyotes examined the previous day, skulls covered with red flesh awaiting the carrion beetles and the ammonia bath. It might be science, it *is* science, but it looked ghoulish to me, and in my mind I can see that mound of small red skulls.

The eastern coyote has reached the Atlantic in Maine at least, and perhaps in New Hampshire, and has probably penetrated inside Route 128, the perimeter highway of Boston, though I cannot prove that. Other kinds of coyotes have reached Florida, the Gulf Coast. H. T. Gier of Kansas has written in the anthology *The Wild Canids*: "Neither altitude nor latitude restricts their survival any more than does vegetation." (However, coyotes do not thrive in the wet vegetation of the tropics.) "The range of no other species of wild mammal extends over such latitude as does the modern coyote." Gier writes that the coyote is a match for most anything except man's technique of destruction.

The coyote can be controlled somewhat by trapping and shooting and den-burning; the coyote might even be exterminated in a certain place if enough frightful poison is used. Carl Ferguson, a federal biologist and trapper working in Augusta, Maine, says there is a way to get rid of the coyote in Maine: "You burn all the vegetation and poison all the rodents. Then let it grow up again. Of course, then the coyotes would move back in."

Coyotes are seldom mentioned in Boston papers; but in

Vermont, where deer hunting is more important than raquetball, coyotes are a controversial matter. I drove north to Northfield to see Ben Day, Vermont's director of wildlife, had a 9:00 A.M. appointment at his home and would have been on time except I missed a shoulder in the snow, my car slipped into two feet of powder snow and I could do nothing but call a tow truck to lift the vehicle out. Though I was late getting to Northfield that morning, and it was Day's day off, he received me graciously and gave me a bundle of papers from his own coyote file, entrusting me with some stuff of value though we had never met. He told me this:

"I don't think there is any great increase in the coyote population. I think it is probably stable and we will have this population until all of us are gone because there is little we can do to control them. . . . I don't know who will inherit the earth. If not the meek, maybe it will be the starlings and the coyotes. We've got 'em living from the most remote areas in the Northeast Kingdom to the outskirts of bigger towns like Burlington [Vermont's biggest city].

"There are two groups who if they could push the button to destroy them, would. First, there are a fair amount of deer hunters. We don't equivocate. There is no way the coyote is a threat to the deer herd. The second group is the sheepherders. They have legitimate concerns. . . . We know he does take lambs, but part of the problem is the husbandry. If a guy is working in Montpelier and his wife is teaching, then when they come home, naturally they find the coyote has taken lambs." Government officials are usually more circumspect.

I could have sat there in his living room drinking coffee and listening to him into the afternoon, but I sensed he had other business and took my leave. He said: "I have been accused of being a coyote lover which I am not, but we have to live with them. Maybe they have some good qualities we could learn before condemning them."

Four million coyotes have been killed by the Animal

–53–

Damage Control program of the U.S. Fish and Wildlife Service since 1915. That is a lot of coyotes, four million, and does not include coyotes trapped or shot or poisoned by ranchers not involved with the federal program. The federal government continues to kill coyotes. In 1976 the government program killed 87,000 coyotes in sixteen states west of the Mississippi: Washington, Oregon, California, Arizona, Nevada, Idaho, New Mexico, Texas, Oklahoma, Colorado, Wyoming, Montana, Utah, South Dakota, North Dakota and Nebraska. Coyotes that year were taken in this manner: 32,000 in steel traps; 34,500 by shotgun fire from helicopters and airplanes; 5,300 by use of the M-44, a device smaller than an English captain's swagger stick (the coyote, attracted to the M-44 by a scent, tugs the end of the stick until a spring injects sodium cyanide into his mouth); 5,500 lured within rifle range by animal calls (often the cry of a rabbit in distress); 5,300 by denning (killing pups in their dens by means of gas cartridges and other means, a practice ended in 1979 because it had become an emotional issue); 3,200 by snares set in places where coyotes habitually travel (for instance, under a pasture fence). Jim Gillett of the U.S. Division of Wildlife Management in Washington, D.C., who gave me these figures, says: "My personal feeling is we do a nice job of cropping coyotes rather than eradicating them. Our goal would never be to eradicate coyotes." No amount of private and government killing has eradicated the coyote, but all this killing may have induced some of his kind to move east.

Coyotes in the west have learned to avoid eating a second time from the carcass of a sheep, thus avoiding poison, and where the attempts to kill it are severe, the coyote has moved on, temporarily. A clever animal is the coyote.

Not all his cleverness is conscious. No one knows what goes through the mind of a coyote who senses a steel trap buried in the ground in front of a piece of bait and then digs the trap up and springs it somehow without getting a paw caught between the two jaws of the trap.

Beyond this kind of cleverness, the coyote is sustained by its reproduction system. Nature has chosen to protect the coyote and let other species, the wolf or the mountain lion, for instance, decline. (Why nature should favor the sparrow over the bluebird is a metaphysical question, and I leave it to others. If the coyote were rare instead of common it would be considered more beautiful, more worthy. The same is true of the sparrow. I am learning to admire the will of the coyote to survive and should admire the sparrow for the same reason. However, I still prefer bluebirds to sparrows.) A coyote pair produces one litter a year, but the number of pups is known to increase where the animal is being hunted heavily. Therefore, if half of all coyotes in New England were trapped and killed, a curious thing would happen. The average litter size would double, and a female coyote who normally does not breed until she is two years old and who sometimes acts as an aunt to another's litter until she is that old, begins to breed earlier. Not all species of animal have that kind of reproductive protection, though man is one who has, and when war and plague kept populations low, women bore children at an earlier age. And in America when the land was empty and the resources of the land were great, families were large. Coyotes can be exterminated, or nearly exterminated by killing 70 percent of the population each year, but the population will recover within five years after the extermination efforts cease, according to G. E. Connelly, a U.S. biologist. The coyote survives not only because it is the fittest but because nature favors it.

New England biologists are unsure if the coyote is increasing in the region. Some of them suspect the population is becoming stable. Nonbiologists, the sheepherders and deer hunters, think otherwise, that coyotes are becoming more brazen as they become more numerous. A Maine trapper tells this story: He found a coyote in his trap and then realized he was partially surrounded by snarling coyotes and also realized he had only one bullet left in his gun. After some indecision, the trapper used the one bullet to kill the trapped coyote, and the others left. The man who retold that story to me said: "I'd believe him if he told me I had a flat tire, but I don't believe that story." I have heard stories that coyotes are entering clearings in the woods where woodsmen are felling trees and displaying no fear of man, and I talked to a woman in western Maine who said her child was frightened by an animal on the road near their house, that the child was frozen with fear. The child, eight years old, could have been frightened by something other than a coyote, but the mother herself is frightened of the animal she hears in the woods.

Henry Swayze, the Tunbridge, Vermont, sheepraiser, had told me he thought the coyotes were increasing and "if there is no natural biological check then people will lose pets and some people may be attacked"; but the coyote is supposed to be cowardly when faced by man; and I wondered about Swayze's perception until I called E. Keith Weeks, a deputy health officer for Los Angeles County, California. This is what he told me:

"Out here coyotes are eating cats and small dogs. The coyote tries to entice larger dogs away, especially those in heat. They're running in packs of eight to ten. In the foothills of the Sierra Madre a man saw seven or eight on his front lawn. They're running up and down golf courses in daytime, very brazen.

"The problem is they are biting people. We have citified coyotes that have kind of moved in. They found it easier to move in [to the city] than out [into the desert]. Animal lovers are putting out food stations and water, and others accidentally encourage them by leaving trash cans open and dog food in the yard. They've found it is easier to eat Alpo in the back yard than to eat rabbits. Once accustomed to living in the city they lose their fear of man.

"We haven't had a coyote biting a human recently [but] in the last year and a half there were about five unprovoked bites by coyotes. Three of them were out-and-out attacks. One girl, seven years old, a coyote ran down a knoll into a group of children, jumped and grabbed her by the throat. It was witnessed by animal control people. The coyote tried to take the child into the woods. Her father heard this, ran out of his house and screamed, and the coyote dropped the child and stood twenty yards off challenging the father. The coyote had knocked the child down, grabbed her by the throat and tried to drag her off. There were puncture marks on her shoulder and throat but no tears.

"There were two others. One was a thirteen-week-old baby in the San Fernando Valley. The mother and child were out in the back yard and when the mother had turned around for a second, a coyote had the baby in its mouth trying to drag it off. The mother threw a barbecue at it, saving the baby who had bite marks but was not seriously injured. A young man, about twenty-one, was hitchhiking to San Francisco. He was just about at the Los Angeles County–Ventura County line at three A.M. and was sleepy and climbed down an embankment and fell asleep. He woke up and found a coyote chewing on his leg.

"The coyote population is really blossoming. There is no bounty. It's against the law to fire a gun in the county. First thing you know, the population is so high they are competing for food and found easy food [inside Los Angeles]. We use the County Agriculture Commission to trap and there's been trapping in the Pasadena area. Nineteen or twenty have been trapped near the Rose Bowl Parade route. But trapping doesn't work. . . . Their only real enemy is the automobile and they're smart enough to learn to dodge the auto."

# – 4 –
# "Oh, They're Very Human"

Helenette Silver had been retired four years as a New Hampshire wildlife biologist when I talked to her at her mobile home in Loudon, a town near Concord. She was wearing dark glasses and said she was unable to finish the last chapter of a book she was writing because of cataracts. She puffed True cigarettes as we spoke. She did not complain about her poor eyesight, and though her name is listed in much of the coyote literature, she has no academic airs. I liked her. She and her former husband Walter T. Silver accepted a litter of coyote pups taken from a den in Croydon, New Hampshire, in April 1960 and raised those pups and their descendants from 1960 to 1966, publishing a monograph in 1969 that established at least two facts: Coyotes would breed with dogs to produce the coydogs people were seeing; the New England coyotes themselves bred true and were coyotes and not coydogs.

"I can tell a tame coyote from a wild coyote. How? Little things." She explained that deer had been her specialty before the coyote work and tame deer had a rougher coat than wild deer whose coats were sleek from food they ate in the wild, but she could not explain specifically how she could tell a tame coyote from a wild coyote except that "they look a little different. I would know instinctively from having handled them." The coyotes she raised were only tame, not domesticated. "One can use force on a domestic animal to tame them, but a wild animal can be tamed only by a system of rewards. If you use force, either they will turn on you or run away. Even a mouse would do it—attack or run. I would hate to try to punish a coyote."

She and her husband raised half the coyotes in cages outside their house in Boscawen. The other half ran free in the house. "Those coyotes had the run of the house. We didn't try to housebreak them. We had so many it would have been impossible to take them out at the same time on a leash. At one time we had seventeen coyotes in the house." The coyotes defecated and urinated in the house, and otherwise were destructive, tearing rugs, curtains, even ripping moulding off walls. The Silvers followed the progress of the outside coyotes and the inside coyotes, trying to discern the difference between the coyotes raised outside by their parents and the coyotes raised inside by themselves. "We kept them [the outside coyotes] in cages with cement bottoms heavy enough to hold a house." They were afraid lest some coyotes would escape. "The neighbors would have nailed our hides to barndoors." Back then, 1960, the coyote in New England was more mysterious a creature than now and was reviled.

They bred female coyotes to a male pointer and to a male mongrel collie. "The first litter of pointers looked like purebred pointer except they were all black. But in winter they grew coyote underfur so they looked like black dogs on a brown cloud." The products of dog and coyote, coydogs, cannot breed with pure coyotes because their breeding times are different. All the coyote books explain it, all the biologists understand it and told me why, but it was in Mrs. Silver's mobile home that I was able to understand. I think I understand.

A male coydog can breed only in November. A female coyote can breed only in January or February.

*"Oh, They're Very Human"*

The male coydog, theoretically, could breed with a domestic female dog, but that union will produce pups more doglike and less like the coyote.

A male coydog can mate with a female coydog in November, but these coydog pups will be born in January or February. In northern New England at least, many of those coydog pups will die of cold, whereas the pure coyotes will mate in late January or February and their pups will be born in April, in warmer weather. There is another reason why coyote pups live. Coyote fathers stay with the mother and help feed the pups. They hunt for the mother and pups while the mother rests; and when the mother goes out to hunt, the father stays with his pups, an admirable quality not possessed by the domestic male dog who cares not for his progeny.

Helenette and her husband took notes on their clipboards and watched their coyotes, noticing, for instance, that female coyotes pulled hair off their bellies before giving birth, perhaps so the young could nurse through the thick hair. "The adults were always leaders over their own pups [but] the pups we took into the house before they opened their eyes thought we were their mother. Then one of these pups would take over as leader, and the others followed. The inside coyotes were very friendly, very jealous. They would fight with each other but not with you."

Males usually fought with their front feet in the air and fought to challenge for dominance. When one proved his dominance, the other coyote backed off. Only one of the Silvers' male coyotes was seriously injured in a fight, and he recovered. Females fought females with more intent, all four feet on the ground, and four females were seriously injured with bites around the face, skin torn off the whole length of a leg; three of them had to be destroyed.

Helenette: "Females chose the mate. In most situations, the male was dominant over the female, but once they take a mate, they stay with them, they get married. If she catches him giving the eye to another female, she would beat him up, and he accepted the beating. Females usually fought for males. If one female wanted another female's male she would fight fiercely."

There was little danger the coyotes would turn on their keepers, but Helenette was apprehensive about Boris. She pointed to the photograph of Boris in her kitchen. "He would play with the back of my hair, and he wanted me to get on the floor and roll around so he could pull on the hair."

Coyotes like perfume, and one inside coyote, a female, managed to get a bottle of Helenette's perfume, open the cap and roll in the contents, causing jealousy among the non-perfumed coyotes who fought with the anointed one. "They loved music and loved to have me play the organ. They would sit on the couch listening for hours, and they liked television music. The one who slept on my bed, Eenie [of an early group named Eenie, Meenie, Miney and Mo], liked TV anyway. A dog leash wouldn't hold them, not even a dog chain, so we had logging chains. Once that broke and the only way to keep Eenie quiet was to put on Oral Roberts [on the television]. . . . They were great thieves. If I would open the ice box door they would grab a steak and run around the house with it. One time the pups caught the cat, several of them, and tried to drag the cat into the den they had made in the fireplace. . . . "

Coyotes like to play the way children might play. When the heating system was being changed in the Boscawen house, a coyote found a workman's tool box in a shed and stole each tool, burying them one by one in a line by the house. It was fun for the coyote. Helenette was fond of her coyotes. "Oh, they're very human." Yet she was careful. When she obliged Boris, let him tug at her hair, she was apprehensive because Boris's jaws were so close to her spinal column.

The title of the Silvers' monograph was properly circumspect for the time: "Growth and Behavior of the Coyote-like Canid of Northern New England With Observations on Canid Hybrids." Scientific works have long titles. I tried for many weeks to find a copy of a new coyote book, having no luck, not at the Widener Library at Harvard, not at Boston's famous public library in Copley Square which had a copy listed in the catalogue. I filled out a slip at the Boston library and sat in a numbered seat in the great reading hall for some proper time until a library worker came by and insouciantly tossed my slip on the table in front of me, the slip marked "book not on shelf," and walked on, saying nothing. The Silvers' monograph was easy to find at the New Hampshire state library in Concord, where the librarian located it in a few minutes and handed it to me politely, and I was able to study it in a reading room where the floor was covered with a thick and handsome rug. I could have found the Silvers' book in Boston, probably, but I would not have learned of the perfume and Eenie's preference for Oral Roberts if I had not traveled north. The monograph contained no stories about the coyotes' liking for organ music played by Mrs. Silver, or Boris's desire to bite her hair. The monograph sticks to the facts.

The Silvers observed: Pups were born from April 1 to May 3 after a gestation period of sixty-one to sixty-six days and weighed from ten to sixteen ounces. Their pups were nearly black at birth, began developing their adult (German shepherd) coloring in the third month and had their permanent teeth at twenty-three weeks. Females went into heat in late January or February. Females breed when they are about twenty-two months old. The male allows himself to be dominated by the female who has chosen him. "When a dominant male and a dominant female mated and the dominant male was greeted by another female, the female snarled at him or threw him to the floor by seizing one foreleg and pulling him off balance and standing on his belly or shoulder in a position of dominance. The male accepted this treatment." How oddly human.

(H. T. Gier wrote that in the wild as many as seven males will follow one female. The female copulates with the male she chooses, and one by one the other males leave to find other females. "So in most cases the elimination of suitors either by discouragement of stronger males or dissipation of stamina or rejection by the bitch has been effective in limiting the sire of the pups to the strongest, most cunning male available . . . . " The coyote pair select a territory, choose a den and then hunt together, sleep near one another, and when the bitch is heavy with pups, the male will hunt alone, bring food to her.)

The Silvers observed that shortly before the female gives birth and while she is nursing pups, the male will allow the mother to finish eating before he takes his food, though at other times the male will eat at the same time as the female and will take more than his share if he could. Father coyotes help the females clean pups by licking them and were seen to take pups into the nest to shield the pups in bad weather; in a litter with weak pups, the sire pushed the weaklings into a position to nurse and growled when stronger pups threatened the weaklings; like good fathers playing catch on the side lawn, coyote fathers played with their pups, leading them in hunting any birds or butterflies that came into the pen outside the Silvers' Boscawen home. Parents began regurgitating food for the young about three weeks after birth. On one occasion a mother regurgitated food for her pups on a box too high for the pups to reach, and she reswallowed the vomit and regurgitated a second time on the floor where the pups could reach it.

(Gier writes that pups stand and claw at the mother's mouth to stimulate regurgitation and pups claw and caress the lips of the male coyote for the same reason. At four to six weeks the parents bring mice to their pups, then rabbits and later, Gier writes, even "leg of lamb." The male helps defend the den, will help move the pups to another, safer den, and if the female dies he will try to keep the pups alive. If the pups are still nursing and cannot take solid food, he leaves them, and they die.)

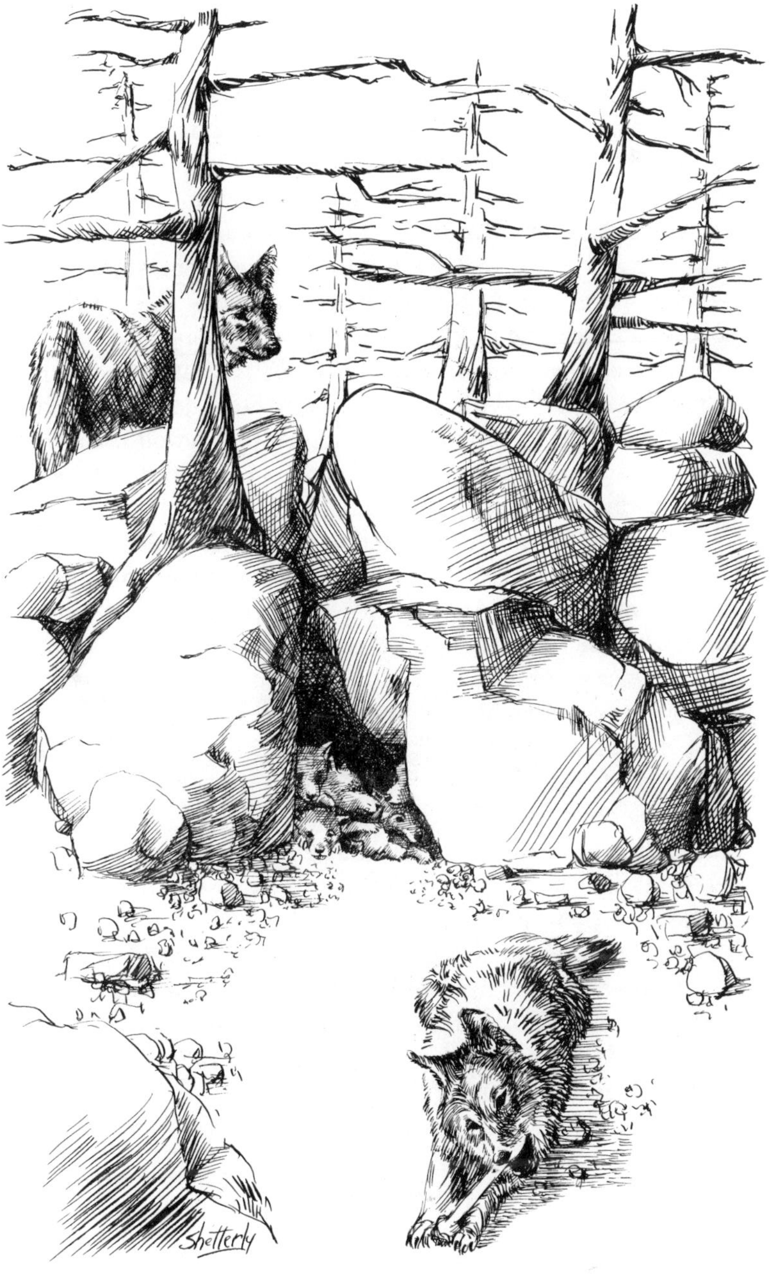
Shetterly

I talked to Helenette Silver at her home February 4, 1981, and put what she told me into coyote notebook number twelve. I still had not seen a live coyote for certain, and I would see the coyotes kept in captivity at the University of Maine in Orono, if my luck did not improve. By that time, February, I expected at least to have heard a coyote, but I was traveling in winter and did not spend nights on the moonless hillsides. I could hear coyotes and see one in spring if I set myself up in a bear stand over rotting meat in western Maine. In the meantime, the Silvers had described the voice of the coyote as lower in pitch than that of a Colorado coyote but higher than a wolf's. Howls of the New Hampshire coyotes tended to be "clear, long howls rising gradually in pitch and volume, then descending slowly." They howled only five or six times a day from November through February (mating season) and two or three times a day the rest of the year. After the Silvers obtained coyotes from Colorado, the New Hampshire coyotes began to howl about fifteen times a day instead of two or three times, an indication that western coyotes howl more than eastern coyotes.

Coyote researcher Philip N. Lehner describes their howls as "growl, huff, woof, bark, bark-howl, whine, woo-oo-wow, yelp, lone howl, group howl, group yip howl." Gier writes that parents howl at least three vocal commands to pups: food, come and get it; lie low, be quiet; follow me. Why coyotes howl more in the west than in the east is uncertain. Perhaps the greater density of coyotes in the west encourages them to howl because they receive answers, and perhaps the sound travels better in open western land than in the east where sound is soaked up by forest. I suppose they howl to one another for the hell of it or, because they have human qualities, howl as some men are moved to cry when, late at night and in their cups, a tenor sings "Rose of Tralee."

Coyotes have canine habits of interest to the clinically

## "Oh, They're Very Human"

minded. Though coyotes prefer to hunt by sight, they have a good nose to smell prey, to smell scent of man on a trap and to smell other coyotes for purposes of procreation and for purposes known only to themsleves. Lehner, who described the different coyote sounds, also describes sacs that lie on each side of a coyote's anus. Ducts on these anal glands open into the anus, and a coyote can secrete substance from the glands into his feces. This anal gland secretes strong-smelling stuff that may identify one individual from another as in mongooses. It may explain why dogs smell the waste of other dogs. This secretion from the anal gland contains materials that sound suitable for a gasoline additive: trimethylamine, ethanol and acetone. Male coyotes seeking mates can discern the breeding state of a female by smelling her urine, her feces and her vulva.

The female coyote may raise a hind leg to urinate, though she does not raise her leg laterally as does a male dog or a male coyote but lifts her leg straight up under her body. Sometimes coyotes raise their legs as if to urinate and then do not, a practice not understood. Coyote urine is used by trappers to lure coyotes because it is difficult for a coyote to bypass such a scent post. A large coyote leaves evidence of his size because he can raise his leg higher and urinate higher on a post, and this may be something another coyote is aware of when it sniffs. Female coyote urine is effective in drawing male coyotes to a trap, especially urine from a female in heat. I have read where a trapper out west used human female urine successfully to trap a particularly cagey coyote, but the author did not give much documentation of this, not that I disbelieve it. There is evidence that menstruating women are more likely to be attacked by bears than other humans. Coyotes often urinate on their food and sometimes on their water supply, perhaps a way of showing ownership. They may also urinate to show disdain for a trapper's set, though that would be attributing human motivation to an animal. Joseph Wiley, the New Hampshire biologist, told me this story: "I was working with a fellow in Corbin's Park [in Croydon, New Hampshire, where the Silvers' original coyote pups were found]. That's an 18,000-acre fenced game preserve. He had a problem with killed deer. He set some traps and had not caught any coyotes. We drove a snowmobile out on a shallow pond to a mound where he had set a trap, and a coyote had set his four feet around the trap and pissed right on it as if to say, 'Piss on your trap.'"

A coyote's tail is about thirteen inches long. It is bushier than that of a German shepherd, darker above than below and shaped like a bottle brush. The tail has a black tip and a black spot of dark guard hairs one-third of the way down from the base of the tail. The dark guard hairs indicate the tail gland. This gland, like the appendix in a human, has no known function. The tail gland has an odor that decreases in strength from the fox to the coyote to the wolf. A coyote entering his den might brush the tail gland on the top of the entrance to his den, marking that place as is own. It is a logical thought even if not conclusive. The study of wild coyotes is scientific but, like economics and the hitting of a curve ball, not yet a science.

Dens are used for delivering and nurturing the pups. Otherwise, coyotes live in the open, taking cover where they choose. They may pick an old fox den or that of a woodchuck for their den or use a blowdown of trees. They will enlarge an existing den or dig a den themselves, an area one to two feet wide and five to thirty feet long. There may be two purposes for the female to pull hair from her stomach: First to bare her teats for the pups to nurse and secondly to use the pulled-out fur to line the den. The mated pair may start looking for a den in mid-March and get more serious about this task when birth of the pups is near. In New England, pups are born in April or early May, an average of six to a litter. In other regions the litter may be bigger, in one case as big as seventeen pups, though that many is abnormal. "Animals do not practice birth control," a biologist told me. That is true of the coyotes as well as other animals if the phrase is changed to read: "Coyotes do not *intentionally* practice birth control." A coyote pair produces only one litter of pups a year, but the size of this litter tends to be bigger where the animal is being hunted, heavily trapped or poisoned. Thus do attempts to eradicate the coyote fail.

Mother coyote, father coyote and the pups travel together that first summer, the pups learning from their parents how to hunt, as did the family that spent the summer in Concord, New Hampshire, hunting rabbits and other stuff in the woods behind houses of the city. Some speculation is needed to explain what happens when the yearling pups are present the next winter and spring when their parents are ready to produce another litter. Marc Bekoff and Michael C. Wells, writing about the coyote in the *Scientific American* of April 1980, said: "Typically only one male and one female breed in each pack.... Packs may also include non-breeding hangers-on, probably also offspring of the mated pair in the pack, that continue to live in the vicinity of the pack but interact very little with it. (It is possible that these individuals benefit from such a minimal association by 'inheriting' a breeding area after a parent leaves it or dies.)"

Eyes of the newborn coyote pups open in nine to fourteen days. They may leave their den the third week or not until the sixth week, and then they play and sleep in the sun, waiting for father and mother to return from the hunt. They will continue to nurse as long as eight weeks but will also eat regurgitated meat after five weeks. The parents returning from the hunt approach a den against the wind, using the wind to carry scents of danger to them (the coyote who was in farmer Babiak's rifle sights in Chesterfield, Massachusetts, was running with the wind at his back towards Babiak and thus did not smell him). If mother coyote senses her den is unsafe she will move the pups. Father coyote will help sometimes, and one male coyote was observed traveling forty miles in one night to move four pups to a den five miles away, according to Joe Van Wormer in his book, *The World of the Coyote*.

Pups are vulnerable to traps because they are curious and

because parents are unable to communicate the danger to them. Most of a coyote trapper's catch is from the young of the year. Pups who have survived the first autumn trapping season and seen their brothers caught will be wary and harder to catch. Pups stay with mother and father through the first winter and gain most of their ultimate weight by this first winter. When these nearly grown coyotes, perhaps six or eight of them, trot along with their mother and father, they constitute a formidable pack. It is not a pack in the sense of a wolf pack because the coyote group will break up eventually and not stay together to hunt moose as wolves do. This coyote pack is enough to make people apprehensive, people who are inclined to be wary of an animal that has evolved over eons with teeth to tear and eat flesh.

At some point, grown coyotes (western or eastern) have to leave their parents, define their own range by urinating and defecating on the perimeter of the range and then find mates by howling and by sniffing urine posts. The question is whether the father and mother have to drive off the bachelors and the spinsters.

Beaver drive off such malingering offspring. Tom Keefe of Pittsfield, Massachusetts, who studied beaver in the Tobiatic Game Preserve in Nova Scotia, explained what beaver parents do. Beaver normally have four kits each year. At one time they have eight young, four yearlings and the four newborn kits. They keep the yearlings for one more year, but when the female is ready to give birth to four more kits, which would raise the number of young to twelve, she drives out the four yearlings, fights them if necessary. The four oldest kits, now two years old, try to find a pond of their own, but if they go back to the home pond, bickering begins between the mother and these two-year-olds. The stress of this bickering affects the mother so that her egg is resorbed rather than dropping into the uterus to become a fetus. A form of birth control has been accomplished.

# – 5 –
# On the Hunt

Carl Ferguson was lying in the back of a truck beside a field in Garland, Maine, waiting for a coyote to show itself. It was a chilly night. Ferguson, a U.S. Fish and Wildlife biologist and trapper from Oregon, lay on his back on a wool blanket, listening for a signal from a lamb, the sound of a bell hung around its neck. It was a clear night, plenty of stars and a sliver of moon. He needed that light to be able to use the night scope on his .243 caliber rifle.

Ferguson was using rifle and night scope because traps he had set on Ernest Stone's fields had failed to get the adult coyotes that were killing Stone's sheep. The cylindrical device called the M-44 had also been used around Stone's land in Garland. The M-44 kills coyotes by injecting sodium cyanide down their throats. Frank Gramlich, Ferguson's superior, explains the M-44: "It does a hell of a lot less damage to other furbearers because only fox and dog and coyote will pull it with regularity. A deer could pull it but is not attracted to it." The M-44 cylinder is about the size of a large candle. It is stuck in the ground, and the end above ground is covered with a substance such as beef tallow. A scent is put over the tallow to attract a coyote which will tug on the cylinder until he triggers a spring that shoots fifteen grams of powdered cyanide into his mouth. This fifteen grams is enough to kill a forty-pound animal, the coyote, but not enough to kill a larger animal, a cow for instance. Gramlich likes the M-44 because it is so selective, whereas a leg-hold trap is not selective, will trap anything that puts its paw into it. Only Gramlich and Ferguson are authorized to use the M-44 in New England, and in Maine they use it only within fenced pasture, and not even there during bird-hunting season when dogs might enter pastures. Though the device has been effective in the west, it has done little in Maine. Gramlich and Ferguson had only one "pull" on the M-44 in 1980, and on that one "pull" there was no confirmed kill. Then, in April 1981, the M-44 worked for sure. A man in Jefferson had been losing sheep for three years, about ninety in all. The federal men trapped six coyotes in the area and then got a seventh coyote on an M-44 placed inside a fenced pasture close to a sheep kill. This seventh coyote was a nursing female and weighed thirty-nine pounds. Gramlich says: "There was no further lamb killing. We were very fortunate to get her. It probably would have been difficult to trap her because she was trap wise."

Gramlich says he had only about three complaints of coyote kills of livestock from 1965 to 1975. Since 1975, though, he has received about six calls a year and always about sheep. He hears of approximately 100 sheep a year reported killed by coyotes. Maine farmers were reimbursed by the state for the loss of 110 sheep to coyotes in 1979, a low figure compared to the Arizona Cattle Growers Association who reported they lost 1,544 sheep to coyotes in one twelve-month period, November 1974 to November 1975. Of course, Arizona has many more sheep than Maine, and many more coyotes.

Gramlich measures the success of his efforts in stopping the killing of sheep, not in the killing of coyotes. In one case the killing of sheep stopped after Gramlich and Ferguson put traps in an area and put up signs "Traps In Area." Because coyotes cannot read, the assumption is that dog owners were careful to keep their dogs leashed to avoid the traps, and the killing stopped because dogs had been killing the sheep, not coyotes. What proportion of sheep kills is done by dogs is not known for certain. Whatever that figure is, there is no doubt that coyotes kill many sheep, because sheep, especially lambs, are easy prey for coyotes and a convenient way for them to feed their pups.

Ferguson twice saw coyotes in a Vassalboro sheep field through his night scope. "I saw the pair come into the field to a carcass they had killed previously." Ferguson could not get a good shot at the pair but continued trapping and caught three pups 400 yards from the sheep pasture. It was October and the pups born that spring were getting big, twenty-three to thirty-two pounds. Though Ferguson had not caught the adults, he thinks by trapping the pups he may have put "pressure" on the adults to move. Another time at another farm, Ferguson trapped a pregnant coyote, the female of a sheep-killing pair he was after. Sheep killing stopped there, Ferguson says, because there were no pups to feed, but eventually a new pair of adults moved in, and the sheep killing resumed; eight lambs were killed in one week. The adult male whose pregnant mate had been trapped remained in the area but did not kill sheep himself. He had no pups to feed.

Ferguson resumed his story about lying in wait with a sniper rifle in the back of his pickup truck overlooking a sheep field in Garland. I tried to take down in my notebook what he said, word for word.

"The first night there was no activity, far as I could tell. There's a lot of eyestrain looking through that night scope. The second night I asked Mr. Stone [owner of the sheep] to put a bell on the one last lamb that was not killed. It was a pretty loud bell. You could hear it several hundred yards. I got set up before dark, about 9:00 P.M. I pulled the truck into where it overlooked the field and had the gun padded so it wouldn't make noise. I was inside the back of the pickup on a wool blanket, listening for the bell. The bell rang twenty after nine, and I rolled over and turned the battery switch on for the night scope. I could see the coyote trotting, stopping, looking back. That usually means not all is well, ten percent concern, probably too much noise from the kids playing a quarter mile up the road. Before I could get the cross hair on the coyote, the coyote had disappeared over a roll of land.

"I kept scanning the area and twenty minutes later I saw a coyote closer to me, roughly a hundred and fifty yards from me, trotting towards the sheep like it was going to the chow hall. There was no hesitating, no stopping, no sniffing, just a fast trot. You could tell it'd been to that chow hall before. Before I could get the sight on it, the coyote had disappeared in the terrain again. A minute later the sheep started streaming. I watched them. The sheep were bunched up in a line running. The bell on the lamb was jingling. The coyote outran the sheep, closed real quick on the last one in line, about a hundred-pound ewe. The ewe wheeled to the right. The coyote had her by the shoulder or by the neck. She dragged the coyote, and the coyote tried to put the brakes on, like a dog pulling a rug. The coyote probably released its hold for a minute to get a new grip. The sheep broke loose, and the coyote stopped an instant. I had the cross hair on it, and in this second I shot.

"The female coyote was four or five years old and was killed by a sixty-five-grain bullet fired from Ferguson's flat-shooting, high-velocity .243 caliber rifle. "I called it quits that night. I went back the next night and all was quiet. The bell on the lamb tinkled nicely, rhythmically, and I could picture the sheep grazing. If a coyote had been around, the bell would have gone 'clang-clang-clang.' That coyote and her mate were probably responsible for thirty-five sheep kills and her death ended the problem for the time being."

That coyote had been trying to bite the ewe in the neck.

Coyotes crush the skulls of lambs, kill them that way, but they grasp bigger sheep by the throat and hang on to the animal, the weight of the coyote and the motion of the attacked animal helping to tear the throat and cause death. Coyotes eat the intestines, the rump, front leg and shoulder. They eat that to begin with, perhaps as much as four pounds of meat. Later, the next day they will eat more, and if they are hungry and the carcass safe, untainted by human scent, they will consume most everything including bones. As with most everything said and written about the coyote, this is not always true. Sometimes they kill a sheep and leave it uneaten, a puzzle because coyotes are not supposed to expend energy without purpose.

A coyote will eat like a dog, gorging himself to the point of sickness, but if chased while full of meat, he can disgorge it and then run with an empty belly. How much meat can a coyote eat? One researcher says a wild coyote might eat as much as twelve pounds from a deer carcass in one day, though he would eat only about two pounds of meat day after day. I suppose it depends on how hungry the creature is. Gier writes that the appetite of the coyote is grossly exaggerated. His penned animals in Kansas subsisted on about fifteen ounces of meat a day, and an adult that ate more than two and two-tenths pounds of meat would not eat meat again that day. Gier allows that coyotes in the wild may eat more. Two other researchers estimate that an eastern coyote requires the equivalent of eight deer and 105 snowshoe hare a year to meet its minimum energy requirements. Much of the food value of those eight deer and 105 snowshoe hare a coyote must find in another form, in something easier to catch.

As I have said, coyotes survive because they will eat anything, including some distasteful things. Although they are supposed to be afraid of man, they have begged food from picnic benches in Yellowstone Park. The western coyote, according to writer J. Frank Dobie, eats: bugs, grasshoppers, rattlesnakes, other snakes, birds' eggs, turtle eggs, crickets, mice, other rodents, rice, wild berries, grapes, dates, peaches, prunes, carrots, sweet peppers, tomatoes, watermelons (coyotes especially like watermelons and some naturalists think they can pick ripe from unripe), plums, pumpkins, oranges, tangerines, bumblebees, flies, beaver (though a beaver is a big animal for a single coyote to handle in a fight, and New England wildlife people say coyotes prefer to avoid beaver), crayfish, any other kind of fish, centipedes, apples, acorns, pears, figs, apricots, cherries, cantaloupes, porcupines, ants, coyote meat, water birds, land birds including the turkey vulture, pine nuts, peanuts, grass, frogs, honey, green corn, bread, sugar and spice, snails, beetles, horned frogs, wildcat, house cat, skunk, armadillo and peccary.

They will also eat manure if it comes to that, and the afterbirth of cows and sheep. They also eat pine needles, perhaps to physic themselves.

Coyote habits are difficult to document because the animal is elusive, but what he eats is evident in the stomach of every dead coyote. Thus, there are many food studies. Ben Day of Vermont did a coyote food study in 1974 and found that the eastern coyote eats these things: woodchuck, snowshoe rabbit, white-tail deer, apples, grasses, red squirrel, grasshoppers, shrews, partridges, gauze dressing and a lunch wrapper. Day's study broke down the percentages of different foods in the stomachs of animals he studied, and found, for instance, that from January to March, coyotes were eating 36.3 percent deer meat, a fact deer hunters would seize upon as proof of the coyote's danger to the deer herd if the deer hunters did not know that many of those deer might have been carrion, deer killed by severe winter. Deer or beaver or rattlesnakes, all three may have been killed by something other than the coyote. However, coyotes *can* kill deer, beaver or rattlesnake, if they choose to expend the energy or take the chance. Coyotes, though, are not famed for their courage but rather for their cleverness. Joe Van Wormer tells this story in *The World of the Coyote*. He is quoting a park employee who saw the incident while on a hill overlooking the Firehole River in Yellowstone National Park, Wyoming. It is the best single story I have read of a coyote's stealth:

"Wild mallards were swimming about on the river . . . the ducks were feeding on underwater vegetation. As they ducked their heads to feed, the current carried them downstream until eventually they were beyond the underwater weed bed. . . . The coyote saw the mallards and immediately stopped. . . . He did not move so much as a hair until the ducks had floated past and were out of sight. . . . Then he trotted forward a few feet and stopped again as the birds left the water and flew back up the river to start their float downstream again. Once more the coyote remained absolutely still until the birds were out of sight. After three tries he reached the water's edge at the point where the ducks came by nearest to the shore.

". . . the coyote stretched out over the water and waited as the birds floated by. However, he was not in the right position and did not move as the feeding birds passed. After they were out of sight he changed his position, but it still did not suit him. He was within a foot or so of the ducks each time they passed, but they paid no attention to the coyote. Finally, after about six attempts, the coyote was perfectly located. As a big greenheaded drake floated under the coyote, he opened his mouth and closed it on the mallard's head. . . ."

Coyotes hunt by sight if they can, something they learned on the plains. A rabbit cannot hide very well aboveground on the plains, and the coyote will see him before it hears him. The eastern coyote does not often hunt on open land and uses his ears to hear snowshoe hare in the thick softwood stands of New England, and when the wind obliterates sound of hare in the leaves, the coyote will use his nose. He is a resourceful hunter and prefers meat to grain. It is easier for him to kill a lamb than a sheep and easier to kill a 100-pound sheep than a deer. The deer is a wild animal, and is fairly equipped to defend itself against one coyote if conditions do not favor the coyote. Maine biologist Henry Hilton writes of an observation made by game warden Rodney Sirois on the St. John River in summer. "The coyote chased a doe out of shallow water onto the river bank, but she turned suddenly and ran back into three feet of water and faced the attacking coyote. At this water depth the coyote was forced to swim, and it discontinued the attack, swam to shore and after watching for several minutes walked away into the woods. The deer remained vigilant in the water for more than thirty minutes before it ran into the woods on the opposite shore." One coyote probably does not kill a healthy deer, but a pair of coyotes can kill a healthy deer, especially in winter. When snow is soft and deep, the long-legged deer, his belly a foot and a half off the ground, has an advantage, but when crust is on the snow, coyotes can run on top, the deer plunges through the crust with each step, and the coyotes win, biting at the deer's legs until the deer is weakened enough so the coyotes can bring it down.

A trapper in Maine told me he counted nine deer carcasses along the Dead River one winter day. He knew they were killed by coyotes because coyotes eat through the ribs first. I told this story to Henry Laramie, the New Hampshire wildlife biologist, and he wanted to know what winter it was, thought it was probably a severe winter and that the deer died of cold and hunger or were so weakened that they were easy prey. If he had been there on the Dead River he would have measured the fat content of the deer bone marrow. Laramie says:

"When we walk through the woods and find a dead deer in winter, one of the first things we do is to take the femur, the bone from the hipsocket to what corresponds to our knees. When a deer starts using its fat reserve, it first uses the fat stored under the skin and in body cavities, around the kidneys for instance. Bone marrow fat is the last fat used, so the standard practice is to break the femur. The deer was in top condition when the bone marrow inside the femur looks like suet, solid white or pinkish. When you go to bend it, it is solid and cracks. Then the next step down is when you can bend the marrow; then, the next step down in the condition of the deer is when you squeeze the marrow and get just a fatty mush between your fingers. Next, that fatty mush will just be oily. The deer was really in poor condition when you squeeze the marrow and it collapses in your fingers, is almost watery rather than oily. What you're doing is visually measuring the fat content. So you break the femur and can roughly gauge the condition of the deer when it died. If the deer was in good condition, you'd be more alarmed about predation. If the condition was poor, the deer probably would have died anyway, from malnutrition.

"We get a lot of flack about coyotes killing deer. We heard the coyotes killed nineteen deer in Pittsburg [a town in far northern New Hampshire]. When anybody can show me nineteen dead deer in New Hampshire, I'll go anywhere to see 'em. I went up in a state vehicle, had a snowmachine in the back. And we went off to see nineteen deer killed by coyotes. They showed me a deer on the shore of Lake Francis, and I had no disagreement with that. And one on Lake Francis that I wouldn't argue with. Then they showed me blood stains in the woods. There was no body. We dug in the snow, but there was no carcass. The next site was similar [blood but no body]. Somebody said a bleeding deer had run down a snowmobile trail. Something didn't look right about that, and after a while it became evident to me that something had leaked out of a snow vehicle, dye or paint. Whatever it was, it wasn't blood. Then we saw ravens circling and found a doe that had been killed by coyotes. I circled the kill and found where the deer had entered the clearing running, coyotes on her track. I backtracked a ways and from what I could see written out in the snow, coyotes killed that deer. You can see where coyotes made contact, got the deer to bleeding. There was a female coyote with three pups in that area, but I don't remember how many coyotes were on that kill."

Of the nineteen deer reported killed by coyotes in Pittsburg, Laramie found three deer killed by coyotes and one other deer probably killed by coyotes. There may have been one or two more deer killed by coyotes in Pittsburg, deer that Laramie could not get to, but the point of the story remains. Coyotes get blamed for everything. Laramie says:

"The day before Christmas last year [1979] we were having a party [in the New Hampshire Fish and Game Department headquarters in Concord] and a guy walked off the street and said he knew where there were ten dead deer near here.

"I said, 'Let's go.'

"He said, 'You mean now?'

"'Yes.'

"'Well, I don't know where all ten are.'

"There's so much word of mouth reports and miscalculations . . . I will never forget my first legislative hearing. It was in the 1950s, and I was fresh out of school, an idealist. The hearing was to repeal the bobcat bounty, and I heard cat hunters tell of deer being killed by bobcats. I made the mistake of saying when I got up to speak 'I don't know how you can separate fact from fiction from what you've heard here,' and the wise old chairman said: 'Young fellow, that's our job.'"

Deer hunters are like golfers or fishermen or horse bettors. They tell stories based on some part of a truth that become just stories in the telling. I came upon a deer hunter by chance in the kitchen of a farmer's house in New Hampshire. The hunter had got his deer that year, 218 pounds, and said all the deer were fat that year, 1980, because the deer were "feeding acorns." He shot his deer back of his house. The deer had come up behind two trees. The hunter felt wind flowing past his head toward the deer and thought for sure the deer would make a dash, but he only walked out from behind the two trees, and the hunter shot him in the neck, killing him. I believed this story but not the story about the time he shot a deer, started toward it and found another hunter beside the deer about to dispatch it with buckshot. "I wouldn't do that, mister, or you might get a faceful of mud, and I swung my rifle. . . ." I told this hunter I was interested in coyotes, and he said he saw lots of coyote manure in the fields, all of it full of deer hair, proof to him that coyotes were killing deer. I do not know if he could tell rabbit hair from deer hair or would separate coyote scat in his fingers to try to see it.

Dogs kill more deer than coyotes in New England. The Vermont Fish and Game Department has a one-page sheet titled "Your Dog Doesn't Chase Deer, But . . . ?" On one side of the sheet are pictures of dead and dying deer. On the other side is a story: Brownie watched the kids board the schoolbus then went hunting with another neighborhood dog. The two dogs found a young buck who had lost his forked antlers and could defend himself only with his front hoofs.

"Quite often they could chase a deer for an hour or more and lose it . . . a lot of times the deer wouldn't survive. . . . After running and struggling through the snow to the point of exhaustion, they will lie down and succumb to pneumonia. A bloody foam throughout the lungs is used as an indicator of this. . . . But today, the dogs had not lost the trail. Brownie and the small, black dog circled the buck several times. . . . Caution was no longer a factor as the scent of blood from the gaping hole [the dogs had] torn in the buck's rear sparked their instincts . . . the dogs dodged [the buck's hoofs] and kept working around the deer, one at the head and the other rushing in from the rear. Mouthfuls of hair soon ringed the deer's last stand. Finally, . . . Brownie feinted to one side and with a rush jumped squarely against the bucks' shoulder, knocking him down. It was the end of the chase . . . and the dogs soon left it to die. . . . Both dogs would be home by noon. . . . The kids would play with Brownie on the living room floor that evening, and he would have a good appetite. No one could ask for a better family pet."

I saw a dog chasing a deer in Buckfield, Massachusetts, in

early winter, about eight inches of powder snow on the ground. I had been talking that morning to dairy farmers in the neighboring town of Ashfield about their loss of silage corn to bears. These farmers told me of another farmer who had also had losses to bears, and I was slowing down on the road to read the name on a mailbox when I saw the deer running right towards my car. The large doe was having no trouble running in that soft snow, but the beagle was struggling on short legs, its belly in the snow. I thought of the opening lines of " The Lady of the Lake," a verse memorized by schoolboys to explain iambic tetrameter.

> *The stag at eve had drunk his fill*
> *Where danced the moon on Monan's rill.*

It was not eve but precisely noon; however, the name on the mailbox beside the road was Walter Scott.

The hunting range of domestic dogs is limited by the distance from their feed bowls. Coyotes normally stay within a certain home area to hunt, also, but the size of their home area increases where game is scarce. Range of the white-tailed deer is determined by edible vegetation and weather. Northern New England is the upper limit of range of the white-tailed deer, but because of favorable conditions deer herds increased in the 1950s and 1960s. Good hunters could take their pick of a good specimen. Poachers could take several deer. Deer liked the habitat, old farms gone to brush, and they proliferated, but in the 1970s these farms were growing from brush into woods. The edge effect declined and so did the deer, because of the habitat and severe winters. Something had to take the blame, something more obvious. The coyote was a logical choice. Henry Hilton of Maine says big populations of coyotes and deer can coexist in an area. "[But] if there is an area where deer are concentrated and there is crusty snow, there could be some waste killing by coyotes. It could happen, but it would not really be wasted. Eighty percent of the critters in the Maine woods eat carrion, and if you find a deer in spring you would see evidence of weasels, fisher, any number of birds—ravens, hawks, owls—coyotes and of foxes who were not in on the kill and multitudes of rodents and insects."

Coyotes may test a deer, make a rush at him. If the deer is healthy, has strength and shows fight, the coyotes may try to find something else. This is conjecture. I found no one who had witnessed such an encounter. Hilton, who studied the coyote in the big woods of northwestern Maine, saw evidence that coyotes traveled alone in December but were likely to hunt with another coyote by January and February, and by March he commonly saw where three or four animals were traveling together. He writes that single coyotes seldom chase deer; paired coyotes pursued deer more often and successfully killed deer in 79 percent of pursuits. He writes this account: "Interpretation of sign at one kill suggested that several coyotes met a single male deer and made physical contact within 25 yards after beginning the pursuit. The pursuit continued for 500 yards with frequent attacks indicated by the presence of deer skin and hair along the route. The deer was killed at the bottom of a steep bank at the edge of the Big Black River; it was nine and a half years old (determined by tooth sectioning). . . ."

Deer prefer open areas of the woods, at least in good weather, though they are easier prey to coyotes there than in deep woods because if the contest is endurance and speed on open ground, the coyotes will win. In severe cold and deep snow, deer seek cover in hemlocks and other softwood trees. Moose, though, do well in the large clear-cut areas because the moose can wade through deep snow and is an animal of the north woods whereas the deer is not. If there is evidence of moose in coyote scats, the moose is assumed to have died without the effort of coyotes. Moose are too strong for the coyote, but much farther north the moose is hunted by the timber wolf. Several wolves hunting moose constitute a wolf pack. Several coyotes, parents and their nearly full-grown pups, chasing a deer are not considered a coyote pack, not strictly speaking, a distinction more obvious to wildlife students than to deer hunters.

There were few deer in New England when the forest went right down to the beach, before colonists first burned back the woods to make farmland and then went to work farming the forest for lumber and charcoal. Deer do not flourish in the deep forest; the branch tips they eat are too far up the trunk of a mature tree. As the colonists made clearings in the forest, the deer proliferated, eating the tips of saplings that grow in new clearings, and in the 1800s the deer population of New England grew until the cutting of the forest had taken 70 or 80 percent of the trees. There was not enough cover for deer, and they declined to the extent that Vermont enacted a law in 1865 to prohibit deer hunting.

The Erie Canal and the railroads saved the deer because the canal and the railroads opened up the west, enabled farmers to ship their goods to market, and the people of New England who wanted good farmland went where the good land was, to Ohio. The forest began to grow back, and now 70 or 75 percent of New England has grown back into forest. Most of this forest is broken by small farms, though the farm be only a cow and chickens and the man works in a paper mill, his wife drives a schoolbus in the morning and works at the town diner in the afternoon. These clearings make a grand checkerboard of clearing and woods, and the deer can reach the choice food at the edge of the clearings as can smaller game, the snowshoe hare. The coyote lives in the deep woods of the White Mountain National Forest, and in the great woods of Aroostook, especially along the rivers there, the St. John, the Allagash, the Big Black; but the coyote prefers the edge, where the woods meet the clearing.

A coyote came out of the woods into a pasture in Sudbury, Vermont, and was jumping into the air and snapping his jaws. The farmer who witnessed this thought the animal was rabid and shot it. The coyote was not rabid but was hunting. Its stomach was full of red-legged grasshoppers. Coyotes chase grasshoppers for food and for the fun of it. If the coyote is smart enough to conserve his energy, he should not expend it on grasshoppers and probably doesn't, not often.

A hungry coyote is not discriminating and will eat porcupine, an animal whose quills repel most animals most of the time, though a starving bobcat will attack a porcupine out of desperation. A young biologist showed me a shack on a road in Washington County, Maine, pointed to the spot where a bobcat had stood poised at the foundation of the shack, so intent on waiting for the resident porcupine to come out that a hunter had time to spot the cat, drive back down the road and return to shoot it. I heard this story only because that bobcat was fitted with a radio collar, and the hunter reported his kill to a biologist. The bobcat would have absorbed some pain had he caught the porcupine because the porcupine's coat contains as many as thirty thousand quills. Godin (in *Wild Mammals of New England*) describes how a porcupine defends itself:

"A cornered porcupine erects its quills, tucks its head between its front legs or under a protective object, turns its rear to the adversary, and rapidly swings its tail or makes a rolling lunge of the body. Once a quill is imbedded it absorbs moisture and expands slightly. Contractions of the victim's muscles engage the tips of the scales and draw the quill in deeper. A quill or quill fragment may travel at a rate of an inch per day, causing intense suffering, and may reach the heart, arteries, or lungs and cause death. Some quills travel back out through the skin, pass out in the droppings, come to rest against bone or become absorbed or encapsulated."

Coyotes in New England eat porcupines, suffering the consequences. It probably takes a pair of coyotes to kill a porcupine because the porcupine could keep turning his protected back at one coyote. A pair of coyotes work together, one from each side of the porcupine, repeatedly charging. Each time the porcupine turns its protected rear towards the charge until it tires of these feinted attacks and does not react. Then one coyote will get a paw under the porcupine's chin and flip it onto its back. The belly of a porcupine is unprotected, and that is what the coyotes eat. Not far from the shack where the bobcat was hunting the porcupine, a group of coyotes killed a porcupine and chewed out its insides, leaving the skin and the quills.

Fishers are not much bothered by porcupine quills and eat porcupines regularly; they are the only animal known to do so. Porcupine quills do enter the fisher's body but apparently do not fester there, and most quills pass through in the feces. Fishers are called fishercats many places in New England, though they are not of the cat family but are weasels. This animal returned to New England in recent years, its numbers growing with the new forest, an animal new to people who often prefixed the adjective fierce to it like damn before Yankee. People were frightened. New Hampshire biologist Laramie told me there were articles in local papers telling of fisher ferocity.

"Trappers themselves thought the fisher was the scourge of the woods. There were reports of horses being attacked and dogs. People would see fisher in their yard and be afraid to let kids out. The fisher still has a reputation for killing house cats. There may be more truth to that than most other stories, but I don't know how much of it is true.

"The fisher is really docile with man. I personally touched on the nose of twenty-five wild-trapped fisher and never got bit. We were trading fishers for turkeys with West Virginia. I did it slowly of course [touching their noses through a cage]. I've taken fisher out of the woods, put them in the back of a station wagon and had one get loose, get out on my lap. . . . I've fed them hot dogs in my kitchen in a cage, then stratch 'em up

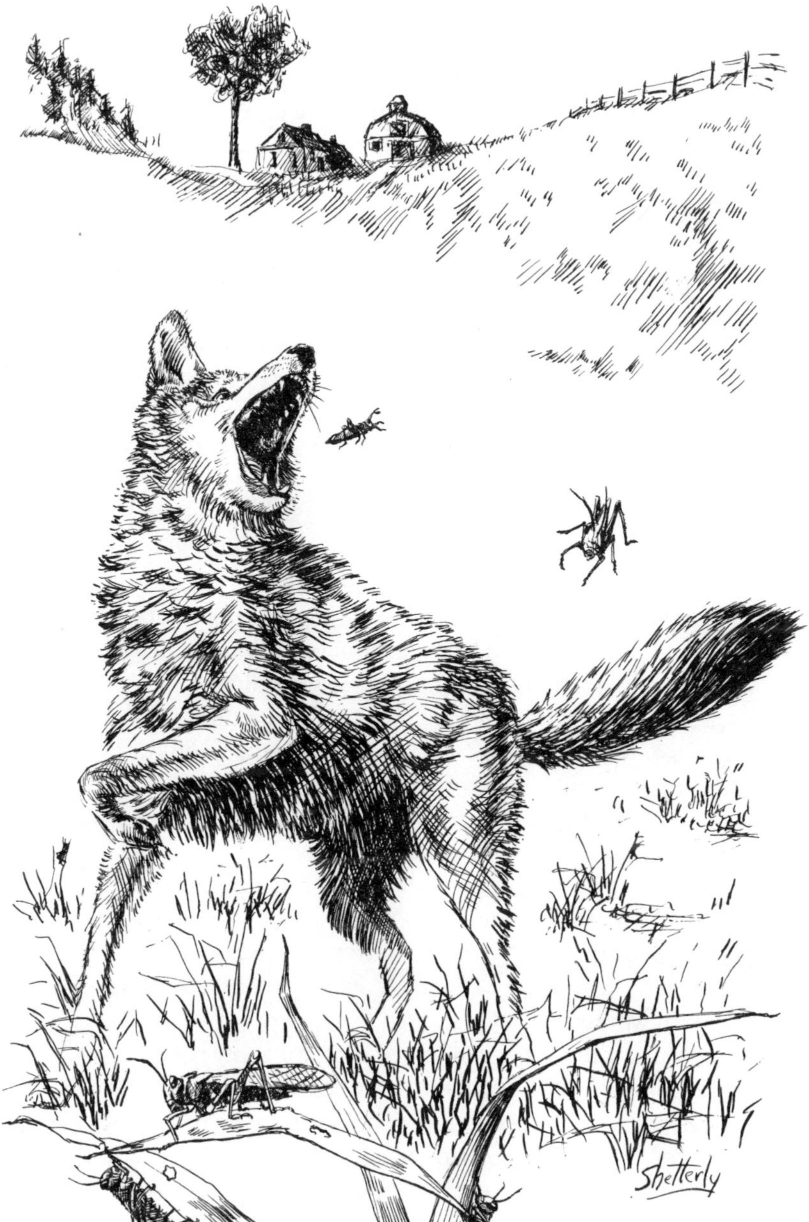
Shetterly

under the chin. So they are not that ferocious. But if you keep a fisher a week, then put your hand in the cage, something else might happen because they become accustomed to man." They might bite your finger off.

Coyotes, too, are often docile when trapped and even later when they are still uncertain of their status with humans. Once they overcome this uncertainty, like the coyotes of Los Angeles, coyotes become less docile, more dangerous. Black bears of New England were considered timid creatures (unless provoked) until recent years when the advent of the backpacker and hiker of the Appalachian Trail has made the black bear more accustomed to man, less afraid and thus more dangerous.

Reputations are easily won and long lasting. The fisher is a good fighter but where the fisher won his reputation for extraordinary ferocity is uncertain; his reputed size is a matter only of ignorance. A suburban Boston newspaper in December 1980 described the fisher as "a big black animal," though a male fisher weighs only about ten pounds, a record animal only twenty pounds. I saw a female fisher caught in a trap near the town of Carthage, Maine. She moved away from me as I walked toward her, not cowering exactly, but her eyes were appealing for solace. I would have let her go, but I can make a living with words and do not have to work in the woods. The trapper I was with shot her humanely enough, with a rifle bullet to the brain. Her pelt was worth about $100 to him, a day's expenses plus a day's pay. In the 1930s when overtrapping nearly extinguished the fisher, a fisher pelt was worth about $90, seven weeks' pay for a mill worker.

Coyotes do not normally eat fisher, probably because fisher can escape by climbing trees or because they fight fiercely enough to dissuade a coyote which prefers easier prey. Coyotes do not normally eat raccoon, either, because the raccoon, like the fisher, can escape up a tree. One trapper I met in 1980 thought coyotes were eating all the 'coon pups before they could mature because he had not been able to trap many 'coon in his area. His view was Aristotelian, based on what he experienced or could see and in disregard of the fact that 31,480 'coon were trapped or shot in Maine in 1979. Maybe disease killed all the 'coons in the woods where that trapper worked. Coyotes are a convenient explanation for many things, and the hunter and trapper are loath to accept other reasons.

Coyotes and fox compete for the same food, and the coyote may be shifting the fox out of its niche as the main predator in certain areas. This is not the same thing as saying the coyote eats the fox. Nothing eats fox, one trapper told me. Often this trapper has skinned a fox he has trapped and thrown the carcass in the woods, returning several days later to find the carcass still there uneaten. Even so, he is not quite correct. Crow or raven eat flesh of the fox, but in summer at least a coyote might avoid fox meat because the carnivorous coyote prefers eating herbivores, rabbits for instance. Perhaps coyotes feel towards fox as some humans regard sea ducks. Sea ducks feed on fish, taste of fish and not as good as ducks that eat grain. Whatever the reason, fox and fisher are not coyote prey, probably, and neither are beaver, not usually.

Beavers weigh thirty to sixty pounds, about the range of weight of the coyote. They have large teeth and are strong animals, the largest rodent in America. Wildlife people I talked to think coyotes rarely attack beaver, but trappers are apt to think coyotes eat beaver kits when they can catch them on land, an idea they get because coyote tracks are often seen near beaver dams. If the coyotes do not eat the beaver, why do they lie in wait for them? Perhaps they are trying to figure out a way to kill the beaver without getting mauled themselves. Beaver is often found in coyotes' scats, but much of this is carrion, skinned beaver carcasses discarded by trappers. This would not explain beaver found in summer scat of the coyote. Henry Hilton writes: "Two wardens . . . flying over the St. John River in early spring, located a freshly killed adult beaver on the ice. There was a blood trail from a hole where the beaver was attacked, and evidence of considerable struggling at the scene of the kill. Several trappers in western Maine have reported similar incidents, but to my knowledge no one has actually observed such an attack."

I know a beaver trapper in western Maine, Gordon Berry. I thought he might have first-hand knowledge of coyotes killing beaver and called him in West Forks, Maine, where he runs a general store. West Forks is a woods town located where the Kennebec joins the Dead River and is not far from the Quebec border. Gordon Berry and his friend, a logger, took me beaver trapping a few winters ago on a clear and cold January day. It had snowed the night before, about a foot of powder, and the woods were quiet, the birds still in cover from the night's storm, and I could hear nothing except the hum of wind in the trees, a sound like faraway highway traffic. It was beautiful there in the woods, and eerie; I would have been uncomfortable alone there.

Berry and his friend the logger carried lengths of poplar to bait their beaver traps. We traveled on snowmachines, one for each of us, and the two West Forks boys made a trail as they went, crashing through brush when they left game paths and logging tracks to reach the flowages where they had set their traps on a previous day. We drove the woods all morning, rebaiting traps, stopping at noon to eat sandwiches on a snow-covered pond where there was not a single animal track. Canadian jays would come near enough to eat thrown bread crumbs, they told me, but this day there was no sound of a bird and not a single animal track on that pond.

Trappers used to snowshoe into these remote ponds, but snowmachines are faster, if less certain. The machines kept breaking down and being fixed with a new spark plug or a lungful of air blown through a fuel line; but one machine failed completely, and when a second machine balked I had thoughts of spending a night in the woods. Berry said not to worry. He had lots of matches to build a fire and then he showed me the compass pinned to the collar of his wool shirt, and a second compass pinned to the collar of an inner wool shirt. They kept their snowmachine going somehow, rode double on it while I followed in a new machine, falling from it two or three times trying to make it jump rills as they had done ahead of me. We reached the woods road where their pickup trucks were in darkness, only two beaver to show for the day's work. Beaver trapping is more for tradition than for profit for most Maine trappers, though if the price of beaver fur goes up, men will trap more, go harder at it, they would say.

That night we drank beer at Marshall's Hotel. Berry told me, tactfully enough, that I could have kept my posterior warmer if I had worn wool pants, that one always wears wool pants when going into the winter woods, because wool has warmth even when wet, and he told me my snowmachine would not have stalled at all if I ran it fast enough to keep the spark plugs from fouling. I learned those two things at least on that trip, and I remembered Berry had been unsuccessful at trapping coyotes, had only caught traces of hair. I wondered if he had learned how to catch coyotes and if he knew coyote were killing beaver. The telephone ring sounded hollow up there in West Forks, old equipment.

Berry had still not caught a coyote, had not gone after them real hard, either, but he and his trapping partner had caught sixty-eight beaver the season of 1981, restricted in the West Forks area to just the month of January. Berry had not witnessed a coyote killing a beaver but is certain they had killed many beaver. "I never seen a coyote on a beaver but come on a pile of scat and checked a number of them and they're full of beaver hair. You can just tell beaver hair after you seen beaver all your life. In October the beaver get out sixty or seventy feet from water. That's when beaver gets feed [to store for winter]. When beaver get away from the lodge, that's when coyotes get them."

The price of beaver has not been good the last six or eight years with the exception of the 1980 season when a large, very good pelt was worth $75. In 1981 the price was back to about $43 for the top pelts. Berry and his trapping partner Colin Bates got to split about $2,500 for their work in the January woods. They saw lots of coyote sign.

"I'm not kidding, ninety, ninety-five percent of the time you'd find coyote tracks all over the smoke holes [holes in the snow leading down through ice to the beaver lodge]. Coyotes try to dig at the smoke hole. Course, they can't get in, but they can smell 'em and run all over [the top of the lodge]. The beaver are froze in [and safe under the ice]." Berry has left skinned beaver carcass in the woods, returning a day or two later to see coyote tracks and the carcass half eaten. He has no doubt coyotes are killing beavers. The proof is in October when there are no trappers discarding beaver carcasses, and the evidence is in the scat.

# – 6 –
# Sign of the Lion

Ashland is an Aroostook County town just beyond the potato country and on the edge of the big woods. I stopped there in early summer of 1979 in search of material for a story I was writing called "Five Faces of Maine." Maine is a big place but has no wilderness, not technically, because wilderness is where man has left no sign, and paper company roads, gravel highways, cross the Maine woods. Still, twenty feet off one of these roads is wilderness, or what city people would call wilderness. A paper company timber cruiser, a man who searches for good wood, left his vehicle one winter and walked off the road. There was snow in the ground, searchers found tracks, but the tracks ended at a brook, and his body was never found.

I was talking of this and other tales with a wildlife biologist and a game warden I found at the Ashland station when I saw a poster on the wall, a poster headed with the word cougar or panther, I forget which. The poster asked people to report sightings of the cougar. This was the stuff of a story. The biologist shrugged. He would receive reports of sightings, but inspections usually turned up tracks of a fisher, an animal one-tenth the size of a cougar. He was dubious. The game warden was young and not dubious about cougars; he was skeptical. But I wonder. The cougar, the mountain lion, lived in New England once. Unlike the coyote, it did not have to migrate one thousand, two thousand miles to get to New England. There is a lot of forest in northwest Connecticut, western Massachusetts, Vermont, New Hampshire and Maine, enough trees and rocks and ridges to provide cover for every foot soldier in the Russian army. There should be cover enough for mountain lions, if even only for a few.

Wytopitlock is a small place in Maine where southern Aroostook and western Washington Counties meet. It is an island in the forest and is not far from New Brunswick. There is no town policeman. The 250 or so people who live along Route 171 really live in Drew and Reed Plantations because there is no town of Wytopitlock, though the U.S. Post Office has that name. People in Wytopitlock think the place was named after an Indian called Pitlock. He died, and when his widow used to walk the railroad track to the crossroads to buy food, people said, "Here comes the widow Pitlock," and thus the name. Etymologists disagree, say Wytopitlock in the Indian language meant the place where "the river is broad and there are no trees on its banks except alders." I like the widow Pitlock story better. I went first to Wytopitlock in search of the mountain lion, not because it has the sound of faraway Timbuktu, but because someone had seen a lion there.

Many people in New England have seen mountain lions, but not all of them are willing to talk about it. Rita Potter came to Wytopitlock from England as a bride and did not realize the mountain lion was Maine's equivalent of Big Foot or the Abominable Snowman. Twice in 1978 she saw the lion cross Route 171, the first time in the morning, the second time in the afternoon eight or ten months later, each time telling her husband, Jim Potter, a logger. In the fall of 1979 she saw the animal for a third time. She told me in her kitchen about the lion and then took me down a road in the woods and showed me the place.

Rita Potter had been hauling firewood that fall day in 1979, loading wood her husband was cutting, taking it to their home to unload, then hurrying back for more. She was traveling in a loaded Luv pickup truck at thirty or forty miles an hour on the dirt road at about 4:00 P.M., driving into the sun, when the lion ran out of an old logging track onto the road. She hit the brake pedal instinctively. The lion swerved from his probable course across the road and ran instead up the road in front of the truck, his fur rippling from the wind he was creating, his rich, dark brown color showing in the sun, his body outstretched in full running stride, his strangely long tail only two lengths of a small pickup truck from Rita Potter's eyes. She had been driving in fourth gear when she braked. Now she rammed the gear level down into third speed and roared the engine to try to keep up with the running creature. "Oh, the feeling of power of the animal you got." The lion was in front of her for one-tenth of a mile, running up an incline too fast for the truck to close on him before he sprang off the road and into the woods. She found one paw mark in a soft place in the road but did not know enough to try to preserve it and later obliterated it with her truck. She drew a picture for her husband of an animal with a long tail that did not taper at the end. Jim Potter had been driving on that same road eighteen years earlier with his wife, had glimpsed a lion and was disappointed that Rita did not also see it. When Rita drew the picture, her husband said, "That's a cougar," and reminded her of his sighting eighteen years before.

Rita also showed her drawing to Blair Yeoman whose farm is on that woods road not far from where Rita saw the lion. Yeoman told her: "That must be the cougar who's leaving tracks around here." She took me to Yeoman's house, but he was not home. We found him a few hundred yards down the road, stooped in a field picking strawberries. He does not farm his place any more. Few people farm in Wytopitlock any more.

Some hippies tried and failed, but Yeoman doesn't blame them for failing because not even the natives could make farms profitable on this thin soil so far north, so far from markets, where the growing season is too short for much except potatoes and hay. His own place was going back to trees. Softwoods, fir and spruce, were beginning to retake the field where he was picking wild strawberries. He used to cut in the woods, used to trap. He has seen the sign of the lion in the snow three or four times over the years, the paw mark and length of stride indicating a cat greater than any he has seen. Ancestors told him of hearing lions screaming in the night woods; the old folks believed lions followed behind humans as if tracking them. Yeoman has not seen the lion, only the tracks, and he believes Rita's story. Wildlife biologists have heard many such stories and remain unconvinced. Biologists are not believers; they are scientists and need documentation, a good photograph, a bit of hair, a drop of blood, a big scat.

Blair Yeoman stood there beside his wild strawberries and said biologists wanted proof when he and others in Wytopitlock said spray to kill the spruce budworm was killing other life in the woods. Yeoman said he could not provide bodies of dead birds and bees but thought it should be proof enough that there were fewer birds in the air and no bees at all. People in Wytopitlock had been seeing coyotes many years before wildlife officials acknowledged that the animal had come to Maine. I believe the mountain lion lives in Wytopitlock because I want to believe, but if I had seen a lion run across the road while we were talking of him, I would not have believed what my eyes saw. Yeoman said if a lion walked by right then he wouldn't believe it, either.

My chances of seeing a lion are almost nil. If the lion exists only in the eye of imaginative people, as most experts believe, my chances are absolutely nil. The fun of it is in the quest. I did see a pair of healthy lions, western mountain lions, at the

Pawtucket, Rhode Island, zoo. The male lay on a bench, his mate on the concrete floor below him. The Pawtucket zoo is an old zoo, not very big, and I had no trouble finding the zookeeper, only a small adventure. I walked into the main building, entered the first room I came upon, saw no one there and looked down to see a tiger lying in a big box. "My God, there's a tiger!" I said to myself. Maybe I said the words aloud. I knew the zoo was shipping some of its cats, and I thought this tiger had been drugged and left unattended for a moment. I leaned towards the box and looked at the tiger's great chest, saw it moving almost imperceptibly to draw breath. Later that morning I learned the tiger was being shipped to Boston for a necropsy. It had been dead and frozen for months.

The eastern lion is not as grand an animal as a tiger, but it is a big cat, the biggest in North America except for the jaguar of the tropics. A male lion may be six feet long plus a tail nearly three feet long, nine feet altogether, and weigh up to 220 pounds, though other lions would be smaller. Godin describes their color:

"The coloration above is dull, dark reddish brown, somewhat darker from the top of the head to the base of the tail . . . shoulders and flanks are paler, and the underparts are dull whitish or reddish white . . . ."

I heard of a farmer near Butternut Mountain, Vermont, who had seen a lion. I spoke to him in his barnyard. He sat on his tractor during our conversation and described the animal he had seen years earlier. He saw it moving in the woods beside a field, a black panther. Though it is certain that mountain lions lived in that farmer's country and might still live there, there is no record of a black lion in North America. But if that is what the fellow saw, it was not my place to tell him there was no such thing.

There are few specimens from Maine to prove what color they were. The last known specimen was trapped in Somerset County, Maine, in 1938 and was brown. A pair of lions was believed to have existed in the early 1920s in Coos County, northern New Hampshire. Vermont's last known lion was shot in Barnard, November 24, 1881, a shotgun round breaking its foreleg at close range, a rifle shot to the head killing it. The lion weighed 181½ pounds and now stands stuffed in a Montpelier museum. The last mountain lion known to have been killed in Massachusetts was in 1858. The eastern mountain lion is considered extirpated in New England, meaning it no longer exists in a certain place. Many mountain lions exist in the west and in South America, so the general species is not extinct, and the subspecies eastern mountain lion may not be extinct either.

People who have seen mountain lions fear ridicule. Yet seeing is believing. Richard B. Stetson saw a lion about 1956 and sent a letter to New Hampshire wildlife biologist Helenette Silver in Concord, a letter dated November 2, 1962:

"About six years ago I bought some acreage at the top of Federal Hill in Milford, N.H., and started to build a house . . . about four years ago I was diligently nailing some trim on the edge of the roof . . . when I heard the blue jays in the woods near the house making a lot of commotion. Looking towards the woods, I was astounded to see a very large cat, complete with a long tail, standing on my stone wall, looking at me. My youngest son, Frank, was at the other end of the house, and I called to him to come and climb the ladder. When asked what he saw there, he replied, 'A great big cat.' The cat looked at us for what seemed a minute or more, walked leisurely along the top of the stone wall, looked again, and then bounded off the other side into the woods. After waiting for about five minutes I grabbed a short length of 2" by 4" for a cudgel, and went up to the wall, looking for footprints. Unfortunately it was all mossy where he left, and I could find no tangible evidence in the way of prints.

"I am an electronic engineer . . . but am interested in nature, and that night I looked up cats in the encyclopedia . . . the only cat I could find that looked like it was a Rocky

Mountain lion, and the book said that they had been extinct in the east for many years. I mentioned the incident to a couple of neighbors, but didn't realize that I was establishing a reputation as the village idiot until one of their children looked me straight in the eye and said, 'Mr. Stetson, you didn't see no mountain lion.' After that I mentioned it only to close friends.

"About two months later the children were watching 'Lassie' on TV and my youngest son called to me to come see 'our cat' on TV. Sure enough, there was a smaller version of the cat that had been on our wall, and in the program they called it a cougar. . . .

"Let me explain again that this was not a shadowy figure in the underbrush or a figure of the imagination seen at dusk, or during the mists of early morning. It was about ten o'clock, on a beautiful, clear, summer Saturday morning. The distance from the house to the stone wall is about 100 feet, and there are no trees or brush intervening. The cat seemed to have no fear of me, and stood broadside on the stone wall watching me. Even when I called my son in a moderate voice, and talked to him, the cat did not seem concerned. He walked at least fifteen feet along the wall before he left it.

". . . Although an estimate of his overall length at this time might be colored by imagination, I seem to remember that he was six or seven feet long broadside.

". . . I might point out that I have never taken a drink in my life, am not subject to hallucinations, nor was the sun particularly hot that day. Neither do I invent tall tales, and, although I am as prone as the next person to stretch the facts a little to make a story sound good, in this case I have done my utmost to set down the exact facts. . . ."

Stetson wrote that the lion he saw was not textbook color tawny but yellowish gray. Mrs. Silver in her reply to Stetson wrote she didn't care if it was pink-striped. If it weighed over seventy-five pounds, had a long tail and was indisputably a cat, then she would accept it as a lion. She told me the same thing when I talked to her in her home near Concord in 1981, and she told me of an old trapper in the town of Henniker who, about fifteen years previously, had "described what no one else even mentioned, the almost frown-like lines around the eyes. It was awfully hard *not* to believe him." And she told me about the woman who called her to report a lion sighting.

"What color was it?" she asked the woman.

"Deer color. I was in the blueberries and saw it the other side of a bush."

"Is the place sand, have open spaces?"

"Yes."

"Well, all right. Go back and if you find tracks, call me." (The woman did find tracks and did call Mrs. Silver.)

Mrs. Silver: "I loaded up a camera and water and plaster of paris [to make a cast of the tracks] and when I got there it was deer tracks," Mrs. Silver said, disgust in her voice.

Joseph Wiley, the New Hampshire wildlife biologist who told me of coyotes living in Concord, New Hampshire, used to work in the Adirondacks and was deer hunting there early one morning and had stopped to rest against a tree. He heard a noise coming from behind a log twenty yards away. "I was convinced it was a bear. I am a very careful hunter, but I sighted the rifle at it—and it was a porcupine. If it had gone away quickly I might still think I had seen a bear." Wiley thinks people, even trained people, see what they want to see. Wiley's colleague Henry Laramie tells this story: Laramie was driving through woods "and as I went by a path, on a knoll stood an animal. 'My God, Tom,'" he said to his companion, "'I think I saw a cougar.' We stopped, backed up. It was a great dane."

Chet McCord is a biologist who works for the Massachusetts Fish and Game Department in Westboro, Massachusetts. I went to talk to him about coyotes but asked him about mountain lions, also, because I asked every biologist I met in New England about mountain lions. He told me he and another man had trapped a cat on a ledge in Idaho, but the cat got free,

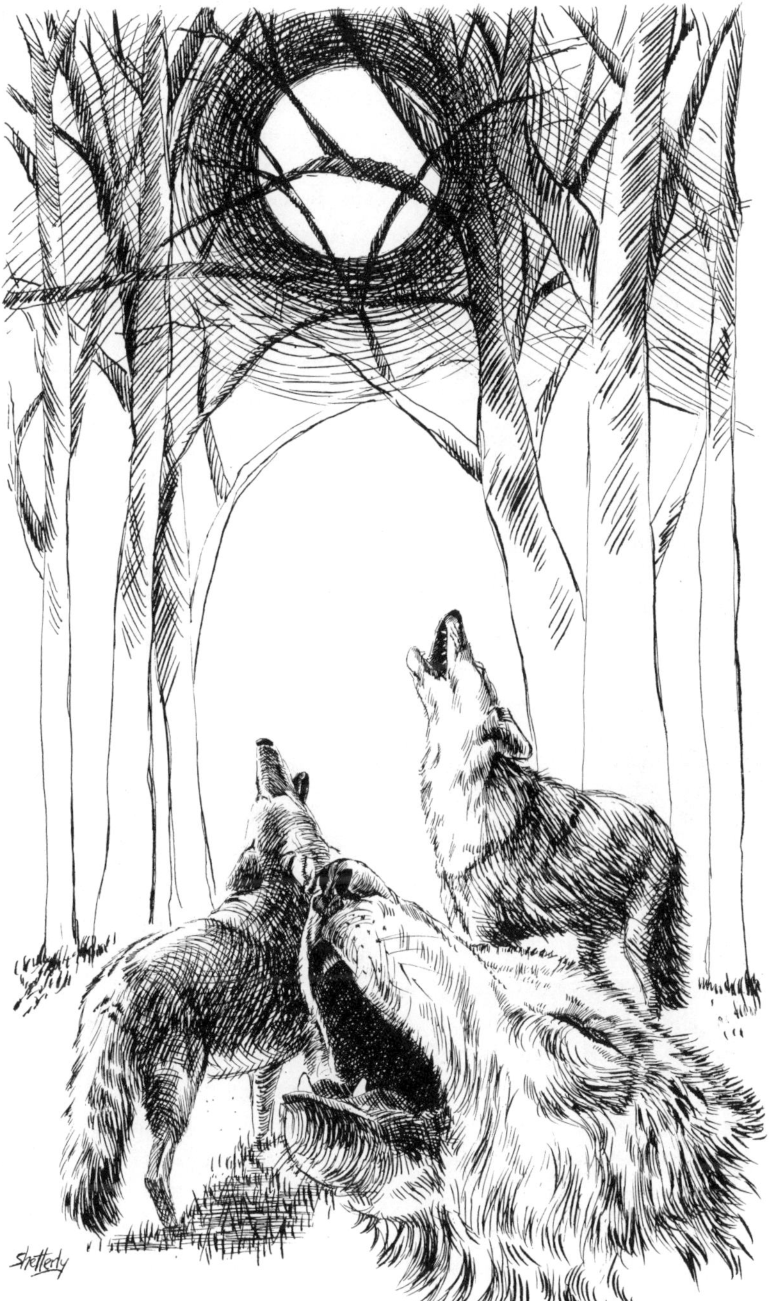
Shetterly

jumped off the ledge and ran away through the snow. "We saw the tracks and both of us said, 'This is a mountain lion.' We were confident we had a mountain lion and we tracked it down into a draw and then into woods. It was a running track in snow, the snow a little bit wet. The sun had melted out [and enlarged] the track. The animal had slowed to a walk in the woods, and the snow was different there because it was shaded. The track became normal . . . the size of a small bobcat." The cat track had shrunk in the shade.

Reports of mountain lion sightings became more descriptive with the appearance of television commercials for the Cougar automobile. Says Wiley: "Now they can give you a beautiful description right down to the little white and black markings like a moustache and the long tail with a curl at the end." If Wiley is skeptical, he is not cynical. "There is no reason why lions can't exist in the White Mountains [of New Hampshire]. There is probably enough deer in the White Mountains to support a few, but not enough to support a large population of cats."

A ski instructor thinks he saw a lion in the Green Mountains of Vermont, in the town of West Wardsboro. I saw Tom Montemagni at Mt. Snow on a day thick with the threat of snow. It snows or rains most times I travel in Vermont. If Vermont had less snow, there would be less skiing; if there were less rain, the Green Mountains would be another color. Snow on the Mt. Snow slopes was in shadow the day I was there, but bright were the cheeks of the skiers because skiers do not need sun, only snow. Montemagni, who, in a sense, skis downhill for a living, skis cross country for pleasure and to keep his running legs in shape. He saw a lion in March 1976, a month before he ran in the Boston Marathon.

"I remember I tried to get my wife to come out skiing with me. It was a gorgeous day, no clouds, the kind of day you could smell spring. She didn't go with me; I don't remember why. I went by myself on an abandoned road. I liked the road because you can find little settlements by the cellar holes. Usually if there are only stone walls it was pasture, but if it had been a main road you find sugar maples. I can remember it so well because when I am skiing by myself, especially before the Boston Marathon, I ski fast, but this particular day I could not go fast because it was too warm, and the snow was slushy. So instead of skiing with my head down, I had my head up and was looking around." Montemagni is thirty-six, used to be a sixth-grade teacher in Springfield, Massachusetts. He related his story well, talking slowly so I could write down his words.

"I saw a movement out of the corner of my eye. I pride myself on having excellent eyes. I saw something in my peripheral vision, and I thought, 'Oh, there's a little critter, maybe a porcupine.' I saw only the movement. So I skied to the wall as close as I could. I had seven-foot skis [so he could get only to within three feet of the wall]. I started to peek over the wall. I had to lean forward on my skis. To my surprise I saw someone else peeking at me. She was on the other side of the wall looking up. She had her head up and was not committing herself, the way cats don't commit themselves. We looked at each other square in the eye. I could hear my heart pound.

"I immediately knew it was feline, and the thing that struck me is she looked like a cat, like my cat, and I thought it looked like a big cat. It was such a shock I don't remember going back to the trail, it startled me so. [Later] I went back and looked at my tracks, but I don't remember backing up. I remember saying out loud, 'Nice kitty.' I was fearful for my life. I thought it was just a bobcat or a lynx.

"The cat jumped on the wall [when Montemagni had backed off fifteen feet or so]. I saw that long tail, and I thought, 'My God, this is. . . .' I don't think I knew, but remember when I was teaching school I took a class to the Boston Museum of Science and saw the [stuffed] animal in the basement there.

"It probably stayed on the wall for twenty or twenty-five seconds, maybe less. It took slow steps, stopped, turned and looked at me, then took slow steps again. It got to a point on the wall where there was an obstruction, or a tree where the wall didn't continue and went off. I didn't follow. I think I was scared.

"I gave a description of its size to my wife this way," and he spread his arms apart as far as he could. Montemagni stood there by the wall trying to figure out what he had seen. It did not occur to him to try to preserve the print in the snow. At first he thought he would try to measure the track by scratching its width on his ski pole, but he had nothing hard enough to scratch his ski pole. He decided to use his finger. The print was as wide as from the tip of his forefinger to the back of the knuckle on the hand.

"I called it a she. Since that time, I've seen a lot of animals. My wife and I are both long distance runners and since then I've seen bobcats so skittish and bears that almost knock over trees to get away, and coyotes like greyhounds." He has seen two coyotes on the same road, an old road that parallels Route 9, the Stratton-Arlington road. "The first one was coming out of the woods toward the road. He looked to the right, then to his left where I was and saw me and continued moving his head one hundred eighty degrees and went into the woods." The coyote had wasted no moment and no motion and had disappeared in the face of man as the literature says he is supposed to do. Montemagni came upon the second coyote while running. The coyote was in the middle of the road ahead of him and began running straight down the road. "He didn't run like a dog, more a loping gait, and then he made a line into the woods, and the way he moved through the woods made me think of beauty like O. J. Simpson running. He went as straight as he could go using the terrain. I'm keen on that because you tell a good skier from a bad one because a good skier will take the good line, instinctively. He will turn in the right place whereas a bad skier makes a bad turn and turns in a bad place. The more experienced skier reads the terrain, and that's what I thought watching the coyote. I like movement and found that beautiful."

Montemagni and I were talking in a main building of the Mt. Snow ski resort. We walked across to another building, to his office, and found a ruler to measure his forefinger from the tip to the knuckle on his hand. It measured four inches, and Montemagni was disappointed. He thought the lion's track had been wider than that. It is a common misconception.

Robert L. Downing says most mountain lion tracks are only three or three and a half inches wide. Downing, U.S. Fish and Wildlife biologist, works from Clemson University in Clemson, South Carolina, and has been trying to find the eastern mountain lion in the southern Appalachians without success. His cougar newsletters explain why woodsmen, bear hunters, 'coon hunters, bobcat hunters may not notice lion tracks in the woods: They may not recognize the track when they see it. Dog tracks are supposed to show toenails; lion tracks are supposed to show no nail except when the cat is digging in for a jump or a quick turn. Downing writes: "I have followed dog tracks more than a mile before seeing good nail marks. . . . A dog with worn nails has to sink one-half-inch into mud or dust to leave nail marks. Cougars on the other hand, can leave nail marks under almost any conditions." Many dogs leave a track more than four inches wide, he writes in his newsletter, and he gives this further description of the cougar track (most people, biologists and woodsmen, call it a cougar, and that is a good name, but it certainly lacks the grandness of mountain lion): "Cougar toes tend to be tear-drop shaped, whereas dog toes are more round. . . . All dog toes are nearly the same size whereas the cougar has a little toe corresponding (left or right) to the little finger of the human hand. Cougar toes are also like the human hand in that they are non-symmetrical, whereas the dog foot is almost perfectly symmetrical unless the dog is turning. . . ." Downing has other hints for the lion tracker: for instance, that dogs rarely travel alone whereas lions often do. (This is also true of coyotes. A coyote often travels alone or with a mate which would have a track almost the same size as his own. A dog in the woods, however, is apt to be traveling with one or two other dogs, dogs of different size that will have different tracks.) Downing writes: "A dog walking a road usually deviates from that path of least resistance only to urinate on roadside vegetation. Bobcats weave back and forth incessantly, and leave the road and return frequently while dogs usually stay in the road for long distances. . . . Dogs rarely walk logs, never for any distance, while cougars . . . seem to seek out logs, wooden guardrails, and rocks, apparently because they can stalk prey from them without crackling the leaves."

Downing's newsletter answered one of the questions hunters and trained wildlife people had asked me: Why are there no lion tracks? (His explanation: People may not recognize lion tracks when they see them.) His newsletter gives a second reason: "If you assume that cougars only make one complete circuit of their home range each two weeks, this means they cross a bisecting road (if there is one) only once every seven days." Rita Potter might have been on the woods road in Wytopitlock on that seventh day. There is another question woodsmen ask, one not so easily answered: The cougar is easily treed by dogs. With so many 'coon hunters and bobcat and bear hunters hunting with dogs, why has not a lion been treed? I asked Downing by telephone. He agreed it was a logical question, one hard to answer.

"They should tree a cougar now and then. A cougar should tree just the same as a bobcat. It is probably how they hunted them to extinction, but they don't have a strong scent. A hunter out west told me he had no luck getting dogs to chase cougar while bear were around [because the hounds would leave the lion scent to chase the stronger scent of the bear]. On the other hand, in the last couple of years there have been three or four reports of treed cougars in the east, most of them in North and South Carolina and unsubstantiated. In some cases they had no gun; in another case they realized it was rare and didn't shoot it [the eastern mountain lion is protected by U.S. law as an endangered species]. A cougar has no stamina to outrun a dog but has the speed to outrun them for a short distance. There is nothing about lions that protects them from man and his dogs. The least little dog that is aggressive will put them up a tree, or at least that's the story we get."

There is always one more question. Ben Day, Vermont's wildlife director, had asked it, rhetorically, of me. Day believes the animal is extinct in Vermont, not for lack of sightings but because "at one time or other a lion has to make a kill and leave specific, unmistakable evidence. A lion kills deer the same way it kills livestock, with a bite to the back of the neck, and leaves a lot of lacerations on the flanks. The fang marks would not be difficult to tell . . . the deer would be dragged away to the closest cover and then fed on . . . and then elaborately covered with snow or branches." Day's rhetorical question to me: Why is no lion kill found? Downing's answer: "Cougar cover a carcass much the same way as a bobcat. The difference is that a cougar carries it farther. A person might go by a cougar carcass because it is so well covered."

Each summer Downing gets new cougar reports in Georgia and the Carolinas, and elsewhere in the east, and his excitement builds while he waits for snow. When snow comes he searches for tracks, but he has learned that snow is not perfect for tracking. "As soon as the snowfall is over, a fifty-m.p.h. wind comes along and blows it so badly that few tracks last more than a few hours. Then the sun comes out and melts the top layer [of snow] which freezes back into a hard crust as soon as the sun sets and before cats come out to hunt." A camera was set up on a trail one summer where lion were thought to be, but the light beam was broken repeatedly by insects; and when the camera-tripping device was changed to solve the insect problem, a bear smashed the whole rig. Downing postponed his

January 1981 newsletter in hopes of reporting his discovery of an eastern mountain lion. He wrote in the newsletter: "Sadly, the winter is slipping away without providing very much snow for tracking nearby, and there is not enough money in the budget or gas in the tank to go farther afield to places that do have snow." This newsletter is limned in doubt but erupts on its last page with hope.

Downing does not have all the optimism he had when he began his project. On the phone he said: "The cougar always seems two steps in front of me somehow, but that is part of the fascination. People report having movies of the cougar, for instance. This individual got in trouble with neighbors and moved out of town. I put federal enforcement people to trace him, and they couldn't find him. Things like that. . . ."

The only lions known for certain to exist in the wild on the eastern seaboard of the United States are in Florida. Biologists are divided generally into two groups, bunchers and splitters, and the splitters categorized the Florida animal as the Florida panther, a separate subspecies from the eastern cougar. There is no proof that an eastern lion exists anywhere. None. If researchers could capture an eastern mountain lion, they would measure it carefully, X-ray the skull, then release it, for it is much too rare a creature to kill. Then they would X-ray the skull of the western cougar, kill that cougar and make conventional measurements of its dried skull. The two sets of measurements could provide a correction factor so that an eastern lion could be identified without killing it. Downing doesn't expect all this to happen soon. I sense from his newsletters and from our phone conversations that the track of the eastern mountain lion in the lower Appalachians is an exceedingly thin track, and yet there is hope. Downing attached a bulletin to his January 1981 newsletter. A cougar had just been killed by a truck in the piedmont of the Carolinas. He wrote: ". . . Where are those skeptics that have been pooh-poohing the existence of cougars in the East with the argument that, 'If there are any, why doesn't someone kill one?" Counting the one killed in Pennsylvania in 1967, one in Tennessee in 1971, and the probable kill in Shenandoah National Park in 1978, this makes four in 14 years. How many does it take?"

His enthusiasm had cooled when I called to ask about the piedmont lion. Apparently, people passing through Rockingham, North Carolina, had hit and killed a lion and asked someone what it was. Two witnesses saw the carcass. Downing went to talk to one of these witnesses, an old-timer who weighed the animal (169 pounds) and sexed it (male). The driver of the truck took the carcass with him. Downing: "What else could it have been unless it was an escaped African lion? I have no way to know if it was an eastern lion." Downing was nearly certain he could find sign of the lion near where it had been killed. He spent six days in the Rockingham area, expecting to find scat and scent scrapes, "and I found no sign whatsoever. Even where I know one occurred I couldn't find sign, which is disgusting."

I can find no reports of lions killed on the road in New England, but a man wrote to me that he had seen a lion in the town dump in Monson, Massachusetts.

Ralph Hicks was running for state representative in 1976 and making the rounds of town dumps, a good place to find voters on Saturdays. In late afternoon "I looked out over the dump, which is an old quarry, maybe four hundred feet away, and thought I saw a large dog. I looked again and said to myself, 'My God, it's a lion.' A chill went down my spine. I saw the line of his back, the tail sloping." Hicks has seen bobcat in the wild and thinks what he saw was a lion. I went up to Monson four years later, a town in west-central Massachusetts near the Connecticut border. No one I talked to had ever heard of mountain lions in Monson. One man I spoke to, a deer hunter and former trapper, said there was a wildlife refuge in town, four thousand acres of forest. I spoke to the woman at the refuge's visitor center, and she said a group of touring children had seen a bear cub there, though bear are not common in Massachusetts, and another group of children said they saw a leprechaun. "They said they saw it plain as day." If I had wanted leprechauns I found the right place to search, but I was looking for something rarer still.

Monson is about fifteen miles south of Quabbin, Massachusetts, thirty-nine-square-mile reservoir, the largest body of water in the state, a lake surrounded by acres of forest where coyote and deer live and where golden eagles and bald eagles are seen and where a mountain lion was twice sighted by trained people. Jack Swedberg, a photographer for the Massachusetts Division of Fish and Wildlife, was driving a road in Quabbin October 12, 1968 when he saw a lion. "There's no question it was a mountain lion. The question is the origin of the beast. Obviously, I would like to think it was living in Quabbin or passing through. . . . I saw that lion for two or three seconds, crossing the road in broad daylight, but a year later a graduate student had a better look. He watched it for probably two or three minutes." The graduate student described into his tape recorder the lion he was viewing, including folds of skin along its side. That was a clue. A mountain lion authority in the west said a wild animal would be very lean, have no flesh hanging in folds. Fat lions live in zoos.

The eastern mountain lion lives in the minds of those who have seen it. It is difficult for wildlife people to believe a breeding population of lions exists, even though there are deer enough in some places to support a small number of lions. There are several explanations for all the lion sightings. One: Some of the sightings are fisher (a weasel with a long tail). Two: Some sightings are seen with imaginative eyes, such as the house cat which was reported as a lion in Shutesbury, Massachusetts. Three: Some sightings are western lions that have escaped from wild animal farms or have been released by owners who no longer wanted to feed the animals or who wanted to reintroduce the breed out of romantic notion. When I am talking to biologists McCord or Day, I believe as they do, that the lion is extirpated from New England, but when I am talking to Rita Potter in Wytopitlock or Tom Montemagni in Mt. Snow, I believe the lion stalks the Maine woods and the Vermont mountains. Wildlife officer Tom Keefe works for Massachusetts in Pittsfield. He has investigated lion sightings in his area, some of them promising, but the lions always turn out to be something else, a bobcat or a dog. He says he would believe in UFOs before he would believe in mountain lions.

# – 7 –
# Bears Do Not Hibernate

In search of the New England coyote, I found track of the bear. Tom Keefe, wildlife officer for western Massachusetts, had told me of farmer Babiak's den of coyotes in Chesterfield, and while talking of that he told me about black bears foraging in corn in Ashfield, a hill town not far north of Babiak's farm. Forest habitat was cleared and bear hunted until they became rare in Massachusetts; but hillsides cleared in the 1800s for sheep grazing now have mature woodlands, and the woods run close to the farms in Ashfield, farms like that of Ken and Wallace Lilly. Bear are creatures of the woods, but hunger moved them out of the forest into the Lillys' corn fields. Bear were using a coyote technique, taking cover in the woods but eating off farmland. It was the edge effect.

The Lilly brothers' farm is up in hilly country off Bear Swamp Road. They were in their barn that winter day; dairy farmers are always in their barns in morning and again in afternoon, for cows must be milked every morning, every night. Wallace Lilly was readying a hypodermic needle, an injection for one of 250 Holsteins the Lillys raise. They were milking 118 of the 1,250 cows this morning. Wallace Lilly was surprised a writer would come so far to hear bear stories. He asked me a second time: "You're from Boston?" He started to tell me about the bears, was joined by his brother, Ken, and the three of us talked up against the milk tank. I put my notebook on the tank, used it for a desk.

A black bear, perhaps a female, entered the Lillys' corn field in 1976. Males range farther than females, but wildlife officer Keefe thinks the first bear might have been a female who taught her cubs about corn and that the cubs returned in later years. The Lillys have several fields. The first field, fourteen acres, had swamp on two sides, woods on a third side. Corn was high. The brothers could see nothing awry from the fourth side, not until they entered the field to harvest the silage corn. They found a patch of corn destroyed, the stalks piled up in mounds. Then they found other, similar patches in the same field. Raccoon forage in corn, and the damage they do is sometimes blamed on bears. Porcupines also like corn. Raccoons eat corn somewhat like humans, stripping the ear, eating the kernels. Porcupines are less fastidious; bears are not fastidious at all. An account of bear eating habits written in 1792:

"He places himself between two rows of corn, and with his paws breaks down the stalks of four contiguous hills, bending them toward the center of the space, that the ears may lie near to each other, and then devours them. Passing in this manner through the field, he destroys the corn in great quantities."

There is an interval between the time silage corn ripens enough to be palatable to a bear and the time it is ripe enough and dry enough to harvest. The black bear in the Lillys' fields gorged itself in this interval and left enough sign so its presence could not be confused with that of raccoons or porcupines. In other Massachusetts towns of the Connecticut River Valley, bear left mounds of vomit in corn fields in the summer of 1980. In the Lilly field the bear ate so much corn it gave itself diarrhea, leaving piles of yellow scat amid the torn-up stalks. Though scatology may be distasteful, it is pertinent. I saw some bear scat in a field of old apple trees in Maine, scat full of apples, and I would see scat in a field in Lunenberg, Vermont, where a mama bear and her three baby bears had only grass to eat, for it was early spring.

It was too late to do anything about the bear in the Lillys' corn that first year, 1976, but the next year wildlife officers tried to scare away the bears with fake cannon fueled by liquid propane. The cannon sounds like a shotgun and can be set to fire at intervals. The cannon did not fool the Ashfield bear for long. At first the cannon merely drove the bear from one field to other corn fields owned by the Lillys. By 1978 the bear in the corn had grown so accustomed to fake gunfire they were sitting in the fields feeding on corn while the cannons fired near them.

Though bear are protected from hunting all but one week of the year in Massachusetts, Ken and Wallace Lilly can shoot bear any time they catch them in their corn. That is not easy to do, for corn grows tall, like jungle, hiding the bear. If they had fewer cows and less work they might have time to sit and wait for bear to come out of the woods and shoot them before they entered the cover of tall corn. Wallace did have a chance to shoot a pair of bear in one of their corn fields that is near a powerline. Wallace had climbed part way up the electric line tower to check for bear in the corn and saw two of them right below him. "I went back to get a gun, but when I returned they were gone." The coyotes in farmer Babiak's hillside pasture were quick enough to run when they saw Babiak reach for his rifle, and the Ashfield bears were smart enough or lucky enough to leave the corn field when Wallace Lilly went for his gun.

A U.S. wildlife official estimated that only ten bear existed in Massachusetts in 1942. Ken Lilly, though he saw what the bear were doing to his fields, did not see a bear the first four years of their raids in his corn, did not see one until the spring of 1980 when he saw two while planting corn, one bear at one end of the field, a second bear at the other end. However, he saw less damage in his fields that fall of 1980, because townspeople began running bear dogs. Bear got used to artificial cannon but could not disregard the dogs; when the dogs had the scent, bear had to keep moving, and that kept them away from the corn. Bear had returned in high enough numbers so that people raised hounds for the sport of chasing them. There were approximately 100 bear in Massachusetts in 1974. There are many more than that now, perhaps two hundred or three hundred. Whatever the figure, it is small compared to Maine's population of six thousand to nine thousand bears, but the Massachusetts population is significant in a state perceived as too urban to have any bears.

Bear in Ashfield may have just stumbled across the corn, following the "Aha!" method of finding food, like the man who first ate an oyster or the Frenchman who first ate a snail. The absence of wild apples and berries may have driven the first bear out of the hills and into the corn. Once there, the bear decided he had found something good, and if the first bear was a she, her cubs would have learned from her, may have returned to the Lillys' field in subsequent years. Cubs also learn from their mothers how to get honey. It is a direct method. Bear smash the hive with their paws to get at the combs of honey, all the while accepting painless bee stings on their hides and some stings on their nose and lips and eyes which do hurt. If bees knew enough to concentrate their stings on those vulnerable places, they could drive off bear, teach them to find other food, because bear remember. Beekeepers' complaints of bear damage are increasing in western Massachusetts, and beekeepers have little defense. Bear love honey enough to go through electric fences to get it.

Farmer Ken Lilly is not amused by the Ashfield bear. "They're just no good. What good are they?" He thinks they should be shot. "Folks up here feel if the state wants to protect bears, it ought to pay for damages." Miles away, in his Pittsfield office, wildlife agent Keefe says: "We play referee. We understand the farmer's loss, but we are in the wildlife protection business. Some say the easiest way is to live-trap and move the animal. We chose not to do that. Other states found you have to move a bear sixty miles. Here that might be to New York or Vermont. Other states don't want troublesome bears." Vermont has enough troublesome bear of its own, including the Crisco Kid. As I would learn later on, the whole of Vermont was not big enough for the Crisco Kid. He was a bad news bear and ended up badly.

In May 1981, several months after talking to the Lillys in their cow barn in Ashfield, I had an appointment with a bear hunter in West Burke, Vermont, at five in the morning. I got to the rendezvous, the West Burke general store, early, in darkness, and could hear a stream a short distance away. Soon robins were singing, a gray dawn breaking. The bear hunter was on time in his pickup truck; his Plott hounds, especially bred to hunt bear, were in cages in back of the truck. The Vermont bear biologist was on time, also. It is important to start early when running bear, for the night moisture holds the scent for the hounds, and once the sun warms the track and evaporates the moisture, the scent is gone. It doesn't matter how warm it gets once the hounds find the original track, for thereafter they will stay close enough to the bear to have a fresh track unless the bear runs across a paved road. Then the hounds can become confused because traffic passing on that road after the bear has crossed but before the hounds arrive can mar the track. Hounds may wander up and down the road sniffing at a track broken by tire wheels. This May morning the bear would come out to the edge of the road once, turn around towards the dogs and reenter the woods, running towards the dogs; the second time the hounds pursued the bear to that road, the bear would cross the road. The hounds were tired after a long hunt so early in the year, and were stopped at the road, allowing the bear to escape.

Duane Smith is the manager of a factory in Lyndonville. He hunts bear with his dogs for sport and in recent years for the

Vermont bear project and its leader Charlie Willey. I rode in Duane's truck. Charlie and his assistant, Will Staats, were in a second truck following us. Charlie had capture equipment in his truck, a dart gun, nets, ropes. He wanted to capture bear, put tags in their ears, weigh them, examine their condition and release them. In 1980 Charlie and his houndsmen, such as Duane Smith, captured thirty-seven bears. This May morning Charlie and Duane were headed toward the town of Newark where a mother bear and cubs had been seen.

Black bear do not hibernate. Woodchucks and chipmunks hibernate, but bear just sleep. Heart rate, respiration, metabolism slow and temperature lowers for hibernating animals. The black bear's breathing slows as does its metabolic rate, but its temperature remains close to normal. A bear will wake up from its dormancy in the den with little prodding and quickly gains its senses. Black bear do not enter their dens because of cold weather; they den up when they can find no food. Biologist Charlie Willey: "Bears will walk through a foot of snow or more searching for food. We've had the whole population [in Vermont] staying out in December going after apples after they cleaned up the beechnuts. In 1980 the beechnut crop was poor and the apple crop was poor, and as a result bears denned early. If there is no food, there is no point in burning body fat looking for it."

Duane led his bear hounds out of their boxes in the back of the pickup truck and set them to stand on top of the boxes. He drove the dirt road where the bear and cubs had been seen. If the bear had crossed that road this morning, the hounds would smell the track from their perches on the truck and begin howling. Duane drove slowly, looking at the soft shoulders of the road for bear tracks. If the bear was coming down the ditch towards the road, Duane would see only the pad mark. If the bear was walking up the ditch away from the road, he would see claw marks. It reminded me of a day in the Arizona desert near the Mexican border. A U.S. border patrol agent was driving a jeep along a dirt road looking for tracks of illegal aliens and told me the tracks were easy enough to read, that only one time was he really fooled. An older Mexican man had crossed this road near the border by walking backwards, leading the agent to think the alien was going towards the Mexican border instead of away from it.

Duane could see no fresh tracks along the road. "Bear will be coming down off the highland looking for green fields. Grass and alfalfa is about all he's got to feed on now." His dogs on the box behind the pickup's cab were standing alertly but had not sniffed a bear track. They had been out once before this spring, three days previously, in Canada where one of his hounds had been mauled by a bear. None of his dogs were in prime condition after the winter. A rabbit crossed the road, and Duane opened the window of the truck and hollered to his hounds, "No! We ain't rabbit hunting." Another rabbit crossed the road and again he opened the window and hollered back to them, "No!" Bear hounds are trained to be "clean" and not run "trash." If a man is running bear, any other animal is trash.

The sun came out in Newark, showing the countryside in green. Duane said: "In the '30s and '40s everybody left the woods. The woods was the bear's property. Now people are coming back and pushing the bear back. Bear's got to live somewhere and there is a new class of people who don't know how to get along with bear. The old Vermont Yankees know how. If they see a bear in the field, they'll send a bullet over his head just to let 'im know not to get used to hanging around. But somebody from Joisey, they see a bear crossing the road and get all excited and get on the phone."

There is a line between a healthy bear population and nuisance population, Charlie had told me. If the population gets too large, chances are increased that bears will wander into town. In the Newark area, a bear had gotten into the habit of walking into an open barn and down stairs to feed at a grain bin. Black bear are not harmless, as is often thought, and this grain-eating bear posed a danger. If someone had walked into the barn when the bear was there, the bear might have taken a swipe at the person out of fright or out of malice. Either way, that person's life would have been threatened because bear are extraordinarily strong. That bear was hunted, shot and killed. Vermont's notorious Crisco Kid would also be shot.

Duane discussed by radio with Charlie in the following truck whether they should continue "roading" for the bear and her cubs or whether they should walk the dogs. They decided to find a green field where the bear and her cubs might be feeding on grass. If the bears had been in the field within three hours, the hounds would find their scent because, as dog men in Vermont say, "Them hounds is awful smart." Duane told a story about a smart hound.

"Ty was so smart he could almost talk. One day I'm in Canada in a bar and Ty is sitting up to the bar drinking milk. This guy comes in and asks Ty to get off the stool so he could sit down, and Ty kind of growls at the guy, and it sounds like Ty said, 'No.' Well, this guy wanted some cigarettes, and I said, 'Ty will go across the street and get you some,' and we put a five-dollar bill in his mouth. About then Ty's owner comes into the bar and said to me, 'Where's Ty?' and I told him we sent him across the street for cigarettes, and the owner is all excited. I said, 'We done that before. Ty can get the cigarettes,' and his owner says, 'Yes, but I'm afraid he might get hit in the traffic.' So he runs across the street and Ty's mixed up with this exotic French poodle, and he said, 'Ty, I never saw you mixed up with a French poodle before,' and Ty said: 'I never had the money before.'"

We found a green field in Newark but no bear track. Charlie was disappointed, for he wanted to capture and inspect a mother and cubs. This day, though, he would have to settle for a dump bear, and we drove to the Westmore dump. There were many bear tracks at the Westmore dump. The track of a hind foot looks almost human. If the tracks were made the previous night, the bear were close by. Duane let Fred, his lead dog, go, then the others, Melvin, JC and Amy. They roared a wheezy howl, a sad sound full of meaning and somehow frightful. All the dogs wore radio transmitters on their collars, and their progress could be followed by listening to the beeps emitted by these collars. Nevertheless, the dogs got away from us. They must have chased the bear over one ridge, and we went by truck over another ridge and out of range of the dogs' radio transmitters.

I was riding with Charlie in his truck now, four-wheel drive, and we went up narrow dirt roads and then onto tracks where two-wheel-drive vehicles could not go, all the while trying to find the location of the dogs by beeps on his radio receiver. Near Dolloff Pond a partridge walked across the road, slowly and stiffly like a peacock. The dogs were not on the hills by Dolloff Pond, and Charlie returned to the main road, Route 5A, driving up and down that road, stopping every little while to make electronic search with his antenna. Twice we passed a marker on the road that indicated it was 1,250 feet above sea level, the spot where water drained one way toward the St. Lawrence and the other way towards the Connecticut River. It was a great divide, of modest New England proportions.

Some male bear leave their dens in March, Charlie said, but females with young do not leave until late April when there is some greenery to eat. Charlie told me this and other things as we drove the roads, "roading" while the dogs hunted alone. Bear pick out one cow in the herd, follow it and whack it with their paw several times. That is fairly common, Charlie said. On rare occasions a bear will come up behind a person and follow him, perhaps taking a swipe at him, especially if the person runs. It is natural but hopeless for a man to try to run from a black bear. "If you ever saw a bear run, you would not try to run away, and if you ever saw a bear climb a tree you wouldn't try climbing. The first time I saw a bear chased by dogs up a tree, my hair stood on end. The bear was just a blur going up the tree.

Black bears are at home in the trees." Charlie has written in his booklet "The Vermont Black Bear":

". . . no animal of equal size is more powerful. A bear in search of insects or rodents can flip over boulders and old logs almost effortlessly. It can also break the necks of large animals with one blow of its forepaw. The strength of the black bear is revealed in its climbing, running and swimming abilities. The black bear . . . has been credited with nearly the climbing speed of a pine squirrel. . . . The front legs are primarily used for clasping the tree while repeated forceful downward movements of the rear legs propel the bear up the tree. . . . It can reach a [running] speed of 25 miles per hour. At every jump the hind legs reach farther and farther forward and outside so that the back arches until the bear looks like a speeding ball. [It] is a strong swimmer and has been known to cross swift rivers and swim lakes five miles in width."

Almost all black bears are harmless and timid of man, but Charlie says they are unpredictable and he would not approach them in the manner of a tourist, for instance, walking up to a bear in a field to take its picture. He told of a day he came across a bear in the woods. The bear started towards Charlie, and Charlie hollered at the bear to scare it away, but the bear kept moving towards him. Normally, Charlie is in the business of protecting bear, but this bear kept moving towards him menacingly, and Charlie shot it.

Duane had located his dogs. They had been running after and harassing the bear for some time while out of radio contact, and Duane went into the woods to be near his hounds, to urge them on and also to protect them if he could, for bear hounds, the best ones, are fearless and will fight a bear who stops running and sits facing the dogs.

We were back near the dump now, where the chase had begun, and the sound of the hounds was coming towards the road. Charlie jumped into the middle of the road to wave down an oncoming car. Hounds chasing bear are vulnerable to cars.

The bear came out of the woods. He popped out of the woods near us and stood there a moment looking at us, Charlie and me. The bear seemed uncertain where the safe route was. He was a small bear, about one hundred pounds, the kind that are all muscle and sinew and can run longer than the dogs can run. In the moment the bear stood by the side of the road and looked at us, one of Duane's hounds came out of the woods, got in front of the bear and began howling at him and making feints as if to attack the bear. Now I knew where the phrase "to hound someone" came from.

The bear turned from the road and reentered the woods, moving towards the other hounds and Duane. We on the road could hear the hounds, sounding like hounds in a movie about a convict who, frantic with fear, claws his way through swamp trying to get away from the hounds. As the convict tires, the hounds get closer. The hounds were chasing the bear up the ridge, and Charlie drove up there to be ready with his dart gun if the bear should be treed. On that road atop the ridge near Lake Willoughby we saw a cow moose, big as a draft horse and just as fast.

Below us in the woods Duane had gotten close to the bear. The bear had taken cover in a blowdown of cedar trees, the dogs on the outside of this thicket bellowing at him. Duane told me later that he walked up onto this blowdown, saw the bear beneath him and tried to hit him with the flat side of his hatchet to get him out of the thicket so that his hounds could chase the tiring bear up a tree. He missed, dropping his hatchet in the attempt, but the bear broke out of the blowdown anyway, and the chase was on. The hounds were getting tired, but the bear was lean, had not been eating all winter and would not be treed. He would run some more.

Soon after the bear broke out of the blowdown of cedar, he ran towards Route 5A again. Charlie and I had driven back there in time to see the bear lope across that main road and into the woods on the other side. We stopped the pursuing dogs at the road. They were tired and did not have strength to harass the bear enough to make him climb a tree where he could be shot with the capture gun. The hounds were slobbering but still willing enough. When Duane came out of the woods, he said: "It don't bother me so much you picked them up. I hate to have 'em starve out."

Duane told us about trying to hit the bear with his hatchet and when I asked him about this he assured me he was not joking. "One time I stuck my hat on the end of a pole and stuck the hat in the bear's face. They don't like that smell. Another time I was pulling a dog off a bear, got him by the back leg. Then the bear came at me. I tried to run but couldn't get going. I took three steps and decided to jump to the side but the bear grabbed my heel with her teeth and was dragging me. My arm got caught on a poplar stump, stopping the bear's progress for a moment, and my brother came up and hit the bear a helluva whack on her back with a length of pine and she leggo."

An hour or two later, after a stray dog had been found and Charlie and his asistant Will had left to drive home to Lemington, Duane and I drove back to West Burke and sat on the front steps of the general store where we drank Pepsis. He told me that in Quebec where he also hunts bear, friends had shown him what is called a coyote park. A line of sticks is placed in the ground like a stockade. Carrion is tossed inside this stockade from time to time and coyotes are able to enter and eat the bait, but in late fall or winter when the fur is good, snares are placed between the stakes, and when coyotes enter the stockade to eat the bait, something they have become accustomed to doing, they put their heads through the snares and catch themselves.

Then he said that bear gall, a small sac of fluid found near the liver, was worth a lot more since the arrival of refugees from Southeast Asia. Each gall was worth thirty dollars, he said, and sold to Asians as an aphrodisiac. I said: "Duane, it would be awful easy to fool me," meaning the stories about the aphrodisiac and about hitting the bear with the hatchet and getting bit on the heel and dragged along the forest floor by a she bear. "You wouldn't be just telling me a story?" And Duane said if he were just telling a story he would tell me it was just a story. I believed him, of course, but I did check the bear gall story with Fred Albiser.

Bear hunter Fred Albiser picked me up at my motel in St. Johnsbury at five in the morning, and we drove to Lunenberg to meet Charlie the bear biologist and his assistant Will Staats. A mother and three cubs had been seen in Lunenberg. On the ride over, Fred said we'd get a bear that day for certain. I thought he might be overly confident in view of what had happened the previous day, but he had reason for optimism. During the preceding year he and Duane and other houndsmen who hunt for Charlie had treed and captured thirty-seven bears in sixty tries, a remarkable percentage, especially if converted to, say, catching thirty-seven striped bass in sixty outings or thirty-seven landlocked salmon on the West Branch of the Penobscot in sixty days, or writing thirty-seven good sentences on a page of sixty sentences.

Mist of the May morning was off the grass when we reached the field where the bear and her cubs had been seen feeding on green grass on previous days. Fred took his lead dog down into the field and reported back to us by radio. "I've got a red hot track here. He started picking scent under the dew." Charlie and I walked down the steeply pitched pasture to the bottom where Fred's lead hound had found the scent. Charlie heard a sound of scratching at the edge of the woods only a few steps away, and we all looked in time to see three cubs, black shapes of fur, climbing high in the tallest tree there, a white pine eighty or ninety or a hundred feet high. I had no way to measure the tree except with my eye. Fred let his lead dog loose and then three more hounds, and they spun their feet in the field, like a car spinning wheels in mud, so frantic were they to get footing and be after the bear. The four hounds went into the woods, their asthmatic howls sounding like the horns of very old cars.

Charlie and I stood in the field a while, listening to the hounds in the woods. Their howls were soon beyond our hearing. Fred was in the woods with his dogs, some distance behind them, keeping track of their progress but not trying to keep up with them, for that would have been nearly impossible. Fred said by radio: "I'm sure she's going to come back to them cubs. I don't think they can make her tree anywhere else." Fred was mistaken. The bear stayed a mile or two away from the pine tree, trying to lose the dogs in alder thickets and beaver flowages along Mink Brook.

A volunteer was left at the pine tree to keep the cubs treed there, and Charlie and I went roading to see how close we could get to the hounds, finally stopping in a field a half mile or so from the pine tree. Fred and Charlie conferred by radio. From somewhere in the woods Fred said: "I don't think she's going to cross the main road." Charlie: "Yes. She's been down close to the road enough times. She's made up her mind not to go across." Fred: "There's a lot of blowdowns in here. This fir is in bad condition, hollow-hearted."

The bear going up and down the brook and in the thickets and blowdowns had an advantage over the dogs. Fred by radio: "Them dogs are not going to have much left in a few minutes." The dogs had been chasing the mother bear for nearly two hours. Her cubs in the pine could keep themselves almost concealed from someone on the ground. Charlie said the mother bear knew just where she was and where her cubs were and how much distance separated them.

Charlie cocked his ear, could hear something I could not. The hounds had treed the bear, he said, and he was right. Charlie and his assistant Will and I and another observer, Dr. Phil Page, a veterinarian, carried equipment from the truck into the woods where the bear was treed. We carried chains to restrain the dogs, saws to cut the saplings from around the tree where the bear was treed, nets to catch the falling bear, the capture gun, a jab stick and other accoutrements, nearly all of which were in heavy backpacks. Charlie gave me the lightest pack, but even so I arrived late to the tree. The dogs had been chained away from the tree when I got there. The bear was up fifteen or twenty feet in an old and fat yellow birch, a birch so shaggy I thought it was a hickory. Will and Fred were at the base of the yellow birch making sounds like hounds, going ha-woof, ha-woof at the bear who was showing signs of trying to back down the tree. A moment later Fred looked at the bear up in the tree and hollered to Charlie: "She's going to come down! Shoot the son of a bitch! Shoot her, you better shoot her!"

Charlie and Will and Fred kept looking up every moment or two while they cut away all the small trees at the base of the yellow birch. They were sawing and hacking at the saplings in a furious manner, trying to get a clearing made around the base of the tree where they could erect a net. The bear got out on a branch and jumped to a fir tree, hung in that smaller, swaying tree a minute or so, then jumped back to the yellow birch. Will got the jab stick ready, a long aluminum rod with a drug-filled needle at its tip. The jab stick would be used if the bear came down the trunk of the yellow birch. The mother bear looked down at all the men below and at the dogs chained to another tree and looked resigned, not that I could read her expression. I guessed she was resigned. A net was erected in the clearing where the saplings had been cut down. Charlie aimed his capture gun up at the bear and fired the dart. There was a snapping sound, the dart flew into the bear's left hip, and she turned to look at what had happened to sting her so. "In four minutes she'll be down," Charlie said. "Not if she gets hung up in the branches," Fred said.

"She run over two hours," Fred said of the bear. She was a small mama bear, all black except around her snout which showed brown in the sun filtering through the canopy of fir boughs. She began to salivate and lose her grip up there in the crotch of branch and truck. One leg went limp and lost its grip, then another and then she came down, falling safely into the stretched net. Charlie punched holes in her ears, as if for pierced earrings, and placed tag number 51 in each ear: She was the fifty-first bear captured by Willey and his houndsmen. "Roll over, sweetheart. This won't hurt much," Charlie said and dug out a tooth with a chisel. He estimated the bear's age at five or six years. When he sliced the bear's tooth in a laboratory he would know exactly how old she was by counting the cementum layers. He tattoed the same number, 51, inside her lip. While he was doing all this I bent to smell the bear's glossy coat. Bears are supposed to have a strong smell, but this mother bear smelled nice enough.

I thought to ask Charlie if bear gall was valued by Asians as an aphrodisiac, said that Duane told me the price was way up on bear gall. The price was up, Charlie said, and he had received a call from an Asian who wanted bear galls, for relief of arthritis, the Asian said. As the hunter, Fred would have been given the gall of this bear if this had been a bad bear, the Crisco Kid for instance, and had to be killed. Fred was laughing. He didn't know how effective bear gall was for an aphrodisiac. "Pig gall might be just as good. We're going to find out."

Fred rigged a pole between two trees. A portable scale was hung on this cross pole. Charlie had guessed the bear weighed 110 pounds. She weighed 93 pounds; minus the weight of the net, only 91 pounds. If the bear had been very large they would have left her to recover there under the yellow birch, but Charlie preferred to have her cubs beside her when she awoke. Charlie thought we could each carry a leg, quartering the effort of carrying the bear about three hundred yards uphill through the woods to the field where the truck was. Fred Albiser, the hunter, looks about the way a Vermonter is supposed to look, tall, wide in the shoulders, lean in the middle, a pretty strong fellow for his age, sixty-two. Fred said the only way to get the bear out was for one man to carry her, and, with help, he hoisted the bear on his shoulders and began to tramp through the woods. It wasn't that difficult, he said, except that bear made his neck awfully warm.

Fred said "She's a nice bear, a nice bear." She was put in the back of a truck and driven to the other field where her cubs were still high in the white pine. Fred began climbing the white pine, going up forty or fifty feet, I could not estimate exactly how high. The cubs kept going up higher towards the tippity top of the tree where the limbs would not hold a man. Fred said he was afraid of heights, a joke of his. "Jesus Christ. I just looked down. Goddamn, it's a long way down." Will, Charlie's young assistant, had taken the mama bear off Fred's shoulders when we were halfway out of the woods, and now Will was climbing up the white pine to where Fred was. Will had the jab stick, its needle filled with a small amount of drug. He jabbed the first cub, the drug took effect almost immediately and the cub fell like a shallow pop fly into Fred's hands. Fred said, "I caught him. I caught him, the poor little fart." Charlie, talking up to Fred from the ground, said: "Tie him high on the chest." Fred: "I'm in kind of a precarious position, a son of a bitch of a precarious position." He handed the cub to Will who said: "He's hopelessly cute," and tied a rope around its little chest and lowered the rope down fifty or sixty or seventy feet to Charlie on the ground below. A net had been strung around the tree in case any of the cubs could not be caught after being jabbed with the drugged stick, but each time Will jabbed a cub, either he or Fred caught the critter. Last year they had captured thirty-seven bears but no cubs. Charlie was excited. The first cub had been a female. Charlie examined the second cub, also a female. "Oh, you're so sweet," Charlie said.

Mama bear was beginning to awaken. Charlie gave her another injection of ketamine hydrochloride and instructed us to move her farther into the shade. Up in the white pine the third cub had been jabbed and caught and lowered to the ground. This cub was also a female. They had been born in

January, and now, the second week of May, they weighed six pounds, six and a half pounds, and seven pounds, three little sisters. Their little ears were punched and tags attached. They were Vermont bears number 52, 53 and 54. Other people had come to the bottom of the field and into the woods to see the three little sisters, and everyone was patting them and saying how beautiful they were, and I thought, They are beautiful, prettier than some babies I've seen.

Charlie wanted the babies to be fully awake and recovered from the drug before the mother awoke, lest she sense something was wrong with the cubs and abandon them. His plan worked. The babies were placed on top of the mother but scrambled away to the nearest tree, either from instinct or obeying the last order of the mother before the hounds chased her. Again the cubs were placed on the mother, and all the men left the field. We watched what happened from some distance away. The cubs sniffed their mother's nose. As she regained her senses she licked at them. At first she could not walk but could only crawl. Then she could get up on her legs and she made her way unsteadily towards the woods, the three little sisters walking beside her.

The three sisters had weighed only eight or ten ounces when born in the den in January, and though the mother was sleeping she was not in a deep sleep and would adjust herself in the den so as not to crush her cubs. The cubs would stay with her all spring and summer and fall and winter, perhaps sleeping in the same den next winter. A mother bear mates only every second year, so the sisters would have no sibling rivals their first winter. The family would stay together through the second spring until the three sisters were about a year and a half old and the mother lost interest in them and became interested in mating. If the three sisters avoid hunters during the two-and-a-half-month hunting season, they will be safe in the woods unless they become troublesome bears.

There were two troublesome bears in the Northeast Kingdom of Vermont in recent years, one small bear and one big bear. The small bear was very strong, and the big bear had a big appetite.

One summer day in 1979 the small bear broke through the screen window of a camp in Lemington and took a freshly baked loaf of bread and a freshly baked cake while the owners were out. When they returned and saw what had happened, they made sure to keep the window closed when they were not there, but the little bear came back another day and tore out the screen, ripped the window loose and ate what he wanted. When the owners saw what had happened they nailed a big piece of plywood over the window, but the little bear came back again and ripped off the plywood and the whole window casing and ate what he wanted.

While the little bear was raiding this pantry, the big bear was raiding pantries in other camps in other towns, and one time the big bear also raided the little bear's favorite pantry. Charlie Willey put bear dogs on the track of the little bear two or three times, one day chasing him for nine hours without catching him. That little bear could run forever, but Charlie spotted the little bear in an orchard one November day in 1979 and shot him dead. The little bear weighed only eighty-five pounds, and Charlie knew he had destroyed the right bear because there were no more pantry raids on the Lemington camp.

The big bear got to like pantry food in 1979, and in 1980 he was breaking into many camps in the towns of Norton, Averill, Canaan and Lemington. He would eat most anything, including cans of shortening, and Charlie named him the Crisco Kid.

The Crisco Kid broke into approximately forty-five camps, especially those around Averill Lake. He would raid the pantry of empty camps and be gone, avoiding camps occupied by people because he could smell where humans were. He was smart that way, broke into camps on weekdays when people were away. He ate a lot of pantry food in May and June and in July until he made a mistake July 26, 1979.

People in the northern towns of the Northeast Kingdom were alarmed, were afraid to go into the woods to pick berries. They thought all the bears in the woods were on a rampage. Charlie knew all the bears in the woods were not on a rampage. He knew the raids were on Averill Lake camps one week, then over to Canaan Hill, then in Lemington. He deduced it was one bear because there were no pantry raids in two towns in the same night. He knew a big bear would fill himself up, then go into the woods to sleep. Another night he might travel six or eight miles to the next town and break into another pantry. He told the camp owners only one bear was responsible and that he would try to catch him if they would call him the moment they saw the Crisco Kid or found out their camps had been raided. They had to call him right away so the hounds would have a fresh trail.

Warden Paul Fink had set up a culvert trap to catch the Crisco Kid, but the big bear avoided the trap. Perhaps he was lucky, perhaps he was too smart to be caught that way. If he had kept to his m.o. he might be raiding camp pantries still.

The Crisco Kid avoided occupied camps, and his break-ins would not be discovered until he was some distance away. However, he did approach one camp in Canaan where a woman lived, and her screams made him run away. This woman placed a line of pots and pans on her porch to warn her if the big bear should approach her porch again, and one night he did, knocking over the pots and pans. Again she screamed and again the Crisco Kid ran away, but this time she knew to call Warden Fink, though it was the middle of the night. And Warden Fink called Duane Smith, the houndsman. Duane called Charlie, and all of them hurried to the camp in Canaan. The Crisco Kid had made two mistakes. He had raided an occupied camp, and this camp had a telephone. He could not know of the telephone, but he should have known a person was inside because bears can smell people.

The warden and the biologist and the dog owner arrived at the Canaan camp about one and a half hours after the frightened woman called Warden Fink. Night is a good time for tracking because the scent of the bear hangs better in the damp air. There could be no reprieve for the Crisco Kid. The state of Vermont was not big enough for the Crisco Kid. Wherever he might be moved he would raid pantries because he was used to that now, and someday somebody might come into a camp while the Crisco Kid was in the pantry. The Crisco Kid would probably run for the door, knocking over that person with a swipe of his paws. The Crisco Kid was dangerous.

Though the track was an hour and a half old and getting cold, Duane's hounds picked up the scent and followed it to another camp and then to a berry patch where they found the big bear and rousted him. The dogs and the men chased the Crisco Kid for about a mile and a half until he climbed a tree to get away from the dogs who were annoying him. Warden Fink shot the Crisco Kid dead in the tree. He weighed 311 pounds.

In his stomach there were jewel weed, unripe blackberries, a white plastic garbage bag, one half of a filter-tip cigarette, two paper towels and part of a Styrofoam cup. He had not eaten well that last day.

# – 8 –
# The Hounds of Sebec

Dover-Foxcroft is in western Maine not far from where the paved roads end and the big woods begin. It is the closest town of lodging to Sebec, and I stayed in Dover-Foxcroft one winter night, leaving early the next morning for my appointment in Sebec with Wayne Bosowicz, a professional hunter. There was a layer of ice on the roads that morning, and traffic had stopped at the top of a steep downgrade. Schoolbuses and trucks were waiting for something. I parked in the line of traffic and walked up to a tractor-trailer truck, surprising the driver who was urinating behind the cover of the opened door of his truck. He pointed ahead down the road and up the other side where a logging truck was stopped halfway up the hill, unable to continue because of the ice. He dug his boot toe into the sand and salt spread on the road, explained that the mixture was working into the ice and that we would be able to continue soon. When I saw the schoolbuses descend that hill, I deemed the road safe enough for me and continued on to Sebec and the Bosowicz home and hunting camp. Bosowicz is one of about twenty full-time guides in Maine, has catered to bear, deer and bobcat hunters for about six years, deer hunters in the fall, bobcat hunters in the winter. In spring he baits bears for hunters who sit in tree stands and shoot the bear with rifle or bow when it is attracted by the smell of the bait. This spring bait hunting is controversial. Critics, including wildlife people, say mother bears are killed during spring hunts and the cubs die. Bears have a slow reproductive rate compared to some animals and give birth only every second year. Spring bait hunting was to be banned in Maine after 1981. In fall, Bosowicz guides hunters who follow his hounds until the bear tires and climbs a tree where the hunter shoots the bear. I was almost on time for my 8:30 A.M. appointment, and Bosowicz came out on the porch to greet me. He has a black beard and is built squarely and stoutly, like a bear. He is used to welcoming strangers, the hunters he guides; he put me at ease, sat me at his kitchen table and poured coffee from a metal pot. It is an old farmhouse with sloping floors. His wife, Donna, likes the old house well enough and said if something spilled it ran only one way on those floors, downhill.

He hunts bobcat many winter days, but there is no hunting in this weather, rain and sleet atop the snow obliterating the scent so that his Plott hounds cannot follow the cat. Bobcats walk on ice on beaver ponds where the scent from their footpads does not hold.

"Snow is another world. Snow really holds the scent. Good powder snow, ten or twenty degrees above zero is ideal [though Bosowicz tracks and kills bobcats at temperatures below zero because snow holds scent even at cold temperatures]. Powder snow is good for scent and for seeing fresh tracks. When you walk out the door and the snow squeaks under your feet, you have good going for bobcat, and when you can make snowballs, you ain't got that good going. Snow's got water and is going to freeze or wash out."

The ancestors of his hounds were brought from Germany to North Carolina in 1750 by Jonathan Plott. The hounds were bred with bear dogs from Georgia in 1780, and it is for bear and for bobcat that Bosowicz uses them. Bobcat have a thinner scent than bear, and a bobcat Plott hound needs a fine nose. "Towards spring when the sun is getting high you put a dog on a bobcat [after first finding a bobcat track in the snow] and about eleven A.M. you hear the dog driving hard and you think you got a bobcat. A half hour later the dog quits. What happened is the sun at eleven gets high and reached that fine line where the track seemed better than it was. The sun melts moisture in the track and eliminates it entirely. Usually a moist day is tremendous tracking, and I've seen high pressure systems reduce the scent [because high pressure systems carry dry air which dries the track]. And fog lifts scent right off the ground."

A bobcat is a small animal, weighs 15 to 35 pounds, sometimes as much as 40 pounds, and because it is light leaves a thinner scent than does a 200-pound mountain lion if such a creature still lives in the New England woods. There is no mountain lion in New England, skeptics say, because there are so many men who hunt bobcat and 'coon with hounds that those hounds would surely tree a mountain lion, an easy animal to tree. Bosowicz should be a skeptic because he hunts with hounds; however, he has seen two mountain lions, has a witness both times, and as a professional hunter should qualify as a reliable observer. He did not see the lions in Maine but in western Massachusetts where he grew up.

"The second lion I saw was in Otis about 1972. I was with the president of the National Plott Association, Del Carlisle of Evansville, Indiana. He was surprised at how wild some of the country in western Massachusetts is. We were 'coon hunting, and we hunted all night, and we were really tired. We were coming out a road by Lake Garfield, and the cat jumped right in the middle of the road and didn't just leave the road but went down the road. The car shook we were so excited. It was just coming daylight. There was no doubt. It was a brown type, nothing odd about it, just pretty. It was really moving. If it went straight across the road, I'd been banging my head wondering what we saw, but he went down the road another bounce or two. We would have put every dog we had [in the back of the truck] on the track, but they had run all night and were tired and we were tired too, and Del had an appointment. And anyway it was illegal [because eastern mountain lion is protected by federal law].

"In Blandford, four or five years earlier, we were checking it out for deer the day before the deer season, and we were snooping out the fields. We had no guns because we didn't want wardens to think we were jacking deer, and there was no drinking. I don't drink. That's the first thing people think. A cat stood right out on the road. I said, 'Look at the deer.' You know, we drove right up and it stayed in the road. Three of us almost had heart attacks. The cat jumped the barbwire fence from the road into the field. We turned the car around and put the lights on him, his great big, round eyes. I said we were going in to look, and we got out and went over the barbwire. John Welch of Southwick [Massachusetts] was with me. We walked towards him and saw his eyes [in the light of the car headlights]. Then he moved his head and we couldn't see his eyes, and we got scared. We never took our eyes off his eyes until he bobbed his head. I'd a run him with dogs just to see him but next day was deer season and we couldn't run dogs in deer season. We couldn't do nothing. . . . I spend all winter hunting bobcats. I get paid to do it, in Vermont, New Hampshire, Maine. There's no barrier, no worry about gas, and I never see anything. I don't know why. If there were mountain lion tracks we should see 'em. I think they just migrate in and are not here in winter."

He thinks he knows why 'coon hunters do not tree mountain lions with dogs, even though he is puzzled as to why he himself does not tree them while running bobcat. "Lions are not likely to be in 'coon country. 'Coon feeds on apples or in corn fields or in gardens, and lion would be in bog or swamp or ledge. Lions would never be in a corn field or a garden."

People who hunt with Bosowicz come from many different places in the United States and from Europe. They see many strange creatures when he sets them out in a bear stand, creatures such as tigers. They tell him about their observations when they return at night. I suspect Bosowicz is patient with these people. I asked him many questions at his kitchen table, and he was patient with me, out of professional politeness and because he enjoys talking about his hounds and about bear.

"No longer do I tell people bear are not dangerous. There's been half a dozen incidents in New Brunswick. I think they are getting used to people, especially in Maine and Ontario where there is vast woods. No other time has there been so many people in the woods, hippies I call them, but I know that's not a very good word. We used to take girls to the movies and now they take them out in the woods. I used to see fifty people a year on the Appalachian Trail; now I see thousands. You see young couples thirty miles in the woods, back in places there's never been humans. Bears start seeing humans and get bolder. Just in the past five years they started killing people."

Some people had been killed in a park in Ontario by bears, Bosowicz said, and many weeks after I talked to him, I talked by phone to Carman Douglas, regional biologist for the Algonquin region of Ontario.

"Three boys were killed two years ago over on the east side of Algonquin Park," Douglas told me. "As far as we know, the attack was completely unprovoked. All three boys in the party were killed so we had to deduce what happened from whatever sign could be found. We couldn't find any reason for the attack unless one of the boys had some fish and the bear wanted those fish, and when others came to distract the bear from the first boy, the bear killed them, too. Eventually the bear was shot, a male, and was well checked out by veterinarians and biologists to make sure the bear was not diseased or was old and had bad teeth. We couldn't find any reason at all to suggest why this animal attacked.

"There was one other instance. A fisherman was coming home with his catch north of here wandering through brush and saw a bear, and the bear started toward him. Eventually he threw his creel away, and the bear was satisfied with that. I have had lots of encounters with bears, but it never happened to me. I don't know whether bears are really and truly becoming more aggressive or less frightened or if there are just more people coming into contact with bears."

Bears kill Bosowicz's dogs, and that is fair enough because the dogs harass the bears, cause them to lose patience, become irritated and climb a tree where they are shot. Often they kill Bosowicz's best and bravest, but it was not a bear that killed Cascade Deacon.

"Two years ago I bought a dog for fifteen hundred dollars plus two hundred to ship him from Florida. Cascade Deacon was five years old. He was flawless." (His wife Donna, who was listening but not participating in the conversation, interjected: "He was brilliant.") "We went into an apple orchard in Sebec, and they run two bear. At some time Cascade Deacon went off on one bear by himself. The other dogs treed the other and we got that bear. I said to myself, 'No problem.' Deacon's got a radio collar. I put the radio on. Nothing. Of course, this was hours later. Maybe he was out of range. We looked for two days in two vehicles, four-wheel drive. The amount of gas we used was unbelievable. Other guides and myself and a hunter who took a liking to Deacon helped me. The third day I went up in a plane. Nothing. The antenna in a plane can pick up the signal for eighty miles. We circled half of Maine in the plane, from here to the Allagash and almost to the Quebec border. That is a good part of Maine and nothing. I said the collar's got to be broken. The bear killed the dog and broke the collar because if the collar is intact we'd hear the beep even if the dog is dead. I thought the bear broke the dog's neck and broke the collar. It has a battery that lasts about a year and a half. So this was incredible.

"I posted signs with a reward, I think it was five hundred dollars for someone to return this dog. A guy going down the

Canadian Pacific track found the dog. He had been hit by a train that smashed the collar. I always said a dog has got to be pretty stupid to be hit by a train, so I checked down south and they told me there's something about a train, whether it's the light at night or vibration that stuns them." Deacon had been found on the tracks in the town of Barnard, about six miles from the orchard where he first began the chase. The man walking the Canadian Pacific track had seen the reward poster and could tell it was the Deacon because all of Bosowicz's Plott hounds have a W branded on one hip, a B on the other. The hounds are shaved down to the skin, and a mixture of alcohol and dry ice is put on a branding iron. This cold brand hurts less than a hot brand, Bosowicz says, and kills the hair pigment in the branded spot so hair grows white on that spot for the rest of the dog's life.

Two weeks after the death of Deacon, a bear killed another hound, Wayne's Buck, bit him to death, gathered him in with her arms and held him close to her chest while biting him. "The worst bear of all is a female, one hundred to one hundred fifty pounds. There's no fiercer animal, and they turn around and fight. If a bear would keep swinging it would put us out of business, but what they do is try to bring the dog in with their arms and bite them. If bears had mouths like alligators we couldn't use dogs, but they have [relatively] small mouths so they are not that effective at biting. They don't know enough to use their arms for weapons."

Bears that do not choose to stand and fight but are smart enough or lucky enough to be near boggy ground can elude the hounds of Sebec. Bosowicz has seen bears running thiry-five miles per hour in front of his truck, and they run quietly. People who hire Bosowicz kill about one hundred bear a year. Many others escape. "Sure it's fun when he gets away, but I'd be out of business if it happened all the time. A dead bear don't mean nothing to me. I'd rather see 'em alive." Bosowicz does shoot some bears himself, bears that destroy dairy farmers' corn. "Beechnuts control New England bears. When there's no beechnuts in the mountains which is every third year or so, bears travel. People say bear are increasing but the next year bears are eating beechnuts, and people say the bear population is down. I've killed fourteen or fifteen bears in one dinky field. They lose their senses, get addicted to corn, and you can't drive them out. It appears that way to me. Once I had some lost dogs before I had radios and I was in a field and came to an opening in the corn and saw three adult bears, and I had just run a bear out of that field." Bears gorge themselves with corn and physic themselves and leave piles of manure, all the time fattening themselves for winter when they go to their den and do not defecate at all, because hair and leaves and pine needles and mucus from the intestines form a plug that blocks the colon and is not purged until spring.

The country around Sebec is good bear country, the woods extending west and north, woods with summer camps but no towns, a place where loggers work but few people live. Bosowicz says logging operations have improved the bear habitat considerably. "Clear-cutting is not good for some game and not good for lots of things, but it is good for bear. Up in where there's miles and miles of fir and spruce now there are roads, and along the roads fantastic amounts of blackberries and raspberries grow, and females are starting to have more cubs because there is feed." Wildlife biologists do not always agree with Bosowicz. The state of Maine does not agree with Bosowicz and shortened the 1980 bear season after 1,058 animals had been killed. Maine has from 6,000 to 9,000 bears, and wants to maintain this population. Black bears sometimes weigh six hundred pounds, though bears that size are unusual in the northeast, and Maine's black bear has become more heavily hunted, drawing hunters even from Europe; the animal that was once considered a pest and too numerous, like suburban squirrels, something to be killed off so they would stop raiding summer camps for food, has become a game animal of importance. When I sit in the offices of wildife biologists, I believe them out of respect for science and for their knowledge, but when I am talking to people who work in the woods, I tend to believe them, for scientists are not always right. Bosowicz has a point of view not usually seen in the *Audubon* magazine.

Bosowicz worries about his livelihood if the bear season continues to be shortened. "We're an endangered species like the eagle. A lot of biologists tend to be preservationists rather than conservationists. They don't like dog hunters. Charles Willey [a Vermont biologist] is an exception, probably because he uses dogs himself." Bosowicz used to hunt in Vermont until about nineteen years ago, when "the ski money showed up. Skiers pay five dollars for socks, a hunter pays fifty cents. There's a changing feeling coming from the new people. They are not bad people. I used to despise them, but I don't any more. They sold their house in New York or New Jersey for a hundred fifty thousand and came up to Maine and got a house for ten thousand, put another five thousand into it and retired. The first three years they belong to the PTA. The fifth year they are selectmen, and after that they're in the legislature. [To their credit] they take an old farm and fix it up, graft apple trees, but they don't want us even to have guns. The natives are working at Pratt and Whitney and Sikorsky in Connecticut. We don't have that good old hunting and fishing code. It's been ten or fifteen years since a man's handshake's been worth anything. God, guns and guts built this country and we got to get back to those. Maine had it [hunting] free all their lives . . . the new people go to all the public meetings. The natives can't afford to go sometimes, and the new people are good speakers. The natives say nothing but when they get out in the parking lot they call the new people sons o' bitches. We hunters are under fire. When I grew up in Otis [Massachusetts] a registered Maine guide was like a Royal Mountie." Now he gets hate mail.

Bosowicz considers new hunting restrictions a threat to his

livelihood and blames the new people from New York and New Jersey. However, the new animal in the woods, the coyote, is not so much a threat as an annoyance. Coyotes do not bother his dogs, nor does coyote scent distract them from their purpose. His dogs are trained to follow the scent of bobcat and 'coon and bear; anything else is considered trash, including coyote. He has noticed coyotes only in the last three or four years.

"I think they are killing bobcat kittens in spring. Lately I see one or two coyote tracks following a bobcat, following for miles and when a cat makes a kill, the coyotes go right in and claim it, a partridge or a rabbit, or a deer. Of course, anything will drive off a cat, even a fox. We found where a cat killed a deer, and I said I would come back in the morning and know there'd be a cat there. The next morning, the deer was gone. Coyotes had eaten it all up. Usually a cat kills, hangs around a while at the kill then covers the kill and comes back in a week or two when finishing her circuit. Now when they come back, there's nothing there, so a cat has to kill more. A cat normally kills fifteen to twenty deer a year, but now coyotes are driving off the cats and cleaning up the deer right to the bone. So it forces the cat to make more kills. In spring when a cat has kittens there's always a high mortality rate. Males kill kittens, porkies kill them [indirectly] because kittens can't eat with quills in their mouths. I don't see kitten tracks, and I wonder if the coytoes are killing them, following the cat tracks to the kittens."

Coyotes are taking the bait Bosowicz sets for bear. He uses road-killed moose, slaughterhouse refuse and scraps from skinned beaver for his bait. He had to find a way to safeguard his bait from coyotes and had a good idea. At first he thought he would not tell me what it was, for it is a trade secret of sorts. He told me anyway. "I use different scents to keep them away. Once I saw where a coyote had weared a track in the ground pacing in front of the bait afraid to go to the bait. I load up at the

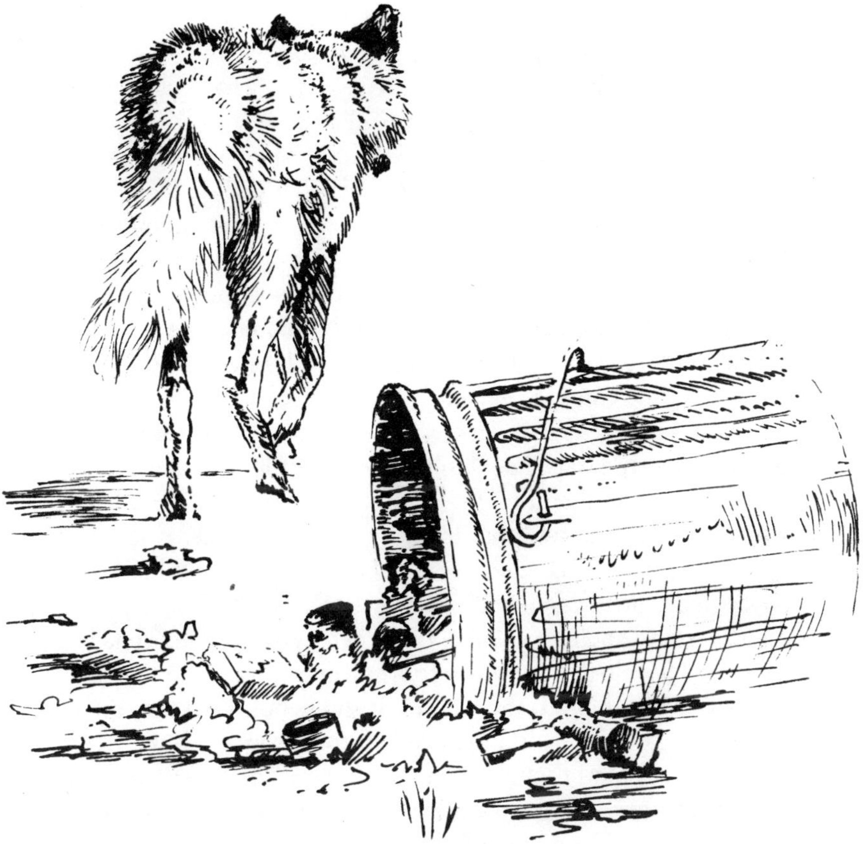

dump on old shoes. The human scent in old shoes lasts a year and fox and coyote absolutely refuse to go past it, but two years later coyote have adapted and will go past the old shoes in some areas. Also I use old rags of shirts, hundreds of them. You've got to stay ahead of the coyotes. When it works, it's like gold, but when coyotes adapt, they could care less. . . . They amaze me in that sense, but I don't particularly like them.

"I wonder if Maine can handle them. They are definitely devastating to deer here regardless of what's said. I've had coyotes drive bear right off a bait. . . . A bear came in on the bait and a guy who'd come a thousand miles [was up in a tree ready to shoot the bear] and here come coyotes yipping, and the bear took off. The guy was so scared he couldn't come off the tree stand. He was petrified. Six coyotes had come in. I've had eight at a time come in on bait.

"I've seen dozens of coyote, I've shot some. I killed a red one in a buddy's trap. I couldn't believe it. It looked like a red fox. I was scared that it might be someone's dog but I could tell when he looked at me [that it wasn't a dog]. I've seen a lot of twos but now I see six to eight at the bait. One night we had six coyotes on one stand and thirty miles away had seven at another stand and twenty miles from there, eight coyotes. I had a fellow that killed three with a bow and arrow from a stand. He pinned two of them to the ground. It shows how bold they are starting to get. I couldn't believe his story at first. I humored him, let it be, but I thought, 'That guy is crazy.' So I went down [after that hunter had left Bosowicz's lodge] and saw the dead coyotes. It was like a fairy tale. It amazes me. You crack a twig and coyotes are gone, but he hit them through the heart and lungs, apparently. I saw two coyotes right by the bait and one about a hundred feet off. I think they'd been eating off that bait for quite a while. I think coyote will chase bear off a bait. It's happened to me.

"There are so many more coyotes than there used to be. I used to believe that two to three coyotes traveled together from book explanations and from my bobcat experience, but now I think different. I've seen seven or eight or ten at a time around bait. I have twenty hunters a week hunting in spring so I have twenty pair of eyes. I have them from Mt. Katahdin to Moosehead to here. I have index cards printed up, and every night I quiz them, so I know six or seven or eight coyotes are at the bait. At real bad areas I go to hanging bait [rather than just set it on the ground]."

Coyotes could become something more than bait stealers and trashy scents for his hounds if Bosowicz could call the animal by another name. He would like to call the animal a timber wolf. "You can't advertise for coyote hunting, because people think of a fourteen-pound animal. Anything with wolf in it's got European interest." Some biologists in New England think the eastern coyote is more wolf than coyote, but they could not agree to the term timber wolf, for that is an animal that once lived in New England but like the mountain lion is believed to be extirpated, gone.

The sleet had stopped outside the kitchen window, Bosowicz would show me his Plott hounds out back, including Princess, one of his more valuable hounds. Princess had been mauled by a bear the previous season. She and other hounds were wearing radio collars one day when they came across a bear track. Bosowicz followed the radio signals of the dogs and found them near a swamp into which the bear had escaped, but Princess was not among them. She had gone after a second bear. Bosowicz found her radio signal and began to follow the beep. "I follow the radio like a compass. I believe it works. I went in with a hand antenna and knew the collar was close [because of the strength of the beep]. I hollered for my dog but got no answer. I waded a brook waist deep and heard a big beep and right under a log I saw Princess. Her eyes were glazed. She was in shock. I picked her up and carried her back across the brook." Princess had been bitten on the back and bitten in the side so badly that her ribs showed. She was stitched up and is almost as good as new. The $190 collar had saved her and "paid for itself. That dog is worth everything to me."

We walked on the glazed surface of snow out behind his barn to where his dog houses were aligned in a row on each side of a path, a Plott hound standing on a chain in front of each house. Bosowicz says, "When I look into a dog's eyes, if he looks me in the eye I like that. Same as when I meet a man. If I shake hands and he looks down at his shoes, I wonder about him." I looked into Princess's eyes, and she returned my gaze. She and the other Plott hounds did not look ferocious, they looked friendlier than some of the dogs on the street where I live in a suburb of Boston. Bosowicz took me into his barn. There were freezers with packaged meat in the barn, bear meat. He would have given me a piece to take, but I had no way to keep it refrigerated. He rummaged through the meat locker trying to find something to show me, an enormous brook trout he had caught, four pounds I think he said it was. He couldn't find the trout, and a few minutes later we said good-bye.

I drove back to Dover-Foxcroft, stopped for a bowl of corn chowder at a restaurant. There was a wildlife biologist at the University of Maine in Orono I wanted to visit. I called him from the phone booth in the parking lot of the Dover-Foxcroft restaurant. When I gave the operator my charge card number, she returned my two dimes, and the dimes fell out of the phone slot to the bottom of the booth and rolled out of a hole in the booth to the parking lot. At that moment a man got out of a pickup truck, saw the dimes and picked them up. I did not get a good look at the man, but his name, Rocky, was painted on the side of his truck, and I did not follow Rocky into the restaurant to get my two dimes back but instead headed for Orono.

# – 9 –
# The Trapper

Some time in the night a coyote living in the woods behind the farm in Carthage, Maine, came into the field and approached the trap buried near a fence. He pawed the loose soil around the edge of the trap until he uncovered the trap, then set it off, perhaps by cuffing its edge with his paw, perhaps just by lifting it. Then he stepped forward past the sprung trap and ate the bait, old bobcat meat. I was with trapper Ralph Griffin early one October morning when he examined this trap. He said: "Can you believe it? That's four mornings in a row." Such incidents nurture coyote legends that the animal is uncommonly smart, smarter even than the animal that is a symbol of cleverness, the fox. No one saw the coyote cuff the trap and spring it that way, though the evidence suggests that's what happened, and no one knows what goes through a coyote's brain when he uncovers a trap. Griffin had trapped some members of this coyote's family in this field, and the surviving coyote may have learned to be careful of the traps by seeing his family members have their paws caught in the jaws of a steel trap. Coyotes often watch the trapped coyote out of curiosity or sympathy or family loyalty, but retreat before the trapper arrives to shoot or club to death the trapped coyote. Coyotes do learn to avoid traps from such experience, proof of intelligence, but I found no evidence they could spring a trap on purpose. A truly smart coyote does not play with traps but avoids them entirely, leaving the trail rather than pass the place where he senses a trap is buried. That truly smart coyote might die of mange or be shot or be hit by a car, but, most likely, he will not die in a trap.

Griffin took me with him on his trap line near Carthage, and at the end of the day he told me about Neil Olson, a successful trapper and perhaps the most active coyote trapper in New England. I found Olson months later, after the trapping season in New England was over. Olson lives in East Bethel, Maine, near the New Hampshire border, and traps in Maine, New Hampshire and Vermont, and in 1981 in Alabama as well. I had heard about Olson in October and November and in December and January while in search of the coyote, heard from biologists and other trappers that Olson knew how to catch coyotes.

We talked one March afternoon in Olson's trap shack, a garage outside his house which is set on flat ground in East Bethel with a view to the west, to Caribou Mountain, Bear Mountain, Goose Eye Mountain. Olson is thirty years old and does not fit the image of a trapper, an image of unkempt men in snowshoes and coonskin caps. Olson did have snowshoes hung on the garage wall, but most trapping is done on bare ground, and he travels by truck except during beaver season, January, when he uses snowmobile and snowshoes. He has caught 118 coyotes in eight years, a substantial number by New England standards.

Olson is a fox trapper, mostly; he caught five coyotes in a row several years ago on No. 2 size fox traps and thought at first that the No. 2 was the right trap for coyotes. He learned it was easier to catch a coyote than to hold him. "In 1978 when I caught twenty-two, I only held half of them. Then I went to bigger traps and I got twenty-eight in 1979 and thirty-five in 1980." He showed me a No. 2 fox trap set apart from his other fox traps on the wall of his garage. A coyote in this No. 2 trap bit the trap jaws so hard that one jaw slid underneath the other jaw, causing the far end of the jaws to open enough for the coyote to withdraw his paw and escape. It is proof of the strength of a coyote's jaws. His new coyote traps are bigger, size No. 3 traps and have a three-foot kinkless chain connecting the trap to a steel stake. There is a swivel where the chain is attached to the trap and a second swivel where the chain is joined to the stake. These swivels prevent a big coyote from wrapping the chain around the stake and pulling the stake out of the ground. Having done that, the animal could drag the trap, chain and stake off into the woods and perhaps pull his paw from the trap jaws in the woods or, when his paw was numb, pull his leg free leaving part of his paw in the trap. There are many incidents cited in the literature of coyotes that have lost paws in traps and continued to hunt while hobbled. I found no stories of peg-legged coyotes in New England, probably because coyote trapping is not extensive in the region and trap jaws with teeth are forbidden in Vermont and Maine. However, a coyote that was securely caught, even in jaws without teeth, might tear off its paw when it became numb and thus free itself. This peg-legged coyote would be trap shy and fresh dirt shy and "circle shy," meaning he would try to avoid any trap more zealously than a coyote that had not been pinched or maimed. There are stories of three-legged coyotes out west, even two-legged coyotes. Olson showed me a picture of a blond-colored coyote he had trapped. The animal's right front leg was missing, but had been cut off by a mowing machine, Olson guessed.

Olson:"I caught nine coyotes in one day in the Colebrook [New Hampshire] area. That's the heaviest area of coyote that I know of. It's in the Connecticut Valley and I trap fox in the meadows there and coyote in the back fields closer to cover [of the forest]. You definitely find more coyote on woods roads than fox. I always set one trap near another for coyote because they travel together more in family groups. People call 'em packs but they're family groups. I feel they run together more than other animals like the fox. It's easier to catch a fox than a coyote, and easier to catch a coyote than a 'coon. What defeats them is their nose. A 'coon doesn't have that sense of smell that a fox or coyote has."

There are many more 'coon caught in traps than fox or coyote, making Olson's statement appear incorrect. But he explained that a coyote or fox finds the trap much faster than a 'coon would because a coyote or fox will smell the lure quickly and from a distance. Also, "There are a lot more 'coon trappers than fox trappers, but once you become a good fox trapper it's easier to catch a fox than a 'coon because a fox finds the set quicker, and once in the trap, the 'coon has a tapered leg and the trap slides off the leg easier. And the average 'coon weighs twice as much as the average fox, so the 'coon has much more pulling power than fox. 'Coon is a much more awkward animal than fox. You can't predict where he'll put his foot. And when it's hibernating season, the 'coon is not there while a fox is there all year around." Nevertheless, nearly 10,000 'coon were trapped in Maine in 1980 and only 4,080 fox, indicating that there are more 'coon than fox and more 'coon trappers than fox trappers. I assume some trappers would say fox are *harder* to trap than 'coon, but Olson had qualified his explanation. He said it was easier to catch fox than 'coon once one had become a good fox trapper. I suspect the discussion can become arcane, as with old-timers who would argue who was the better second baseman, Bobby Doerr or Joe Gordon.

Olson's daughter, a toddler, came into the garage with a toddling friend, and they puttered about a while then left, taking an instrument Olson would miss later. Olson's wife and third-grade daughter were in the house. Olson grew up on this rural road a short way from his present house. He first went trapping when he was eight years old, with his father, for muskrat. Later, when Olson was ten or eleven, he and a friend used to check their muskrat traps together on the Androscoggin River. "We loved it. We stayed out trapping one night until ten or eleven and when we went into the store, the man said 'They found you!' My father and my friend's father had been searching for us and had found our two knapsacks by a log where we crossed the river and they were worried." Olson loves his work, trapping, and has been trapping full time, or what amounts to full time in the limited New England season, for ten years. He was working seven days a week and grossing seventy-five dollars at first. "People who worked in a mill would say why didn't I go to work. I *was* working as hard as I could. As luck would have it, the price of fur started going up." In the 1980–1981 trapping season he worked seventy-three days (including the time in Alabama) and caught 118 fox, 21 raccoon, 33 beaver, 35 coyotes, 4 bobcat, zero fisher, zero mink, zero otter and 70 skunk. "There's nothing blacker than a skunk. You put it up beside a black bear and makes the bear look brown. I got three dollars for skunk. Some don't bother with skunk, but I think you should use it if you kill it. The essence is worth almost as much as the fur." When trapping across the state line in New Hampshire, Olson leaves his Bethel house about four in the morning so he can arrive at his first trap one half hour before sunrise, the legal starting time in New Hampshire. He works setting and resetting traps and gathering his catch until dark. He runs a line of 75 to 115 traps. "I'll trap twenty farms for four or five days then pull up and do the same on twenty different farms like checkers, from Colebrook to Lancaster [New Hampshire]. I went forty-five days in a row one year and lost only eight hours daylight from trapping."

He doesn't spend time trying to get a specific smart coyote; he says it is better to move one's traps down the trail a few miles and catch the dumb or brave coyotes there. "The average trapped coyote acts cowardly when you approach. That coyote don't even want to look at you. That's one feature that makes it hard to trap. They are afraid and high strung." However, he does not believe that a coyote once pinched cannot be caught. "You catch a coyote because he's bold or stupid and you catch him again for the same reaon, because he's bold or stupid. Coyotes are just like people. Everything related to a coyote can be related to man. Man is an animal. Young people get into accidents and three weeks later they get into another accident. Two years later they kill themselves."

Olson is primarily a fox trapper. He says there aren't enough coyotes in Maine, New Hampshire and Vermont for anyone to call himself a coyote trapper. There were 739 coyotes trapped in Maine in the 1980 season as compared to 4,080 fox. Also, fox was worth about sixty-five dollars to a trapper, coyote only about thirty-five dollars. Olson averages 100 foxes a year but has caught only 118 coyotes in eight years.

Western coyotes, though more numerous, are worth more because of the quality of the fur and the uniformity of color. In 1981 top quality Montana-type coyote pelts were worth about one hundred dollars; Wyoming and Utah types about seventy dollars; pale-colored Nebraska coyote about fifty dollars and smaller size Western coyotes about thirty dollars. Not all New England trapping is done soley for profit, however. Some of it is for sport; and because a coyote is harder to trap than a fox, some trappers take more pleasure in catching coyote even though fox fur is worth more. Though Olson traps for a living, he also traps because he enjoys it, a fact that antihunting and antitrapping people could not understand. Olson must tend every trap every day by law. Some days he tends the last trap at 2:00 P.M., and, because he began work at 4:00 A.M. when he left his house in Bethel, he has to push himself to set new traps until darkness rather than head home to rest. "Every day the fun, the *fun* is checking your traps. At two P.M. I've checked all the traps and the fun is over. I've got to set more traps from two to five. If I don't set more traps then I can't check those traps tomorrow." I know lobster fishermen who must feel the same way, though they haven't said so, exactly. A lobster fisherman once told me he would rather catch more lobsters when the price was low than fewer lobsters when the price was high because of the disappointment, the lack of pleasure, of fun, of pulling empty traps from the water. Though much has been written about the cruelty of trapping animals, nothing is said about trapping lobsters. Lobsters are trapped painlessly enough, but they die in boiling water.

"What makes a fur trapper I can't tell. Some are millionaires, some you might call bums, and they are. The first thing a trapper is is a worker. It's one of the few jobs left today when you can get out of it what you put into it, but a mill worker will say of a trapper 'He ain't workin'.' To be a good beaver trapper he's got to love beaver, in a way. Same as a fox. You have to study them. To catch a coyote you have to think like one. Maybe the word is not love, maybe the word is respect. Maybe the word is appreciate. A real dedicated trapper loves or respects the animal more than an antitrapper. . . . I buy fur, sell trapping equipment, and some trappers get so busy at that they stop trapping, but that never happens to me. The biggest reason people don't trap is public relations. It's no fun knocking on farm doors, asking permission to trap, like a salesman. Who likes getting doors slammed in their face?"

Olson keeps a ledger of his fur catch year to year like certain record-minded golf addicts who post every score on the insides of their lockers. Olson caught his first coyote in Grafton Notch State Park, Maine, in a cubby set, a trap set inside a pile of rocks and intended for a fisher. Not many coyotes were caught in the 1960s and early 1970s in New England, and those that were, were caught on No. 2 size fox traps. Trappers and game wildlife biologists ascribed great wisdom to the coyote for its ability to evade capture, and it was thought special skill was needed to catch coyotes. The federal government sent a man to Maine to instruct native trappers. Olson debunks the idea that a coyote is abnormally smart. A good fox trapper can catch coyote, he says. The trick is to hold the coyote once he is caught, by using the bigger No. 3 trap with the chain and a steel stake. A wooden stake will hold a fox but not a coyote. However, the question recurs: Is a coyote smarter than a fox?

"The difference between a coyote and fox is the coyote can associate faster. You put a hundred traps out and catch fifty coyotes. You catch the stupid or the bold. The fifty smart coyotes are uncaught each year. The luckier and more educated remember year after year [and don't get caught], so in a slight way they gain knowledge year to year. The [state wildlife] report that ninety percent of the coyotes caught are young is probably true. . . . The coyote can associate the trap with trouble faster than the fox. Some considered the coyote smarter but it's because he's bigger. If a fox is caught in a coyote trap, he's there, but a coyote caught in a fox trap, he's gone. If you catch a fox in one spot, that's a good spot to catch another, but you catch a coyote and it's a lot harder to get another there." It is a mistake to give a coyote too much credit for intelligence, Olson says. A coyote may avoid one trap through knowledge and cleverness, but a second trap in the same place may get him because "no coyote alive can count to two."

Olson had a stack of photographs of animals he had trapped, forty or fifty photos, mostly of fox and coyote, a few bobcat, and he showed me a picture of a trapped fox that had been killed and eaten by coyotes. "When coyote come on a fox in a trap they are going to play with it. This was the only time they actually ate it." Coyotes and other animals do not normally eat flesh of the fox. Coyotes and other animals like beaver meat. So does Olson. "In Alabama we ate a lot of beaver. There's not much meat on a forty-pound beaver, about enough for a good meal for two trappers. We fried it in onions. If you didn't know what you were eating you'd think you were eating a beef critter. Course, the fellow I went with was an awful good cook."

*The Trapper*

It was nearly April when I talked with Olson in his trap shack. He was getting his traps ready for the new season the following fall. He had approximately one hundred coyote traps that cost eleven dollars each, complete with chain and stake and swivels. He had more than two hundred smaller No. 2 traps for fox, and about one hundred fifty size 1½ traps for fox and raccoon and fisher, and seventy beaver traps. Olson looked on his workbench for something to show me. I asked him what he was looking for and said I would help him search, but he said, no, he couldn't describe it. His little girl must have taken it, he said, and he walked out the door and found his fox trackmaker where the girls had been playing.

The fox trackmaker was a stick with the wooden form of a fox track on its end. Olson made some tracks by pressing the stick into the March mud outside his trap shack. The track mark could have been coyote or fox. Only woodsmen who are very sure of themselves pretend always to know fox from coyote. A fox track is somewhat smaller than that of a coyote and a coyote has a longer stride, about nineteen inches compared to about fourteen inches for a fox. The fox puts one foot in front of another, putting his tracks almost in a single line. Coyote tracks are not so much a single line as a fox. A dog leaves a double line of prints. I asked Olson if he could tell fox track from coyote all the time, and he gave me a state-of-Maine answer. "If I was in country where there were no dogs and no fox I could tell coyote track ninety-nine percent of the time." Then he said: "I can't tell, not always. In springtime you get an adult fox track and a coyote pup track and they're similar. On fluffy snow where a coyote and fox urinate, the way to tell—it sounds barbaric—is to smell it. I can tell the difference, not that I'm a urine expert."

Coyote lore makes much mention of urine because urine is the best single way to lure coyotes to a trap. Some western trappers believe urine from an old coyote is best because younger coyotes are less wary to tread where older creatures of their kind have stepped: Some trappers believe urine from the bladder of a trapped coyotes gives off the fear felt by the trapped animal. H.T. Gier has written that males are attracted to traps by female urine and vice versa and that urine from a female in estrus is very effective.

Ralph Griffin of Dixfield was using fox urine the day I accompanied him on his trap line in Carthage. Griffin had his own source of fox urine, a fox he had trapped and had penned behind his house. The flooring of this fox pen was sloped so that the animal's urine flowed to a particular point where Griffin could collect it. Griffin would have liked to have done the same with a coyote but had decided it would take a strong pen to hold a coyote and for this reason, and in deference to his wife's apprehension, he did not keep a live coyote penned behind his house. Fox urine will attract coyotes to a trap, and Griffin used fox urine both for fox and for coyotes. Says Olson: "You can catch coyote on fox urine but fox might be afraid of coyote urine, though that's not always so."

Trapping is not a science. Some trappers say it is an art, and for that reason many things believed by one trapper are disbelieved by another, in the way some fly fishermen prefer small nymphs rather than large nymphs and in the way some who trap lobster prefer round traps to square. As in all these things, the equipment and techniques used by one are similar to those used by another. However, in all my reading and in all my conversations with trappers I had not come upon the cow manure set before meeting Olson and reading a description of it written by him.

We had been talking two or three hours that afternoon before we left his trap shack and found the fox trackmaker outside. I was going to come back the next morning after going over my notes that night in a Bethel motel, and Olson gave me something he wanted me to read, a draft in longhand of a handbook on trapping he is writing. But on the car radio that

## The Trapper

afternoon while driving into Bethel I heard of the assassination attempt on President Ronald Reagan, and I watched television coverage of that drama that night as I studied my notes. I did not get to read Olson's manuscript until the next morning after breakfast at 5:00 A.M. at a Bethel diner where loggers were drinking coffee and sucking on cigarettes in preparation for their day's work.

A cow manure set is used by Olson especially for fox. Fox look under cow flaps for bugs. The trapper cuts a wedge out of a dry cow flap and buries lure at the top of this vee opening. A trap is buried in the earth under this vee. Olson writes of this set: "Many foxes become dirt shy instead of trap shy. A fox that has been pinched at a dirt hole set will become shy of fresh dirt because that is where he was pinched. The cow manure set when made correctly has no fresh dirt showing. The final thin layer of covering [over the buried trap] consists of dry manure and a few blades of grass. In most cases you can't use green grass at all [in other trap sets] for covering because it dies and takes on a dead yellowing look. [But] remember under this dry cow flap [the grass] already looks like this and is thusly not unnatural."

A drawing of the cow manure set plus the text made it clear to me. I think I could catch a fox with that information if I had a trap, rubber gloves, rubber boots and the lure. Lures differ. Some trappers buy their lure, others prepare it themselves. A lure for coyote or fox might contain these ingredients: fish oil, coyote or fox urine (depending on the quarry), muskrat musk, ground-up beaver glands and a few drops of skunk essence. That is the real stuff, skunk essence. I smelled it, or thought I did, in Olson's trap shack and other places where I talked to trappers. Olson writes in his trapping book: "There is nothing stronger than skunk essence and nothing more natural. . . . A fox is a hunter and when a skunk sprays, something has happened. . . . When a fox approaches your set he's thinking skunk and not human." Olson describes other effects of skunk essence, possibly introducing Maine hyperbole into his otherwise straightaway guide to trapping. "After a hard day on the line I decided to stop into a restaurant. I thought people were looking at me rather oddly. When I made my final decision to leave was when cook stuck his head out of the kitchen and started sniffing. At least I knew my lure was working."

(Six months earlier I had been following trapper Griffin up a track that once was a wagon road to a farm in the woods. That farm had gone back to brush, good habitat for coyotes. I noticed a peculiar smell, asked Griffin if I smelled the Boise Cascade paper mill in Rumford, and he said no, probably not, that I was smelling his trapping clothes.)

Griffin was using dirt hole sets, a common method to catch fox or coyote. He placed a piece of bobcat meat in a small dirt hole, put some lure on the bait itself and more lure on the side of a tree or some other place near the trap. The strong-smelling lure is to attract an animal from a distance. The trap is buried in front of the bobcat meat bait the right distance away so that a coyote bending down to eat the bait will place a paw on the trigger that springs the jaws of the trap shut on its paw. The trap is set in a hole and then covered with waxed paper to keep the covering soil from getting into the trap mechanism and making it inoperable. Griffin wrinkled the waxed paper to take the noise out of it before fitting it over the trap because a coyote is so wary he might withdraw his paw in time if he could hear the paper rustle. The waxed paper that covers the trap is covered with dirt sifted through a screen. This sign of fresh dirt might make a coyote think another animal had buried food there. Griffin could have added something else, coyote prints on the sifted dirt, using the end of his trowel or a molded print of the kind used by Olson. A coyote is more likely to step in a place

---

Coyote trap, shown here in a cutaway view, would be covered first with waxed paper to keep the mechanism from fouling, then with loose dirt. The coyote is lured to the general area by a trapper's scent (either essence of skunk or coyote urine), then attracted to a wad of dry grass (to look like a mouse's nest) by a piece of meat. To get the meat he must step on the trap.

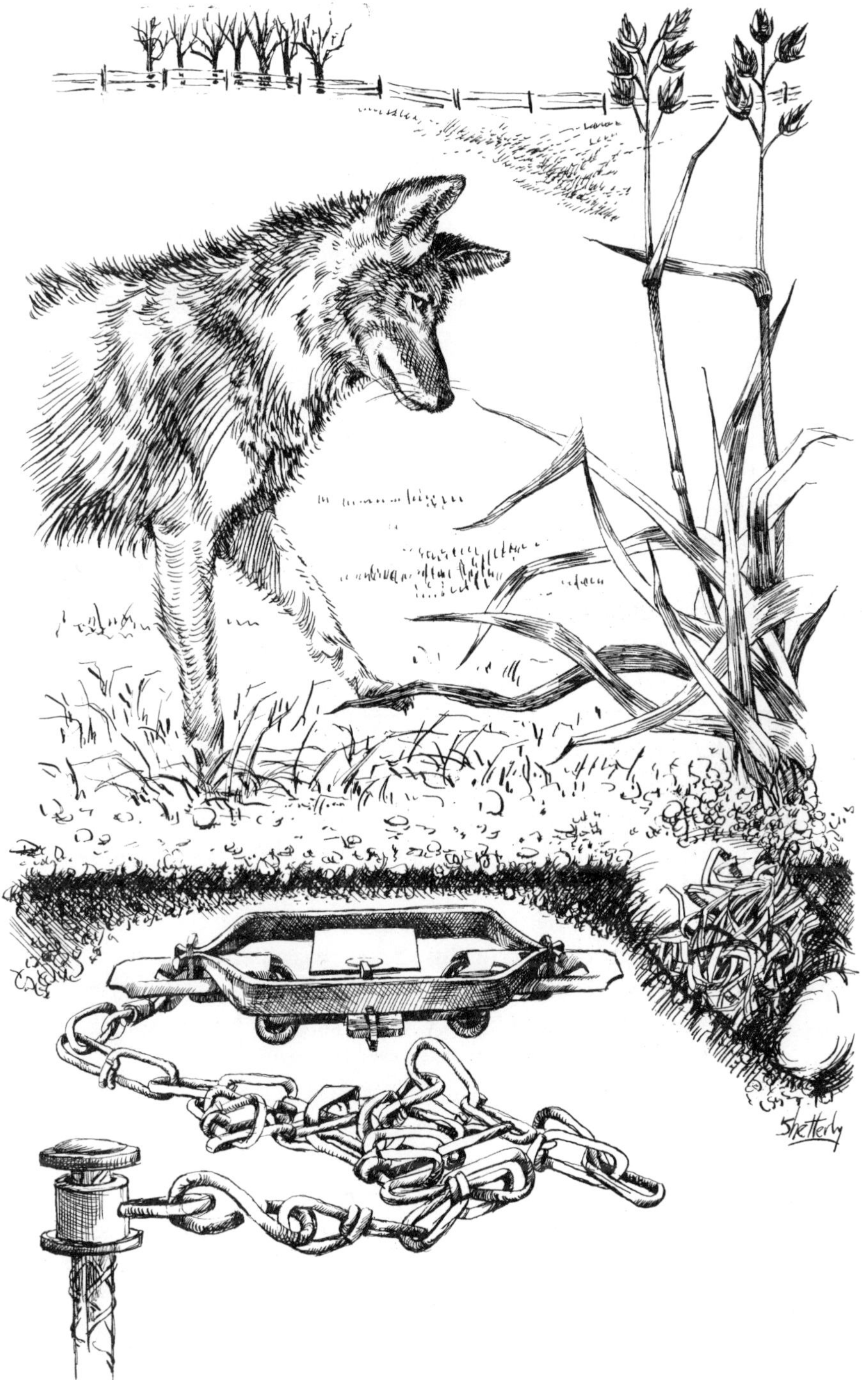
Shetterly

where he sees the print of another coyote.

Olson would make a dirt hole set about the same as did Griffin. Olson once used brown paper bags to cover his traps rather than waxed paper because the brown paper would not show up as quickly as the white waxed paper when rain partially uncovered the set. He no longer uses the brown paper because it absorbs water whereas the waxed paper repels it. The dirt hole set is a common set and used to trap many animals. If a coyote cannot be caught on a dirt hole set, there is another way.

Olson says a coyote once pinched in a trap can be caught and held a second time, though it is written and said by knowledgeable people that a coyote is too smart to be caught again. Olson; "A coyote may become fresh dirt shy and dirt hole shy but can be caught on a post set." Coyotes urinate on fence posts, hence the name of the trap set, but a scent post could be any place a coyote urinates, on the edge of a log, on a rock as well as on a post. A trap is buried eight inches or so from the post or log or rock where the trapper sprays urine. When the coyote lifts a leg to urinate on this spot, he steps into the trap with the other foot. Olson: "If a coyote is afraid of that post set he is afraid of himself, because the urine odor plays a big part in his life. We write notes to each other on a pad, they urinate." Though a coyote is drawn to a post set by the smell of urine sprayed there, he could walk up to the wrong side of the post, the side away from the trap. "You have to make it so the coyote stays on one side of the post. Just by putting a pile of leaves on one side will make the coyote go on the other side because the coyote is a hunter and doesn't want to step on dry leaves and make noise."

Old-timers tell Olson they used to catch fox on snow. Olson mentioned this several times. It was an important point, but at first I failed to realize its significance. At first he said, "They said they caught thirty foxes on snow," and he would shake his head and say, "Maybe they did." But at some time during the two days of our conversation he implied the old-

## The Trapper

timers were telling stories. He didn't believe anyone could catch thirty fox on snow. "If a dirt hole or scent post set is done right, there's no way an animal can tell that man has been there, but in snow you leave tracks. Rain washes the dirt off a trap so he can see it. Coyotes don't know how the trap works [but know enough to avoid it]. . . . And freezing makes a trap harder to spring. . . . If the snow stays fluffy you can work on it, but the top of the snow freezes so the coyote can't reach the trap."

There is one good thing about trapping in snow. "Trappers are always guessing what happens, but in snow like last year when I was in Norton, Vermont, you could see what was happening. On bare ground you don't know. On the snow you see the animals knew a set was there. Sometimes they would come so close and I'd say 'Oh, just missed 'em,' and others would come no closer than from here to the road [pointing outside his house] and no closer. I relate it to them and people on thin ice. Nine times you don't step on the thin ice, but the tenth time for some ungodly reason you do."

He sets his coyote traps in many places: a rock pile or sandy place in a field; where a logging road enters a field; on a bridge from one field to another field; near phone poles in a field where a farmer cannot cut the grass with his mower and a coyote might find mice; on the edge of fields; along brooks or the edges of farm ponds. Traps are not used as they come from the factory but are boiled in a mixture of water and ground-up bark. The boiling rids the trap of the odor of man; the bark dyes the trap. Then the trap is waxed, which seals in any remaining odors and speeds the action of the trap, like wax on cross country skis.

Coyotes usually pull their paws free of the trap in the first moment, Olson says, for there is a moment after the trap is sprung when it has not firmly set. That is his theory. There is another moment when they are apt to escape. "I had three coyotes this year escape when I approached. They had been fighting the trap all night, then rested. Then they saw me and made one last effort. It's like stories you hear of a man, his adrenalin pumping, picking off a log from somebody." If there is blood about the trap, Olson says it is from the coyote's bleeding jaws, the result of the coyote trying to bend steel with his teeth, something I found hard to believe until Olson showed me proof, his bent traps. A coyote normally escapes by pulling at the trap hard enough to bend the fasteners that hold the jaws. The animal has great strength for its size, and its size is often overestimated. The biggest coyote Ralph Griffin ever caught weighed fifty-two pounds; the largest coyote Olson has seen weighed was forty-seven pounds. Olson says: "The animal is smaller than some people think but look bigger because of the length of fur, and they are long-legged. But some can be short and fat and others are long and lean." Olson does not think a sixty-pound trapped German shepherd could be mistaken for a coyote, at least not for very long. "Because of the higher price of fur there are new trappers and new fur buyers. There's a learning process. I won't say it is not happening, but at some point [in the fur market] someone will recognize it as a dog." There were 1,648 trappers in Maine in 1970, a figure that grew to over 5,000 by 1980, but while summer people in Maine probably know a man as a lobsterman or a logger or a blueberry grower, few know of him as a trapper because the trapping season is short and trapping is part-time work.

Cats and dogs are caught in traps meant for coyotes and fox. A Maine trapper and taxidermist told me: "I've released a lot of dogs. I can't tell you how many cats I've released." His own dog had been caught in the garden where the taxidermist was trying to catch a raccoon. The dog was released and an hour or two later showed no effects of the trap, the taxidermist said. Trapper Griffin had released a dog from a trap in the vicinity of Carthage some days before I traveled with him. A dog will accept the restraint of the trap and wait to be released. Dogs are not supposed to be in the deep woods in deer country unless attended by their owner, and stray dogs in Maine woods are traveling unfriendly territory, endangered not so much by trappers as by deer hunters, although the deer hunter may be a trapper as well.

Dogs kill deer for sport; coyotes kill deer for food and for sport. Those who are most certain that the coyote endangers the deer herd of New England often have the least knowledge of the animal. Trapper Olson is uncertain how many deer are killed by coyotes. He was asked one winter to catch coyotes that were attacking deer in a deer yard in the town of Newry. Olson obtained the special permit required for trapping out of season. He caught a fox and a fisher but no coyote; a good example of why fish and game departments do not allow year-round trapping of coyotes, not to protect the coyote but to protect the valuable and easily trapped fisher that is making a comeback in New England. Olson thinks he failed to catch the coyotes in Newry because the coyotes had gone back towards the mountains. "That's where the coyotes go in winter. In fall I catch them in corn fields where they catch birds and mice. Mice are harder to get there in winter and coyotes go back towards the woods and go after rabbits and deer."

Olson released the fox and fisher he had caught out of season in Newry. "There's no animal I know of that can't be released, but releasing a bear takes some effort. I stopped at a landowner's property one summer to ask permission to trap and that fall I set some traps. He called me one night and I went over there, and he said someone had shot the mother bear, and a cub was caught in a trap. The cub had pulled the trap out of the ground and climbed a tree to about shoulder height. I went back and got the landowner, and he held the bear pinned with a forked stick while I pulled out porcupine quills from the cub's face with pliers." Olson released the cub's paw from the trap, and the thirty- or forty-pound bear climbed higher in the tree where it felt safe.

"I probably give skunk more respect than other trappers who say they release them simply by talking to them. But I never've gone to the extent to talking to one. To an extent it's true with coyotes. If you talk to a coyote in a trap in a low voice sometimes they calm down. Lots of times they might be thrashing and hard to get a good bead on them. If you talk to them, calm them down, it makes for a better shot."

Olson traps about seventy days a year, trying to catch fox, coyote and beaver. He could trap longer if he followed the beaver season more from place to place. When he is not trapping he is working on his fur and fur he buys from other trappers, occupying himself about eight months of the year with fur. The 1980–81 season did not produce an abundance of fur nationally, he says, so fur brokers were active and Olson sold nearly all his goods by the end of April.

In summer he puts on a trappers' convention in a field near his house. "It takes a lot of effort. About two thousand trappers came last year." He knows of one Maine man who might be truly called a professional trapper because he earns four-fifths of his total income of $5,000 by trapping and lives way back in the woods without electricity or other comforts. Olson himself comes close to being a professional trapper by New England standards and is familiar with tracks and with other sign.

There was a question remaining and I asked it. He said: "People ask me about mountain lions. I have a hide in the house and visitors look at it. I say the mountain lion came from within three miles of here, which it did. They ask me where. I say I don't tell you because there's another one there, which was true, the Rumford Animal Farm. I say a bobcat killed it which is true. The cougar put its leg out, got clawed by the bobcat in the next cage and got infected." Trapper Olson has seen no sign of the lion.

# – 10 –
# The Fur Dealer

Tom Stevens is a fur buyer for the Mark Mowatt Fur Co. in Holden, Maine, a town near Bangor. I was talking to Stevens about bears and bear claws, and he began his explanation with this fact: Bears have twenty claws. "The front claws are much larger than the rear. Usually you have ten large claws and ten medium size from a large bear. A big bear is two hundred fifty pounds. Most people think bear are bigger, weigh five hundred pounds, but bears that size are few and far between. I saw one last year that was close to four hundred and had bigger claws. . . . A hundred fifty pounds is average. Fall cubs weigh forty or fifty pounds, a yearling seventy-five to eighty, adults two and a half years old weigh one hundred to two hundred. Bear are shot or can be caught with a spring-activated bear cable trap. The cable is thrown around the leg [when the bear steps on the spring] and the bear tightens the cable by jerking at it. It doesn't hurt them. Cable traps are used to catch and release bear. Good quality claws are unbroken. You might have broken nails on one that has been killed in the road. Or one that has been trapped might dig and dig, wearing down the claws, or maybe a bear's a digger anyway and wears down his claws naturally.

"Bear ivory is not nearly as valuable. There are just four canine teeth and if you get two good ones out of a bear you're lucky. A bigger, old bear might have good claws but have worn-down teeth. When you buy a bear you get the claws but not the head and the ivory. . . . I got a shipment of four feet in the mail today.

"I would go four years and not see a bear, then see ten or twelve in one year in the woods. The big thing in bear sighting is the food supply. If there's no food in the woods they come out to beehives or orchards. Two or three years ago they were shooting bear on this road [Route 1A, the main road from Bangor to Ellsworth]. A fellow shot one right behind here in an orchard."

Stevens heard a vehicle park outside the one-story fur plant. It was a hunter with a load of raccoon skins. Stevens thought he recognized him, that he would not sell his fur but had come only to see what Stevens would offer. Stevens was mistaken. The hunter was from Hartland, wore green wool pants held up by suspenders, a red and black plaid wool jacket and new leather boots. He wore a hat of phosphorescent orange, for it was November, deer season. The hat would keep him warm and might keep him from being shot. He spread his fifteen 'coon pelts on the floor, and Stevens began grading them, putting the better ones in one pile, the poorer pelts in another pile. "The market is not too good," Stevens said. The hunter replied that the market is never any good when a man wants to sell. He said this without mirth but without malice, either. He and Stevens were doing some fur trading, and Steven's opening remark and the hunter's reply were traditional, I suppose, like car buyer and car salesman sparring. Stevens tried a conversational approach, asked the hunter if he had gotten his deer this year. "Oh yeah. We [he and his group] got six." A man entered the shop then with a deer skin. Stevens looked at it, paid the man five dollars. Deer skin is not worth much in its raw state; its value increases with processing and it is worth about fifteen tanned. Mark Mowatt, Stevens's employer, sells hides he buys to tanners in Gloversville and Johnstown, New York. Deer hunting is for sport and for meat, not for profit from hides, but raccoon is hunted and trapped for its valuable fur. In 1979, a total of 31,480 'coon pelts were sold in Maine; in 1980 the figure was 23,638, of which 13,413 were shot, 9,899 trapped.

Stevens kept looking at the 'coon skins on the floor. He had separated them by size and by quality and measured them with a yardstick and tested the condition of the fur with a steel comb. Some of the skins were prime, others less so. Stevens flipped each skin on the floor one more time and said: "What price were you thinking of?" The hunter must have heard that question before and anticipated it, and said without hesitation, almost blurting the words: "What will you give me?" Stevens said, "Three hundred eight dollars." Hunter: "Three-twenty-five, and you've got a deal." Stevens said he might go up a few dollars on the prime skins, but, gee, the others weren't worth much more. He flipped the first batch of prime skins another time on the floor and said, "Three-twelve." The hunter said "Three-fifteen." Stevens accepted that figure, and then he and the hunter talked a while about deer hunting, and now that business was done it was not just small talk but genuine conversation. After the hunter had been paid and left, Stevens said: "He was probably hoping for three hundred, probably would have sold for three hundred if I held my ground. But he went out happy and that's better."

Raccoon is a long-haired fur and peaked in value in the winter of 1979–80 at fifty dollars for a large prime pelt, up greatly from the late 1960s when raccoon fur was worth only two or three dollars and once sunk as low as fifty cents. A large prime pelt was worth about thirty-two dollars in November 1980 when Stevens made his deal with the 'coon hunter from

Hartland. That hunter would have received the same price if he had delivered the 'coon whole because Stevens and Mowatt would rather have their own man skin the 'coon to insure quality work. Bob Defarges was working on raccoon on the other side of the room from where Stevens had purchased the Hartland 'coon. There was a strong but not obnoxious smell of animal flesh in the room. Earlier that morning a visitor had said he could separate a skunk's odor sacs, the rectal glands at the base of the tail that a skunk can utilize as a repellent by contracting his anal muscle, squeezing the sacs and discharging the spray. This visitor's efforts to separate the glands a new way was unsuccessful, and the scent of skunk heightened the smell of 'coon fat and flesh and fur.

Bob Defarges wants to learn how to become a fur buyer and was learning how while working for Mowatt skinning and fleshing 'coon. Defarges says he's not as good at skinning as he is at fleshing because he is light, only 155 pounds. "I could flesh twenty-five small 'coon in an hour, can average about sixteen an hour. I did seventy-two the other day within four and a half hours." Fleshing means separating the fat from the fur with a special knife, a fleshing tool. Skinning is the process of taking the pelt from the carcass. In Maine or New Hampshire or Vermont, most woods people use only one form of the verb to skin. They skun a beaver, or just skunned a beaver, using a past tense not normally heard but found in the dictionary as a dialect past tense. Defarges, though, is from Philadelphia and did not use the verb skun in our conversation.

"I have long arms, and I'm tall, six-two, and got leverage and strength in my arms, but I don't have the weight so I can't tear a skin off a carcass as well as a heavier man. When the carcass is fresh, it's easier. When it's been frozen and thawed, the fat becomes like a hard brick of lard and harder to pull. Fresh ones I can tear off fast as anyone." He described how a skin is cut and then pulled off a carcass, a process I had seen before in the garage of a trapper. The process is difficult to describe in words, not that it is complicated. Defarges is asked what he does for work sometimes, at a bank for instance, and "I get a kick out of saying I'm a 'coon skinnner. The ladies especially do a double take."

Defarges sees old wounds on the legs of 'coon he skins and fleshes, an indication the 'coon has been retrapped after once escaping from a trap. He has not seen coyotes with old trap wounds, an indication that most coyotes who escape are trap shy and trap wise; and he has seen steel traps bent by coyotes and teeth marks in the steel of the trap. I think Defarges meant the coyote's teeth have scratched the surface finish of the steel and not the steel itself. Whatever the strength of the coyote, its teeth are made of enamel.

Defarges grew up in Philadelphia but wants to be a country boy. Already he has the open manner of a country boy, but whether that characteristic is learned or innate I do not know. He sees animals native state-of-Mainers never see, the marten for one. "People don't know pine marten exist because they're nocturnal, same as flying squirrels. Flying squirrels are common, but people don't see them. Of course, if you go up to a tree and bang on it in daytime, the squirrel will come out and fly to the next tree." Flying squirrels do not fly, exactly, but they get from one tree to the next by leaping from a tree and using their winglike membranes to glide downwards and across to their target. It amounts to flying, almost.

Mark Mowatt is thirty-one, owns the fur company in Holden, says he sells several thousand pelts a year, worth over one million dollars. He sells to dealers in New York and in Europe and Asia and operates a branch of his fur business in Nova Scotia where he was born. "In New York fur dealers call themselves skin dealers. I don't like the sound of that. We call ourselves raw fur dealers."

Mowatt grew up in Nova Scotia in a place called Shubenacadie, which means land of the wild potato in the language of the Micmac Indians. His father trapped and hunted, made his living as a logger. "I was constantly in the woods. One summer I went to a guide school for boys where they taught us things like how to use a map, shoulder a canoe. I met two fellows, graduate wildlife students, there. I realized for the first time a man could get a job working with animals in the woods." Mowatt went to Acadia University in Nova Scotia, earned a biology degree in three years and then went to the University of Maine at Orono for graduate work. His project there was moose disease.

"I was still interested in trapping. I paid part of my tuition each year by trapping. I trapped almost full time in Maine, had a two-day run, a sixty-mile trap line on the Airline [Route 6, the road, much of it through deep woods, between Bangor and the Maritime Provinces]. I trapped near Aurora and along the Narraguagus River and north of the Airline and in T-24 [an unorganized township in the woods designated by a number instead of a name]. I tried to schedule my classes and graduate student teaching assignments to leave a day open to go out and run my trap line, but often I'd go at night with a headlamp." He earned his master's degree in wildlife management in 1972 and received a grant to study the marten while he worked on his doctorate, but he became restless. "I left school in 1973 and went trapping full time in the fall of 1973 on the Airline and other parts of Maine. I started buying fur, and in the fall of 1974 I concentrated on buying. I started to travel to fur centers in 1975, and in 1975 I hired my first employee, Tom Stevens, who'd been an A student at Orono. I hired him to skin 'coons."

Mowatt led me towards his fur storage room and talked about the fur business. "Fox and 'coon and mink fur reach full prime in November to December. The guard hairs are full length when the pelt is prime and the underfur becomes more dense. Any time from mid-January to mid-February, depending on the weather, 'coons and fox get overprime. The fur starts showing wear on the ends and becomes discolored. Fox sit on the snow. The heat of their body melts the snow and tips of hair freeze. They leave small patches of fur on the snow several times a day and get bare spots on their rumps. Also, the color fades after mid-December and becomes paler because of the sunlight, and the fur is not as desirable. In summer the guard hairs are shorter and the underhair thinner. The guard hairs tend to cure in late winter and shed out in summer.

"Our market is London, Milan, West Germany and Scandinavia, Japan (especially fox), Paris, too (especially fisher). Almost all the fox in northern Maine is red. There are a few grays in southern Maine. There are a few cross fox in Maine. That's not a hybrid but is caused by a recessive gene in red fox. Cross fox is worth the same or less than a red fox in Maine."

A cross fox is a color phase of the red fox as is the silver fox. The cross fox, though mostly reddish brown, has a band of dark guard hairs down the middle of his back and another band across his shoulders to form the cross that gives the cross fox its name. The only fox I have seen in Maine was in a field on the edge of the Penobscot River near Lincoln the day I was on my way to see Rita Potter, the woman in Wytopitlock who saw a mountain lion. It looked very small. Red fox only weigh ten or twelve pounds.

Mowatt told me: "Fox averages fifty to seventy dollars. Last year [1979] it was worth eighty dollars. We're seeing a shift back to short-hair fur, mink, 'rat, beaver but not otter. That's unusual because the otter price is usually good when the beaver price is good. The long fur is fox, 'coon, fisher, bobcat and marten. Raccoon and fox were especially popular when 'fun furs' were worn by younger people. Older people wear more conservative fur such as mink.

We passed the skinning beam used by Defarges, the 'coon skinner. A skinning beam is shaped something like an ironing board made round and fat. They used to be made of maple and oak, but Mowatt made his of pine, a wood easier to shape and smooth but too soft for scraping. He covered the pine with fiberglass. "It works beautifully because the fiberglass is harder than oak." Fat is scraped off the pelts on this skinning beam. Foxes have little fat, only pockets of it under what would be the underarms of a human and in the genital area, but 'coon can have an inch or two of fat from their tail to their nose, fat they use while lying dormant in winter in a den or hollow tree. A 'coon may come out on a mild winter day and thus is not a true hibernator as are woodchucks. 'Coons are clever, though not clever enough to avoid traps. Their curiosity militates against them, but, as trapper Olson says, they do not have a good nose and do not find a trap as quickly as a coyote, a fact that works in their favor in that respect at least.

We entered Mowatt's fur locker where he had approximately 1,200 raccoon skins stacked in separate bins according to size and quality. This batch was scheduled for Milan. Raccoon pelts are measured from the nose to the base of the tail. Pelts over thirty-three inches long are referred to as XXXL (for extra-extra-extra large), and they range down to XXL to XL (which is twenty-seven to thirty inches long in Maine but would be only twenty-four inches in Texas where the raccoon does not grow as large) to L (for large). Each size grade is further graded into ones or twos according to the quality of the fur. A "two" may have been trapped a week or two before the fur grew out and became prime. Maine raccoon have heavy fur and are used for trim, collars and cuffs and borders at the bottom of a coat, whereas raccoon from the central United States or Texas has lighter fur and raccoon from those areas are called coat 'coon.

"A person might wire and ask for one thousand medium small Number Twos coat-type northern Pennsylvania raccoon. That's an exaggeration but an example of how business is done. We put up large matched lots of furs. I know the manufacturers so I can deal over the phone. They wire cash, and it gets here in one day. When it hits the New York bank and is transferred to my bank in Bangor I have the furs on a plane that night. It has to be fast because of the amount of money involved. A man who pays thirty or forty thousand dollars wants the goods. Also, the market can change in a day if a large auction goes bad. It happened last year [1979] when a large auction in eastern Canada and a large quantity of long-hair fur, coon and lynx, was offered for sale. All of a sudden there were no buyers. This can cause a big drop in price. The price can also go up, a fifty percent drop or a fifty percent rise in a day, but that is not normal. The fur market last year got grossly overpriced because it's unregulated. Country fur buyers [and Mowatt does not consider himself one of those] were paying higher prices, competing with each other, while the manufacturers had reached the point where they couldn't move the garments.

"The reason it's so up and down is the time lag is so great. It takes nine months from the time a fur is trapped until the coat is made. Last December my European customers were refusing goods while my competitors in the woods were still buying. In February things fell apart. A lot of small dealers sold off before Christmas. Anyone who held high-price furs except beaver and 'rats were in trouble.

"For example in Canada. We are active in eastern Canada. Last year in January and February small country buyers were paying three hundred dollars each for bobcats though they were only worth a hundred fifty in Europe. Eventually they lost over one hundred dollars a pelt. Previously they'd been getting as much as three fifty so they were willing to pay three hundred or three fifty in expectation the price would go to four hundred."

He had fox fur next to the bins of raccoon pelts. He picked one out. "These are jacket foxes, have a nice smooth, flat finish, good color and light weight. Nova Scotia fox are caught later in the year and are heavier, are used as trim. . . . Maine fox would be heavier if trapped in December. . . . One reason there is no December fox trapping in Maine is to prevent catching fisher or bobcat by mistake, and those animals are not plentiful."

Fox were almost worthless in Maine in 1955, worth as little as fifty cents a fur. Only 300 were caught in a long season because trappers had no incentive. Foxes proliferated because there was no pressure on them, and as the population became dense it became susceptible to disease. A fox with mange or rabies transmits its disease simply because it comes in contact with many foxes. This is accepted wildlife theory among biologists. Mange does not concern the general public much, only trappers; but rabies is another thing. When fox proliferated in the 1950s and rabies broke out in some areas, poison bait was set out in the woods to kill them.

John Hunt questions this accepted theory of proliferation and disease. Hunt is an old-timer in the Maine Department of Inland Fisheries and Wildlife and works out of Bingham in the western part of the state. I spoke to him by phone some months after talking to fur buyers Stevens and Mowatt. Hunt says: "A lot of people with a lot of education subscribe to the theory that if predators become dense it leads to mange. It's not proven. I've been in this part of Maine for years. Fox were free of rabies for lots of decades and when rabies came in it was in the northwest wooded country where there are not so many foxes. We spent prodigious amounts of man-hours trying to control rabies but without success, using strychnine. It had no effect at all. It was a smoke screen. I have no idea why there was no rabies before and just hope those [good] days come back. Right now in areas between the Kennebec and the Penobscot where there's hellish high trapping pressure we have rabies among foxes, a minor epidemic in a small area. . . . When animals get sick, how the hell do people know why." Hunt says there is no danger from rabid foxes unless the fox bites a cat who bites a member of the family, and under Maine law all pets are supposed to be inoculated against rabies.

"Right now," Mowatt said, "I doubt you could get an explosion of foxes because trappers are getting fifty to seventy dollars. This year [1980] the fox is definitely down." [As it turned out, the 1980 fox harvest in Maine was 4,080, down from 6,214 the previous fall.] "But no one can tell you why. It could be the heavy trapping or the influence of coyotes. Trappers feel coyotes are driving out the fox, but there is no biological evidence. People too often are quick to make a conclusion that the coyote is responsible. Trappers generally flat out say coyote is responsible for the reduction of fox, and one trapper did see evidence in the snow where two coyotes had run down a fox and killed it. That is the sort of thing that people react to and believe because it has a flare. . . . I see no evidence that the coyote is making an impact on the raccoon. If there is an impact it would be on fox because 'coon are mostly vegetarian and are not competing for the same food. The fox is after the same food as a coyote, and a fox can't climb a tree to get away from a coyote as a raccoon can.

"There are two things wrong with Maine coyote fur. The texture of the fur is very coarse. The best fur should be silky." He picked a coyote pelt from his fur locker and said: "The big drawback is the coarseness. A western coyote is silky. The second problem is Maine [and all eastern] coyotes are a very dirty gray and the belly is a dirty brown. It is not very beautiful. But a western coyote has a very pale belly and the top is a clear color. There is more contrast in its lights and darks. . . . Maine coyotes run from dark gray to red like a fox and our coyotes are used in inexpensive coats or for trimming. A Maine coyote coat might sell for twelve hundred dollars whereas the same coat of good western skins would cost five thousand dollars and be sold at a place like Nieman Marcus or a Paris fur salon. When we buy fur from a trapper he wants so much for the lot, no matter how it is broken down, and we'll take the coyotes to accommodate him. . . ."

This trapper with coyote skins might be disappointed with the price because, Mowatt says, the trapper does not realize that the fur industry is global. "If there is a scarcity of coyotes in Maine, Texas has a zillion coyotes. [But] a thousand or two thousand fishers are trapped in Maine and very few states produce that many, so one thousand fisher is significant in the fur trade because the total harvest in the United States is about twenty-five thousand a year. [The Maine fisher harvest was 1,912 in 1980.] Local trappers might say they only caught a hundred bobcat in Maine and hold them for a price, not knowing that several hundred were taken in New Brunswick. There is no secret place to get a good price."

The hunting and trapping of bobcat and otter are regulated by federal law, and fur dealers require a special license to export fur from those two animals. An otter pelt is worth thirty to fifty dollars; but while otter are not rare they are difficult to catch, and most trappers prefer to concentrate on muskrats, always called 'rats. Although 'rats are worth only about eight dollars a pelt, they are plentiful and easy to catch. A trapper in central Maine told me of a woman who trapped 100 'rats on the Androscoggin River near Rumford. "She's a young, attractive woman," the trapper said, "and she like to trap. She keeps a good house, too, and likes being outdoors. You don't find many like her."

Mowatt told me about Maine 'rats.

"A trapper would rather go after 'rats than try for the two otters [in a particular flowage]. The average 'rat house has four or five 'rats. Commonly, on one acre of marsh there would be four or five houses, so there would be twenty to twenty-five 'rats per good acre of cattail marsh. Maine has a lot of beaver bogs where there is acid feed [in the form of poplar trees] but not so much good 'rat marsh. In good marsh condition like Montezuma National Refuge in New York you might get fifty 'rats per acre whereas a good acre in Maine there would be only twenty-five. But in a common Maine marsh you might get only one 'rat. 'Rat trappers might trap in a place two or three nights, and then move on, whereas otter might not come to that place for several days. 'Rats only travel a few hundred yards.

"'Rats are easy to skin and stetch. A trapper can do a good

job whereas on a 'coon, chances are he'll ruin it." Mowatt held up a muskrat pelt. "This 'rat has a hole, probably a bite. When they're breeding, they chew each other. Bites would be only on adults because they have been through a breeding season.... 'Rats have two litters in this latitude. They eat aquatic vegetation, and their favorite is cattail roots and freshwater mussels. They also eat the center stem of the cattail. They love wild rice and from here on north on the Penobscot there are a lot of 'rats because there is a lot of wild rice, same as ducks eat.

"The Maine 'rat is desirable, has a good blue-gray color contrasted with a pale belly and is very silky. It's not a large 'rat, but if I said to a trapper that Maine 'rats are smaller he might be insulted [or think he was being snookered], but Montezuma 'rats are huge, maybe eighteen or twenty inches long. Anything over fifteen inches in Maine is considered extra large."

In addition to 'rats and 'coon and fox and coyote, Mowatt had one bobcat and several marten pelts in his fur storage room. Skins well scraped of fat will keep months or even years in a room with controlled humidity, but some furs become discolored if stored too long. Mowatt: "Foxes have very little fat and will keep for years if kept in a cool room with low humidity. When fox was down to a dollar, some men kept them for years and did sell them at a good price eventually. 'Coon will age, the leather turns yellow because of the fat. Any stale pelt you see you wonder how it was kept. If it was kept in a barn rather than cold storage it might not tan properly. For instance, if it got wet the pelt would start to decay, the hair would fall out, and if the pelt was redried, it might not tan correctly. When it was put in the [tanning] chemical the hair falls out. Tanning removes the natural oil and it is replaced with artificial oils which don't decompose."

We had reached the place where marten fur hung. The marten, American sable, is worth fifteen to twenty dollars, about one-tenth the value of its cousin, the Russian sable, which is almost jet black. The Maine marten is smaller than a house cat, weighs a pound and a half to three and a half pounds. Marten I saw at Mowatt's fur locker and other places were colored pale orange with darker streaks. The marten likes the dense forest, but its secretive habits do not mean it is smart in the way a coyote is smart. Marten are easy to trap, and 2,252 marten were taken in Maine in the 1980 trapping season.

Mowatt had one bear hide in storage, and while talking about it he said he was the largest bear claw dealer in the country. I did not know there was a market for such a thing. He told me about his bear claw coup that afternoon and retold the story the next morning at a restaurant in Brewer, down the road a few miles from his Holden fur plant. He had to catch a flight to Nova Scotia that morning and could see me at 5:30 A.M. I arrived before he did, anxious to hear how he had cornered the market on bear claws.

Mowatt says he was a one-man show, "not two cents to my name," before the possum deal which preceded the bear claw deal. He had no business experience, for his experience was at the university and in the woods trapping, but he began to buy fur from other trappers and had some success fur dealing before his first coup, the possum deal in 1976. He met a Korean in New York at a fur dealer's shop, a Korean who wanted a lot of possums, a fur not usually handled in Maine. Mowatt remembered where there were a lot of possums, in Winnipeg at the storehouse of a dealer who in order to get a batch of fox and raccoon skins from the Dakotas had had to buy some possum that had been trapped in Iowa. Mowatt quoted a price to the Korean he met in New York and then called the Canadian dealer.

"I had never handled possum so I took a one-day crash course in grading possum and spent the next day [after that] grading eleven thousand possum in Winnipeg. I sold nine thousand to the Korean and two thousand to another dealer. I made two dollars a skin, bought for two dollars and sold for four. ... The fellow I got the possum from was a wealthy, established trader, but he had a sleeper in his cooler and didn't know it. He probably made a little on it but doesn't know the price I got."

The possum market went through a big price range in the next few years, rising to twelve dollars a pelt in 1979, then falling to three dollars. "One friend of mine is stuck with seventy-three thousand possum. I saw them stored in Montreal.

"I developed the bear claw market. In 1974 and 1975 the market was quite good, dealing directly with jewelry manufacturers in New Mexico, Arizona, southern California. The jewelry business got bad and the demand disappeared. Meanwhile, I was buying claws from hunters and had several hundred, and I had a couple of thousand in Canada. I called [to the southwest] and there was no interest in my claws but in 1976 I started to get calls: 'Got any bear claws?' and I would say, 'I got some,' or 'at this price I might.' Obviously the market was ready to come back. Canadian dealers didn't know about it because they were not dealing directly with the manufacturers. A week or ten days after the phone calls I was able to get in and buy the claws. You can't produce bear claws overnight, and I bought them in June, and there would be no more until the bear season."

Mowatt made several phone calls to Canada to locate the bear claws, then flew to Canada, making six stops. He made two stops at fur dealers in Montreal; he bought several thousand claws in a town in northern Ontario; he bought four thousand from a taxidermist in western Quebec, and he made three stops at dealers in the fur center of Winnipeg, buying fourteen thousand claws in all. He remembers what he paid for the claws and how much he sold them for but is reluctant to quote the price for fear of antagonizing the Canadian dealers.

He brought the claws to Maine in June 1977 and began to process them, cleaning, polishing and trimming the claws and grading them as he does his furs, into extra large claws that measure two and a half to three inches; large claws that measure two to two and a half inches, and medium claws that measure one inch to an inch and a half.

He continued to receive calls from the jewelry manufacturers in the southwest. Finally he named his price. The manufacturers called Canada, found Mowatt had bought them all. They had to buy from Mowatt. He had cornered the bear claw market. "In three months I sold the whole inventory. With that money I built my first building, fifty feet by twenty-two feet, in Orono. . . . So that's what the fur business is like. The only time you speculate is when something is very low. Never speculate on something that is high. An old fur buyer told me once, 'When everyone wants to buy, that's the time to sell.'"

# – 11 –
# Rusty and Sawyer

One thing leads to another in the story-writing business. Several years ago I was in Eustis, a small town in western Maine near the Quebec border, a place Benedict Arnold went through with his half-frozen, half-starved troops on their way from Cambridge to a defeat at Montreal. I had spent part of two days working on a story about a man and wife and their two children from Boston who had moved to Eustis Ridge where they lived in a cabin without running water, without electricity but with a view of the mountains. They had sought the simple life, found it, and evidently liked it well enough. After leaving these people I stopped in the town of Stratton for lunch, debated whether or not to have a beer with my sandwich, for it was a long drive back to Boston and beer would make me sleepy. I thought, the hell with it, and had two bottles of beer because I couldn't make it home that night anyway, probably could not get farther than Auburn by dark. Because I lingered over lunch I overheard a traveling salesman telling a story. He said he had run out of gas near Bingham but had several cans of dry gas in his trunk, had poured that substance in his empty tank, and his car "she run hot, but she run good." I talked to him after he had finished his business and made an appointment to ride with him later in the fall to write a story about a salesman who travels rural Maine. While with him on that sales trip, I met Gordon Berry, the beaver trapper and West Forks storekeeper. A few months after the sales trip, I went with Berry on his beaver trap line. That experience led me eventually, some years later, to coyotes and Ralph Griffin, the Dixfield trapper who took me with him on his trap line near Carthage, Maine, in the fall of 1980. It was Griffin who told me about Neil Olson of Bethel, a trapper who went at it real hard. Tom Stevens, fur buyer for Mark Mowatt in Holden, Maine, told me about Wayne Bosowicz who runs the hounds of Sebec. And while I was in Vermont for the mystery of Magic Mountain, Vermont biologist Walt Cottrell told me about a predator project led by Dr. James Sherburne at the University of Maine at Orono. I called Sherburne from Dover-Foxcroft after talking to Bosowicz, and it was then that a man with the name Rocky painted on his truck took my two phone call dimes and got away with it.

Sherburne is a U.S. fish and wildlife biologist. The February afternoon I talked to him he was wearing an L. L. Bean chamois shirt and khaki pants, and looked well dressed that way. He was supervising seven graduate students on a study of predators, utilizing radio-collared animals to dispel myths about the coyote, bobcat, fox, marten, fisher and bear (though the bear is not a predator, strictly speaking). Sherburne rates the coyote at the bottom of this list in terms of aggressiveness. Bear guide Wayne Bosowicz had told me coyotes routinely run bobcat off their kills, but I did not argue with Sherburne; it was not my place to do so. A little knowledge is an impediment, and I tried not to impede the interview with what little I knew.

Sherburne and his students had thirty-eight coyotes fitted with radio collars. It was not difficult to trap the animals, he said, though trappers had told him how difficult it would be.

"We immobilized the coyote with drugs then checked the

sex, size, whether or not it was adult or juvenile, weighed them, marked them with an ear tag, fitted the radio collar and released them. Now we don't bother always to immobilize them because we can pin the animal's neck or use a catching noose and tie a rag around its jaw. As long as it's held, the coyote won't struggle and when you let go, the coyote runs off."

Sherburne had three groups of students in three different areas of Maine, one in the big woods of the St. John River in Aroostook County; a second group in the mountainous area of western Maine near Flagstaff Lake and Bigelow Mountain; and a third group in Cherry field, a small town in Washington County on the edge of the blueberry barrens. In the first year and a half he and his students had learned that: The coyote is active 65 percent of the time, "and that's more than the other animals"; the coyote family has a close social structure; they stay in a fixed home range; they will defend their territory against another coyote and do not normally cross into the range of another coyote family, a range marked with urine scent posts or a line of scats; they do not travel in large packs (he has seen no group larger than four adults); if they have a choice of habitat, of hardwood, mixed woods, softwoods, they will live on the edge of the softwoods because small game hides there and the softwood evergreens give more cover to the coyote. Other predators, the marten and fisher, also prefer the softwood and will travel the periphery of a field in the softwood cover rather than cross the open field.

The Cherryfield coyotes eat a lot of blueberries in season but leave the barrens for the woods when berries are green. Coyotes and other animals avoid green berries because green fruit are toxic to them. "Bears eat green berries," I said, forgetting myself, and Sherburne thought a moment and said bears might be an exception. He does not believe coyotes in New England are becoming brazen. "When our animals see us, they go off with their tail between their legs, literally."

The New England coyote is just a coyote and not a subspecies of coyote, he says. "For my money it's just a plain coyote." He is skeptical of the idea that the New England coyote is getting bigger and evolving into a wolflike animal. Most of his adult radio-collared coyotes weigh between twenty-nine and thirty-five pounds. The biggest coyote he knows of is a five-year-old coyote kept on the Maine campus, an animal weighing forty-five pounds. He was going to show me this animal but couldn't just then, and I was not really disappointed because I wanted to see my coyote running free. Certainly I would see a coyote, if only in the distance racing away from me on the blueberry barrens of Washington County.

Cherryfield is a town made pretty by the handsome houses near the main crossroad and by the Narraguagus River that runs through the place. The Narraguagus is as hard to pronounce as it is to spell and is one of the few rivers in the United States where the Atlantic salmon still runs up from the sea. Cherry field calls itself the blueberry capital of the world.

Maine blueberries grow on bushes a few inches high, handy for coyotes and small children who eat them. Growers of low-bush berries follow a sequence of burning and insecticide and, when the berries are getting ripe, heavy irrigation to make the berry fat with moisture. I was talking to a blueberry farmer in Kennebunk, way south of Cherryfield, a few years ago, before I thought much of coyotes, perhaps before I knew they existed in New England, and I was making a little conversation with the fellow and said Maine's state blueberry expert had an unusual name, Amr Ismail. "Not for an Egyptian, it ain't," the blueberry farmer said.

Suzanne Caturano, the student I was to meet in Cherryfield, told me an eagle often roosts in a tree beside the main road near the center of Cherryfield, and I looked for the eagle without success but saw two boys waiting for the schoolbus, baseball gloves on their left hands, schoolbooks in their right. It was the last Tuesday in February, no snow on the ground and bad luck for me because there would be no snow tracking of Sawyer and Rusty, two coyotes that had been trapped and fitted with radio collars and by luck turned out to be mates.

Maine students Suzanne Caturano and John Major were loading their four-wheel-drive Chevrolet trucks when I pulled into the yard behind their house, a state building next to the forest ranger's house. They had trapper's wicker baskets filled with gear and three-wheeled all-terrain motorcycles with fat, comical tires. The cycles are good on bare ground or muddy ground and even on packed snow. In deep snow they use snowmachines, called snowmobiles in Massachusetts. The language is the same, north or south New England, except for nuances and a few different words. For instance, someone in East Conway, New Hampshire, is described as being "hot" or "very hot" not to describe his temper but the state of his intoxication. And the Maine farmer who was losing sheep to coyotes was not angry; he was wrathy.

Caturano, twenty-four, is from Connecticut, received her undergraduate degree at Virginia Tech. She drove the truck down Route 182, the scenic highway from Cherryfield to Ellsworth. She like this open country on the edge of big woods and modest mountains, Tunk Mountain, Lead Mountain. She stopped along Route 182 and tried her radio antenna. She heard no signal from Sawyer and Rusty but was nearly certain we would find them even though it had been several weeks since she had tracked them. She had been monitoring the pair of coyotes since the previous April, about ten months, and always found their radio signal.

She handled seven of the nine radio-collared Cherryfield coyotes when they were trapped, and she named Rusty for his color, Sawyer after a female biologist whose work she admires. She set some of the traps herself and learned what works through trial and error and from the instruction of an accomplished trapper. "They're all so different, the color, the behavior. While I handled them they took on certain characteristics." She hasn't seen Rusty or Sawyer since they were trapped, fitted with the transmitters and released, but: "I get a feeling for the coyotes, especially when I'm snow tracking. It excites me to be on a fresh set of tracks. I have never seen a coyote while tracking, but I imagine them just ahead of me."

Sawyer and Rusty have lived in the same area of Franklin, a town just south of Cherryfield, since April 1980. Rusty was only a year and a half old and weighed only twenty-six pounds when trapped six miles from the spot where the female Sawyer was trapped. Caturano lost two other collared coyotes to trappers in the 1980 season. "I had hoped they would know the scent the trapper used and avoid being caught, but the trapper noticed the coyote getting so close to a dirt hole set and then backing off. So he got her on a scent post trap. The second animal was also caught on a scent post." This tends to corroborate what trapper Olson told me in Bethel, that a coyote might become shy of a dirt hole set but cannot avoid a scent post set because if he is afraid of coyote urine he is afraid of himself. Fortunately, the mated pair, Rusty and Sawyer, have avoided post sets; or perhaps no coyote trapper is working in their area.

Suzanne Caturano's Cherryfield coyotes seem most vulnerable to trapping when at the edge of their home range. She does not know why unless it might be because coyotes are more curious there. Sawyer, in her third year, had a litter of pups with Rusty as sire in spring of 1980, but that litter did not survive for reasons uncertain. "We trapped that area heavily last fall and there was no sign of pups." She stopped the truck on the Relay Tower Road on Martin's Ridge and stepped on the truck bumper for added height while holding an antenna and listening for the signal of Rusty and Sawyer on her earphones. She found Sawyer's signal towards a swamp of cedar and softwoods. John Major, in another truck behind Suzanne, was in radio contact with Suzanne and was trying to triangulate Sawyer's position but could get no signal from his location.

We drove on to an old hillside farm on the verge of lapsing into forest. It was a summer retreat for a seaman. We walked past the uninhabited farmhouse and headed into the woods on a trail part mud, part ice and snow. Suzanne stopped to examine a scat. It was coyote, and she poked it with a stick into a plastic bag. She could be certain that Sawyer and Rusty were out there because she could find them on their particular radio frequencies, but the scat was solid proof. Later this day she would promote me from observer to student and give me a trail to scout for scat.

We talked as we walked up the trail. Suzanne had been antihunting at one time but had come full circle and understood the value of hunting. She did not say, as Wayne Bosowicz had said, that a hunted animal was a healthy animal. She meant that in the absence of predators controlled hunting maintains a population of animals at a level in balance with the habitat. We reached a clearing, a blueberry field, perhaps two acres, a field ringed by birch and spruce and beech. On summer nights she has howled in this field and been answered by coyotes, presumably Sawyer and Rusty. She turned her radio receiver to Sawyer's frequency and heard the clock-clock sound, the signal. She marked the time and compass bearing in her notebook and then tried Rusty's frequency. "He's not around." If I had not been with Suzanne, she would have used her fat-tired, three-wheeled motorcycle to get to this hillside field. In heavy snow off the trail she leaves her snowmachine and uses snowshoes. Trappers take snowshoes not only for use off the trail but in case their snowmachines fail completely. Suzanne has been lucky. She can perform some field maintenance on her snowmachine (change a fouled spark plug, for instance) and has been really stuck only once, and that time in summer in her truck. "When you're stuck in a four-wheel drive, you're really stuck, and it was black fly season, too."

It is easy, or at least easier, to see coyotes in the west where there is open land than here in the forest and field of Franklin,

Maine. I wondered if I would see a coyote except by chance or in a trap. Suzanne could not find Rusty on her radio although, she says, the two coyotes are together 80 percent of the time. "They seem perfectly in touch. They meet, they make the same loops; one goes one way, the other goes the other way. I know for sure they were together in April [1980] and I'm nearly certain this is the second breeding season for them. A female is in heat in January, and I could see blood in her urine in mid-January. I started to notice pairs of tracks [in the snow] more often, almost all the time. One time they rested together, and the next day I crawled in and found where they had been atop a boulder and saw her blood there. I'd like to find their den. We monitored them twenty-four hours a day for five days in May [1980] trying to find the den. There were two areas they spent a lot of time. . . . If she had pups she was moving around. I tried to find the den. I'd like to find the den this year, but it's hard for one person. If several people scour an area, you'd have a good chance to find it. I'd like to find the den mostly for my own reasons. I'd like to see the pups."

Suzanne did not seem concerned about rusty's absence this day, though she said she worried Rusty or Sawyer might be killed crossing Route 182, though that road is lightly traveled by any urban or suburban standard. Her receiver could find Rusty's signal if he were within three or four miles unless there were a hill between him and the receiver. Coyotes are supposed to be loyal mates, according to the literature, but coyote literature contains many things that are not strictly correct. Rusty could have copulated with Sawyer in January and now at the end of February gone elsewhere in the way of a dog. She turned again to Rusty's radio frequency and this time heard his beep at the same compass heading as Sawyer's position. "So he's just showed up." Rusty will stay with Sawyer and help her rear the young and will stay with her even after the pups have become adults, and Rusty and Sawyer will have a few months alone together before they begin raising another family of pups.

Rusty had been hunting, presumably, and probably for snowshoe hare. In summer he might be sitting in a blueberry field stuffing himself, but even there coyotes are not easy to see because they do not always run into a clearing but stop and look about with, Suzanne says, "that curious look on their face. I've found that in summer they're most active from four to 8:00 A.M. and again 4:00 P.M. to midnight. The rest of the time, they're fifty-fifty, active or inactive." She has seen four coyotes running free, none of them her collared animals (she thinks); and two of the four she saw in the middle of the barrens where a coyote has little cover.

We left the small blueberry field in the forest of beech and birch and spruce. Suzanne would keep moving this day, taking different compass headings on the position of Rusty and Sawyer, compiling the information later to form the basis of her master's thesis. One thing she learns is how far they move each day. "It might take us half an hour to get around that ridge, Little Hardwood Hill, and by that time they may be gone. I always wonder how they move so fast in the woods. Then I realized they use snowmachine trails in winter for certain and probably use them in summer. They move over that hardwood hill very fast." And when the coyote pair leave the snowmachine trails I can imagine them moving through the woods as Tom Montemagni, the Mt. Snow ski instructor, had described it, the coyotes reading the terrain like an expert skier and moving around obstacles with speed unbroken by hesitation.

We walked back through the woods and past the summer farm to Suzanne's truck. She drove around several miles of woods to a point on a road on the crest of Sugar Hill. Sugar Hill overlooks Molasses Pond. People driving onto that sweet scene slowed as they passed the two University of Maine trucks driven by Suzanne and John. The antennas elicit curiosity. People wonder what they are listening for through the earphones. Suzanne: "You're practically in people's front yards with antennas, so naturally they are curious." John: "When they find out you're biologists studying coyotes they want to know 'Why don't you do something about them?'" Their meaning: Why can't the biologists kill the coyotes, all of them?

I joined John while Suzanne went ahead to get another compass bearing on Rusty and Sawyer. I had trouble finding a place for myself in his truck because of all the gear piled there and the books. He was reading a textbook on sociobiology, and on the floor, atop his field gear, was a book entitled *2001 French Verbs*. He is studying for his doctorate and reading some accounts of animal life in French. He does not normally work in Cherryfield but at Sherburne's radio tracking operation near Flagstaff Lake in western Maine where the country is heavily forested, not broken by blueberry barrens as are Washington and Hancock Counties. Coyotes at Flagstaff eat raspberries because that is what grows there, John said. They also eat snowshoe hares. "There is a lot of logging and the cleared areas are good for snowshoe hare. In the cleared areas, first come the raspberries, softwood thickets of good cover, and then aspen and maple. The snowshoe hare eat the cambium layer of hardwood especially. They won't eat this from the big maples because they would be out in the open and not in a thicket. . . . Moose and deer have no upper incisors and break off the tips of new growth of fir whereas a snowshoe hare has upper incisors and strips bark and twigs cleanly." Small evergreen softwoods grow in the clearings made by loggers, and here the snowshoe hare is out of sight and safer from predators; but not entirely safe from the coyote, because if the coyote cannot see his prey he has the nose of a hound to seek the hare that way.

John stayed on Sugar Hill and was in touch with Suzanne by radio, and he helped her trianglate the positions of the two coyotes, so that by drawing lines of the compass headings on a map, the position of Rusty and Sawyer could be determined more or less accurately. However accurate radio tracking is, it lacks the certainty of snow tracking. John had little snow for tracking even in his Flagstaff Lake area in the winter of 1980–81, though that inland area beneath Bigelow Mountain usually gets more snow than the coastal area of Cherryfield where Suzanne had some snow until February when I arrived and the ground was bare.

Suzanne returned in her truck to Sugar Hill, and we traveled a few miles and turned off into a field where new radio readings were taken. The beeps were strong here. Rusty and Sawyer could hear the radio beep but had been hearing it for months now, whenever Suzanne got close, and presumably had learned the beeps were no threat to them. Suzanne unloaded her three-wheeled cycle from the back of her truck, running it down to the ground on planks before I could offer my help. She was twenty-four and could manage for herself. In winter, though, she has trouble loading a snowmachine onto her truck alone and sometimes accomplishes this by building a bank of snow behind the truck, then driving the snowmachine onto the bed of the pickup. Suzanne taught me how to use the antenna and receiver and compass and left her notebook with me and gave me instructions to make periodic readings of both coyotes and make entries in her notebook of time, strength of signal and compass bearing. She mounted her motorcycle, then dismounted to get an extra spark plug and a spark plug wrench. She would run some of Rusty and Sawyer's trails looking for scat, and when I had taken enough radio readings I could walk a trail and look for scat myself. She gave me several plastic bags in case I should get lucky.

I did as she told me and stood in the field by the truck first listening to one coyote, then switching frequency on the receiver to hear the beep of the other animal, each time moving the antenna to where the beep was strongest and then taking a compass heading for that spot. I believed the coyotes were there, only 400 yards away, resting or lying in wait in cedar for snowshoe hare, but I would never see coyotes this way. I put the radio gear into the truck and walked the trail Suzanne had asked me to scout for scat. It was away from the coyotes' position, and I would not see them on that trail. Maybe I would see their sign. I had been in the Wytopitlock woods with Rita Potter who showed me where she had seen the lion; I had been in the nameless flowages beyond West Forks with beaver trappers and in the woods of Vermont's Northeast Kingdom with bear biologist Charlie Willey; now I was alone in the Maine woods walking a muddy path towards a lake and entrusted with scientific duty, to pick up scat of the coyotes Rusty and Sawyer. There were tracks on the trail, the marks of a hunter's boot. I think the other track was that of a dog and so was the scat I found that of a dog, but I did not want to come back empty-handed and picked up the stuff with a stick and pushed it into a plastic bag. I walked a half mile until the trail ended at water, hoping all the time to catch sight of something, and saw nothing, not a bird. Later I showed my plastic bag of scat to Suzanne, and she judged it dog, and then, only feet from the truck in the field where we were standing I saw better stuff. Suzanne examined the coyote scat with interest. "There's a lot of feed in this," she said and put it into a plastic bag. It would be catalogued with notation of date, location and estimated age (of the scat, not the animal). She and John can tell the hair of the deer from that of the snowshoe hare in the coyote scat. Dried seeds are proof of the berries they eat. Deer hair is very coarse and crinkly and is hollow; snowshoe hare has hair that is finer textured and longer than that of smaller animals. Unidentified hair can be compared to a chart of mammals' hair. There is real knowledge in scatology.

We had begun the day's radio tracking on Martin's Ridge; then moved to the summer farm and the blueberry field in the woods near the summer farm; then to Sugar Hill that overlooks Molasses Pond; then to the field beside the dirt road where Suzanne first used her motorcycle; and we took one last reading from a cemetery to confirm that Rusty and Sawyer were at the northeast side of Scammon Pond bog. We had covered many miles by truck and some afoot, but the coyotes had moved perhaps only two and a half miles and always within their home range of about fifteen square miles. Suzanne believed no other coyotes existed within this range unless it might be the year-old pups of Rusty and Sawyer. A man in Maine, who was experienced in the woods, told me that the coyotes in the woods behind his house moved every so often after they had eaten all the available game, that they moved five miles to an area of new game and after hunting there moved still again another five miles. The work of Suzanne and John, all their radio and compass fixes and scatology, proves a coyote pair does not hunt hundreds of square miles.

We were going over the day's work at the house in the forest service compound in Cherryfield. John was explaining how to examine scat. Suzanne told me the six radio-collared animals she and other students were following were located in the towns of Franklin, Deblois, Cherryfield, Eastbrook, Osborne and Beddington and in the unorganized territories, the townships of T-9, T-10, T-16 and T-22. I was wearying of the search. They invited me to supper. John would bake bread. I suggested a restaurant instead, the Red Barn in Milbridge, and we went there, Suzanne ordering scallops cooked in wine, John ordering beer and fried fish. I had beer and something I have forgotten. What I remember was how John and Suzanne appreciated restaurant food after cooking for themselves, and while we ate John mentioned the danger of chasing coyotes in winter and referred to a time he nearly went through the ice on a snow-machine.

I was invited to breakfast the next morning at their forest service house in Cherryfield. John had baked bread the previous night after our dinner in the restaurant, and Suzanne used it to make French toast. I asked John to tell me again about chasing coyotes across ice on the other side of Maine from Cherryfield, at his station near Bigelow Mountain.

"The first time I nearly went through the ice was on Upper

Kilgore Pond. The ice was real good. I tested it around the edge, stamped on it and tamped it with poles. Out on the pond I got off the [existing] snowmachine trail on the ice because I was looking for coyote tracks and felt the back of the snowmachine drop down. I hit the throttle. Ice was breaking under the machine. For twenty yards or so I could see the water behind me. I'm quite sure it was water and not slush and I don't know if it was shell ice atop the water and ice under that. It was quite a sinking feeling. It had been cold for weeks and I had no reason to be concerned.

"The second time, I was crossing a road we call the carriage path that connects Carrabassett Valley to Long Falls Dam Road. Normally there's a tiny stream crossing the road, six inches to a foot. Normally I drive through it, but there was an ice dam that flooded the road. Water was flowing over the ice. I probably should not have gone across, but I knew there was a moose carcass and knew that would probably attract coyotes. And a snowstorm was coming that would have covered the scats. That's what I was interested in, the scats, and in locating the coyotes probably feeding on the moose carcass. I decided to go through though I might get a little wet. I got a running start—you can cross some distance of water on a snowmachine if you're going fast enough. You can plane across. I was going too slow, the water slowed the machine, and ice started breaking up around me. The water was deeper than I thought, waist deep. I was afraid if the machine gets wet, it would be inoperable. I was standing in water over my knees and holding up the rear of the snowmachine so water wouldn't get in the carburetor. The nose of the snowmachine was through the ice in the water, and I pulled it out backwards so it wasn't in such deep water. I got the snowmachine up on the edge of the ice and gave it one pull and it started. I walked it over the ice and water to solid ground about thirty feet away and drove it to the truck, about two miles. I was starting to get cold. I had insulated felt boots and several layers of wool and a snowmobile suit over all the wool. It was about zero. My boots were full of water. If the machine didn't start, people knew where I was, but it might be three or four hours before they would get to me. I was carrying waterproof matches, and there was a locked camp right there. I would have tried to get inside. I imagine there was a wood stove there. I would not have tried walking out until I got my feet dry.

"It's an occupational hazard, that kind of stuff. If you're out for recreation you wouldn't take the chances we do hoping to get another day or two to check on our animals. We try to work in pairs if it's a long-distance trip or hazardous, but can't always do that. What can turn from a nice day in the woods is when you pull on the machine and it doesn't start. You get sweaty. All of a sudden you realize you got to get yourself out quickly or build a fire. But wild animal attacks, that's not where the danger is."

John took pictures of a bear in its den once. "I don't know if I would do that again." This reminded Suzanne that she had accompanied biologists on a seach for a bear's den and that the bear awoke and came out of his den, though one biology student tried to cover the den hole with a snowshoe until the net could be located. The bear ran away leaving a terribly pungent smell in its wake. Sometimes, alone in the woods, Suzanne imagines she smells that pungent, musty smell of bear. "Then I get nervous. That's one thing I worry about."

It was about three months later, in May when bear are out of their dens, that I traveled to Vermont to accompany men running bear and when the bear fell out of the tree into a net, I remembered what Suzanne had said in Cherryfield. I put my nose right into the mama bear's fur, and she had a nice smell, hard to describe and not very strong. Of course, Suzanne's bear had been in a den for some time and the mama bear in Vermont had been running through the woods away from the dogs and had splashed across Mink Brook several times.

Breakfast was finished, and we left for Deblois, where the blueberry barrens are and where Rebel, Ginger and Silver had been trapped and fitted with radio transmitters the previous year. Rebel had dug around the leg-hold traps without setting them off. There is a way to catch such an animal with a foot snare. Snares are illegal for commercial trapping. Rebel, an adult male, was caught in a foot snare placed in a trail where he was known to walk. It was a blind set so called because no bait or urine was used. Suzanne had been out of radio contact with these coyotes for four weeks. She thought Rebel might have gone across the Narraguagus River on the ice and might now be on the other side, separated from his normal territory in the blueberry barrens by the torrent flowing down the Narraguagus. The barrens are flat, not in an Arizona sense, but flat for Maine, and there are few trees. The blueberry plants were dormant as a sleeping bear and nondescript. I could have walked on them and not known what they were unless I stopped to think where I was, Washington County, Maine.

John and I had gone ahead to the barrens in Deblois in John's truck while Suzanne stopped in Cherryfield at the post office. John parked his truck on a dirt road leading into the barrens and stood outside the truck holding an antenna in his hand, trying to find the signal of Rebel or Ginger or Silver. A beat-up pickup truck came towards us, up the dirt road out of the barrens, and the driver looked at John, his antenna, the University of Maine truck; and the look on his face was of hostility masked. He was of the band of unlettered natives who think anyone who works in the woods or hunts there knows all that needs to be known about coyotes and that wildlife biologists are superfluous. He drove past John's truck very slowly, turned onto the hardtop road and slowed down even more so he could lean his head out of the truck window and shout, referring I suppose to John's antenna: "Stick it up your ahhse."

Rusty and Sawyer are together still. Suzanne wrote me a letter with the news:

"We found Rusty and Sawyer's den on April 28, 1981 with the help of a golden retriever and a lot of praying! She had six puppies—five males and one female nestled under a large boulder (six by six feet) in an ex-porcupine cave. She has dug out a little hollow over six feet back under the rock where the puppies were when we found them. Less than ten days old—their eyes just barely beginning to open. Quite well furred and mobile. In the week or ten days prior to this she and Rusty had been at the den constantly. She would venture a mile or so away for short periods of time when Rusty returned from his longer (time and distance) ventures.

"It started out to be an exciting day as Sawyer was at the den at 5 A.M. and Rusty was making his way to it from south of 182. (Oh, yes the den was on a ridge along Martin's Brook, west of the Relay Tower Road.) I 'knew' he would be crossing 182 and had a spot picked out in a brushy softwood patch along the road that looked good to me. I waited as cars and trucks buzzed by. Then as I was thinking to myself during a long stretch of no vehicles, 'Come on, cross now,' he stepped out of the woods onto the shoulder of the road about 100 yards away and just stared at me for a couple seconds then nonchalantly loped across the road and up to the den where he and Sawyer both stayed until we got close enough to spook them. Rusty stayed in the area of the den all the time we were searching 10 A.M. to 2 P.M."

(Suzanne could tell Rusty was nearby though she could not see him because of the strength of the beep signal she was receiving from the transmitter on his collar.)

"Sawyer left and came back before we left the den site. We were with the pups from 2 to 3 P.M. She may have moved them to another cave, but it doesn't appear to be far from the den we found, within a mile. All the pups were dark-bodied with a lighter brown head except the 'runt' which was very dark all over. . . . The den was immaculate and free of any coyote sign. The pups looked very healthy."

Rusty and Sawyer had done well by their progeny and would care for them spring and summer, teach them to hunt in fall. Then the young adults should move out on their own. Rusty was two, Sawyer at least three years old. They will remain together for their lifetime, ten or twelve years, or until a post trap set or Route 182 traffic do them part.

# – 12 –
# The Coyote and the Wolf
## (Cousins or Brothers?)

There was a man named John Hayden who lived on the North River in Hanover, Massachusetts, and earned his living from trapping beaver and otter and muskrat and mink along the river and in the swamps and woodlands that bordered the river. One day in February some year between 1720 and 1740 Hayden was tending his trap line, on ice skates, and by midafternoon he had ten or twelve beaver and otter skins on his back. It began to snow. He checked one more trap, found an otter there and then began to skate downriver towards his home in the snow and the gathering dark. He heard the howling of wolves somewhere behind him, and he began to skate faster. A deer crossed his path, and Hayden thought the howling wolves behind him might be on the trail of that animal, but soon he realized the wolves were not after the deer. They were after him. The snow storm worsened; the wolves got closer. Hayden reached his cabin and did not stop to remove his skates but ran up the bank, breaking his skate blades on the rocks there. He reached his cabin, entered and shut the door just in time, because at that moment the wolves were clawing at his cabin door. He could see eight wolves and shot three of them through his window, killing two, wounding a third. The other five wolves escaped into the night. The wounded wolf crawled away from the cabin and climbed on a rock where he howled in his torment until he died in the night. Thereafter the rock was called Wolf Rock.

This story has the elements of a good wolf story: a snowy night on the frozen river; a man alone; a cabin; a narrow escape. Moreover, it *might* be true, though there is at least one thing wrong with the story. Wolves hunt in silence. Apologists of wolf behavior belittle man-eating wolf stories, but they also realize wolves are capable of killing man. Erik Zimen is an admirer of wolves, writes that they are an endangered species and that much fear of the wolf is based on myth. However, in his book *The Wolf*, Zimen writes:

"My own guess is that attacks might occur if natural prey were lacking, if wolves were too numerous to be able to live on domestic animals, and if human beings were poorly armed, so that they were not very dangerous, and the wolves had got used to human flesh as a result of eating corpses. Such conditions seem to have prevailed above all in the Middle Ages, and most of the episodes of that kind can be presumed to have actually taken place. . . ."

There is no record of how many North American Indians were attacked and eaten by wolves because the Indians did not leave written accounts, but it is logical to assume that wolves in North America have killed some men. The wolf is a shy animal, afraid of man, but hunger makes an animal bold. Firearms kept the wolf from becoming too bold, but the Inidans did not have firearms.

Wolves and coyotes and dogs, all canids, have the same chromosome number and can interbreed. Wolves are being bred to dogs to produce a wolf-dog for those people who want the biggest or the fiercest animal in their town. Female coyotes in heat entice male dogs out of backyards and breed with them.

The first coyotes to enter New England from Canada and from New York State probably bred with dogs because there was a scarcity of coyotes in New England. The product of this mating was the coydog, and coydogs confused scientists and the public. Scientists are less confused now and consider the coydog population unimportant. They feel certain the creature in the New England woods is a coyote, though a somewhat unusual coyote. Only the uninformed continue to call the coyote a coydog or call it a coydog out of perversity in the same way they call a fisher a fishercat, though that animal is not a cat but a weasel. The New England coyote bred with the wolf in Canada on its way from the Great Lakes region to New England; at least that is the theory. No one saw the coyotes and the wolves copulating, but there is evidence of a remarkable and mathematical kind. This union of wolf and coyote would account for the greater size of the New England coyote and the changing shape of its skull.

Vermont biologist Walt Cottrell had a report of a wolf in Newport, Vermont, in October 1979. "What do you think of these pictures?" a trapper asked him. Cottrell looked at the pictures, and the trapper said: "Goddamn, if it's that big it has to be a wolf." The carcass was not weighed, Cottrell did not see it. The trapper was calling it a wolf on the basis of size, as most people would do. Few people can really tell the difference between wolf and coyote. Hampshire College zoologist Jay Lorenz, who tried to trap coyotes in farmer Babiak's Chesterfield farm and failed, but who successfully trapped coyotes in Vermont, had told me in the first months of my search for the coyote: "In Ontario they call fifty-five-pound animals wolves. Over the border they a find thirty-five-pound animal and call it a coyote. In between they find a forty-five-pound animal, and there is no way, through skull analysis or any other kind of analysis, you can tell a cross coyote or wolf or a big coyote. There is no precise way to distinguish. . . . It is mostly on the basis of size that we set up the eastern coyote as a coyote rather than a wolf. So I go along with that because it is easier to communicate with people that way, but I'm not convinced it's true."

Coyotes and wolves are similar in several ways. Wolf parents are monogamous, and so, too, are coyote. Sawyer and Rusty stayed together at least two breeding seasons and will probably remain together. The average litter size is similar for wolf and coyote, four to six pups, as is the gestation period, about sixty-three days. The largest wolf may have been the 175-pound animal killed by a government hunter in 1939 in Alaska. A 172-pound wolf was killed in Canada's Jasper National park in 1945. Coyotes do not grow that large, the biggest on record being 74.8 pounds, an animal killed in 1937 in Wyoming. A small timber wolf weighs 60 pounds; a large New England coyote about 50 pounds. If the difference in size is the best way of distinguishing wolf from coyote, it is not a particularly good way, not a scientific way.

It is uncertain why the wolf left New England, though his departure was caused partly by the efforts of farmers who wanted to protect their farm animals by killing all the wolves. Helenette Silver, who was to take the New England coyote into her house in 1960, wrote in 1957 that the wolf was hunted in an organized way. "Occasionally as many as 500 or 600 men assembled for these drives which were often effective in cleaning up a whole township." She thinks wolves disappeared in New Hampshire before 1900. A wolf was killed in New Marlborough, western Massachusetts, in 1918. The last bountied wolf in Maine was taken in 1908. Well organized though the farmers may have been in the hunting of wolves, they could not have killed them all that way. They killed off the wolf by clearing 70 percent of the New England forest, destroying the habitat of the wolf's prey, caribou and moose. The last native caribou seen in Maine was in 1908, coincidentally the same year the last bountied wolf was taken. When there was no prey in the woods, the wolf came to the farmyard for domesticated animals, and when the wolf got that close to man, the wolf was vulnerable. The wolf does not adapt the way a coyote does, and the wolf is a meat eater, mostly. If he could live on blueberries as the coyote can, the wolf might have done better in New England. If the mountain lion could eat corn, he would have done better, too.

Wolves travel in packs of five to eight and sometimes up to twenty animals. Wolves are more social than most coyotes and have pack members who do more hunting than other members. There is this theory: If one of these hunting wolves is killed, the pack may suffer, but if a coyote is killed, it just means more food for the other coyotes in the area. There is another theory: New England and the middle Atlantic states were the southern end of the timber wolf's habitat to begin with, and when the habitat was cleared of trees and the elk and caribou and moose shot out, the wolf moved north to Canada. Those which stayed behind were killed, unless a few moved so far into the woods of Coos County, New Hampshire, the Northeast Kingdom, Vermont, or Aroostook County, Maine, that no one saw them but the loggers who talked of *les loups*, who still talk of *loups*. There may be a stray wolf in New England still, just as there may be a mountain lion. Duane Smith, the bear hunter from Vermont who tried to hit the bear with the flat of his hatchet, has trapped north of St. Johnsbury and told me he never saw a lion track, did not believe lions existed there, but several times he did see a big canine track. He and a friend used to refer to the animal as the "thing." They saw where the thing had made kills. Smith thinks it was a wolf.

A sixty-pound wolf trapped in Norton, Vermont, or in the St. John River valley of Aroostook might be taken for a coyote. No one could be certain what the animal was unless its skull was meticulously cleaned and many measurements of the skull taken and the measurements put through a computer. A sixty-pound animal is suspect, however, because it is big for a coyote. Henry Hilton, the Maine wildlife biologist, told me: "I've looked at and weighed an awful lot of animals. I accept fifty or fifty-five pounds but after sixty I'd be looking closely at what it could be. When you get into a fifty- or sixty-pound coyote it is an incredibly large animal because they do not have a big frame. That much tissue and fat and muscle on the frame is very unlikely. If it had the bone structure to support that much weight it would be getting out of the coyote strain." Hilton says the line between wolf and coyote gets indistinct. He says it is not as if elephants left New England and giraffes replaced them.

The coyotes came to New England in substantial numbers only after the wolves left, but pioneering coyotes probably came earlier. The coyote, traveling alone or in pairs or in small family groups, does not stand up to the larger wolf. Coyotes had moved across Lake Superior ice to Isle Royale and lived there an undetermined length of time until timber wolves began breeding on the island about 1950. Then the coyotes had to leave, find some other territory. The coyote has been finding new territory ever since its home range on the American plains were taken over by farmers and sheepherders and cattle ranchers. The poisoning campaign against the coyote began as early as 1847 with the use of strychnine. Wolfers killed the buffalo wolves by poisoning carcasses of bison, but the coyotes were more resourceful and survived, by learning not to eat certain carrion and by moving to where there was no poisoning.

Hilton explains the migration east in his graduate research paper this way: Large coyotes of a subspecies probably began their trek east from the American and Canadian prairie states about 1900 under pressure of poisoning campaigns. One route took the coyotes into southern and southeastern Ontario at Sault Sainte Marie, Michigan, and brought the coyotes into contact with the small Ontario wolf sometimes called the Algonquin wolf. These Algonquin wolves were few in number and bred with the immigrating coyotes to produce an animal nearly indistinguishable from a large coyote or a small wolf.

"As the true wolves continued to be pushed out of southern

and eastern Canada the more adaptable and resistant coyote-like animals continued to maintain breeding populations which, in the absence of wolves and pure western coyotes, and through natural selections of the most beneficial traits, rapidly evolved to become a true breeding animal similar to the eastern coyote of today."

I talked to Hilton in his office at the Maine Department of Inland Fisheries and Wildlife in Augusta. He said some scientists were critical of the idea that evolution of an animal could take place so quickly, in less than a hundred years. He said the new coyote with the Algonquin wolf gene was bigger than the typical western coyote and this increase in size helped it survive in New England's more severe climate. He thinks the hybridization with the wolf hastened the evolution, but "I don't like to quibble over the point of whether it is really evolution when hybridization is involved."

There are biologists in New England who say the eastern coyote is just a coyote and no different from coyotes in the west, but Hilton found that Maine coyotes' skulls averaged 6 percent longer and 11 percent wider than skulls of western coyotes. Thus he agrees with Dr. William Bossert, a Harvard scientist. With his associate Barbara Lawrence, Dr. Bossert measured Helenette Silver's New Hampshire coyotes and proved to his satisfaction these new animals were not dogs, not wolves, but big coyotes of a new kind. I made an appointment to see Dr. Bossert, mathematician and biologist, at his Harvard office across from the Peabody Museum.

Bossert took me to a faculty room where he poured coffee for me into a cup with saucer, and we sat at a long table talking about coyotes. He introduced me to a colleague at the table, an astrophysicist I think he was, who spoke with a European accent and was smoking a cigarette. Small clouds of smoke hung around his head. Later two other Harvard professors came in and began talking to the astrophysicist, and I overheard just a phrase of their conversation. They were discussing the origin of life, and for a moment the faculty coffee room seemed like a scene from a movie, Hollywood depicting Harvard.

Bossert and his Harvard associate Barbara Lawrence examined about two hundred and twenty-five skulls of coyotes, deciding to use fifteen measurements, nine measurements of skull shape and six of tooth form. These same fifteen measurements were made of wolf and dog skulls. The measurements were used in a process called linear discrimination. Bossert said he would explain linear discrimination to me, went to the blackboard of the faculty coffee room and began to teach me. Bossert was so knowledgeable and so full of good humor that I made an effort to understand linear discrimination and almost did.

If I could not understand the mathematics, I could understand what Bossert said to me: Barbara Lawrence measured twenty wolves, twenty dogs, twenty plains coyotes. The skulls were from museum shelves and the identities known. The measurements were weighted differently and put into a number. The final number was placed on a chart, and the dog figure fell in one place on the chart, the wolf figure on another place, the coyote figure on a third place in the chart. When the number of the New England coyote was put on the chart it fell between the dog and the wolf and close to the plains coyote. Bossert said:

"If this graph really measures genetics, hybrids [coydogs] should fall between dog and coyote, and they did, exactly half way between dog and coyote . . . this convinced us that this technique really tells something about the genetics of creatures."

The skull of the New England coyote is changing, Bossert says, because the coyote has assimilated a wolf gene and because it is eating larger game in New England than on the plains. In order to crush the bones of larger prey, the New England coyote needs a bigger skull, a wider snout. The long snout of the western coyote is good for grabbing grasshoppers and birds but does not provide enough leverage for chewing on deer. And the

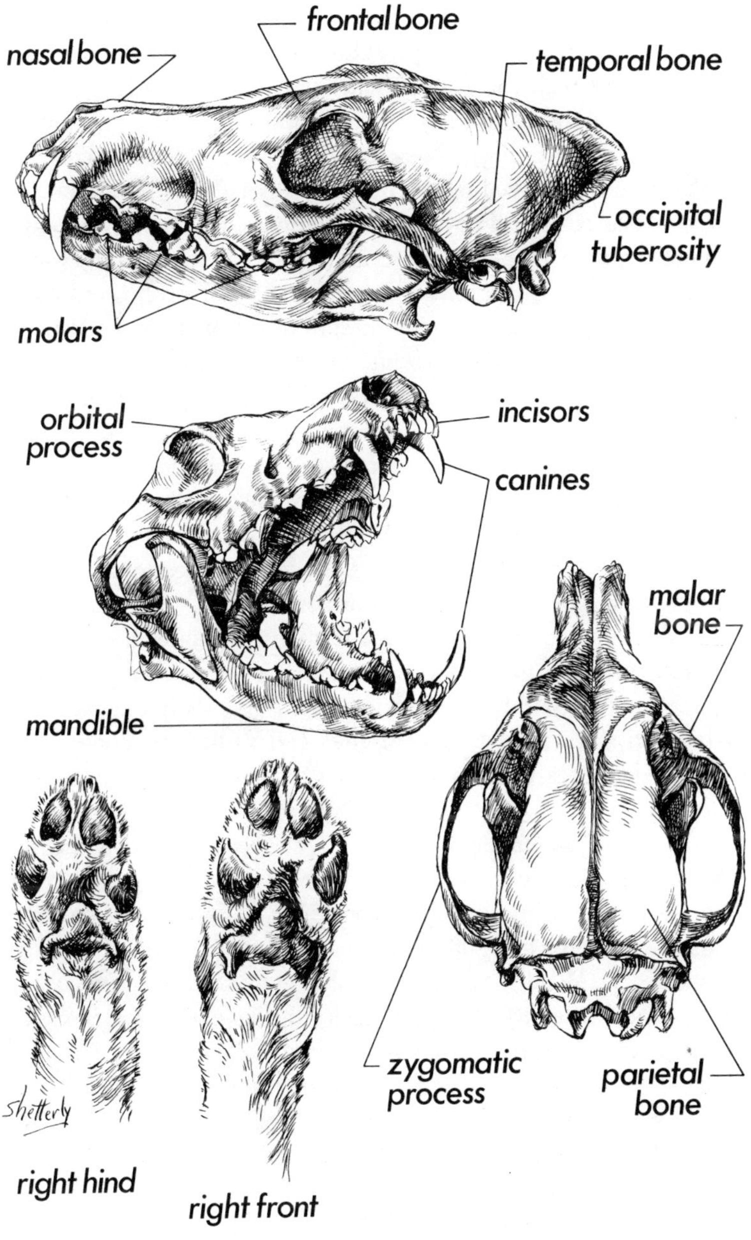
frontal bone
nasal bone
temporal bone
occipital tuberosity
molars
orbital process
incisors
canines
malar bone
mandible
zygomatic process
parietal bone
Shetterly
right hind
right front

animal continues to change. There is a wider range of skull measurements in the New England animal than in the plains animal, an indication of hybridization with the wolf (and maybe with the dog). Bossert agrees with Hilton that this hybridization is speeding the process of evolution. This hybridization has produced coyotes of different colors, blond and red as well as the more normal color, that similar to a German shepherd. As evolution continues, the color of the New England coyote will become more homogenized. Bruce Bellemeur, the Tunbridge, Vermont, storeowner who shot two coyotes in his town, says the animal is too big to be called a coyote. "I call 'em the eastern wolf." When farmer Babiak's wife looked out the window into their pasture in Chesterfield, Massachusetts, and said there was a strange animal there, farmer Babiak said maybe it was a wolf. Maybe Babiak was right, because Harvard Professor Bossert says the new creature in the New England woods is growing towards a wolf.

A coyote by any other name might be more acceptable unless the other name is wolf, for a wolf is the symbol of danger and of savagery. All canids are savage, if that word can be used to describe the actions of an animal. Erik Zimen, author of *The Wolf*, describes Cape hunting dogs attacking a wildebeest in Kenya:

"The dogs had picked out a younger gnu, about eight months old. They separated it from the herd and soon overtook it. Two bit its hindquarters, causing it to stop, and one immediately went and bit the animal's snout, causing it to yelp loudly. . . . While the victim was held fast in front by one dog, the others tore large lumps of flesh from its hindquarters. One bit a large piece from the anus and swallowed it immediately, while the dog next to it tore out the intestines. The animal was still standing with wide-open eyes, uttering low, moaning sounds. Eventually it collapsed to its knees and then on to its side; it died after about eight minutes . . . we drove slowly back to our camp, feeling very weak in the knees."

## The Coyote and the Wolf (Cousins or Brothers?)

Dogs that live in living rooms do a similar job on deer or sheep, though I have seen no description quite as vivid as Zimen's. Domestic dogs often eat the anus of sheep. Coyotes are no less savage, though coyotes can kill sheep more efficiently than dogs, by cutting off the windpipe. Sometimes live sheep are partially eaten by coyotes before escaping or succumbing. A pack of hungry domestic dogs gone wild would frighten me as much as a pack of hungry wolves or a pack of coyotes.

Every wild animal is potentially dangerous, even those animals smaller and cuter than coyotes, raccoons for instance. A pet raccoon in Ann Arbor, Michigan, climbed into a baby's crib in 1980 and tore off the infant's scalp, chewed off part of her nose and mouth and bit the fingers off one of her hands. The baby died of those wounds.

Dogs and wolves run in packs; coyotes usually run in family groups. Coyote pups are nearly full grown by fall and still with the parents and thus constitute a group, but by that winter or the following spring the pups should be out on their own and the group disbanded except for the parents and perhaps a malingering daughter who might stay as an aunt and help the mother with the next year's litter. However, there is some evidence that the New England coyote is becoming more social, like the wolves, and may be hunting together in groups more like packs, at least in winter. This could be because coyote are more apt to eat big game in winter than in summer and need the numbers of a pack to bring down a deer, or it could be because the coyote now has the gene of the wolf to guide its behavior.

The coyote outlasted the wolf on the prairie and has replaced the wolf as the biggest predator in the New England woods because it could adapt to local conditions. If there were no prairie dogs to eat, the western coyote would eat something else, watermelon; the New England coyote which cannot find deer carrion or live snowshoe hare will eat blueberries. If the New England coyote evolves into a creature too much like the wolf and grows a snout too stout to grab grasshoppers, it could go the way of the flesh eaters, to extirpation.

Several animals are extirpated in New England, including the wolf (probably), the mountain lion (probably) and the wolverine, American elk and eastern woodland caribou. The coyote, on the other hand, was not here when the Pilgrims landed (unless, as Helenette Silver says, not as a theory but as a thought, the coyote was here all along, in small numbers, waiting for the wolf to leave before emerging to proliferate; but that would be another story). A new animal has appeared in New England and is evolving into a different creature not in Darwinian time, but in our lifetime, a fascinating thought.

❧

The story of the New England coyote is told by the underinformed, and it is told by biologists, some of whom are overinformed and rigid in their perceptions. They are like the far left and far right of political opinion. The overinformed, the far left, tend to debunk anything those who work in the woods say. The leftists tend to believe that coyotes kill only deer or sheep they wish to eat and never kill for the atavistic canid hell of it. The far right, the underinformed, like the man in Washington County who hollered to the biology student to stick the antenna "up your ahhse," tend to believe every dead deer they come upon has been killed by a coyote. The truth lies between the extremes. Coyotes may pick out a slow, old deer rather than chase a healthy deer, but coyotes do kill healthy deer and sometimes kill more than they eat. Nevertheless, it is not true that coyotes kill everything in the forest. The coyote kills only what it can catch.

Coyotes are shy creatures who survive on stealth, but they also survive by being brazen. If coyotes could make unprovoked attacks on children and adults in Los Angeles County, California, the same could happen in New England, though that possibility is remote. Of Los Angeles coyotes, Henry Hilton says: "There are several million people with coyotes living among them. It's a wonder there aren't any more incidents." Hilton thinks it is misleading to suggest that coyotes might attack people in New England, and he is probably right. No one I spoke to about coyotes knew of a person attacked by a coyote in the wild until the incident in North Amity.

Hazen Hall is fifty-nine years old and has lived all his life in North Amity, Maine, near the New Brunswick border, and made his living from farming and cutting wood until taken ill with cancer of the lung. He still cuts some wood and was planning to do that the afternoon of August 20, 1981, about one mile north of his house. He tells this story:

"I went down to swamp a road, cut the brush out so you can get in. I wasn't there much more than half an hour. Two coyotes come out in the grass and bushes coming towards me. I didn't pay no attention to 'em. I was about fifty feet from the car and they were seventy-five feet beyond me. These two come out and I just kept walking. I seen two the night before. I wasn't afraid. I paid no attention to these. The next time I looked up there was four of them. They was in kind of a circle ten or twelve feet apart. They was coming toward me, not running, just kind of creeping. I tried to start the chain saw to scare the coyotes."

Hall had not used the saw in a day or two, and the saw does not start well, anyway. It would not start this August afternoon, and the coyotes continued moving towards him.

"So I just chucked the saw towards them. It didn't slow them. I didn't look. I run to the car, jumped on the hood because I didn't think I had time to open the car door. One grabbed me by the pant leg as I was getting up. He had a piece of thread. When I got on the hood I tried to work off one side. Three was on one side of the car and one on the other. I tried to get all four of 'em on the same side of the car so I could get in the

–213–

car but he wouldn't go over. So I jumped down on the ground, opened the door and got in. I got the gun loaded, an Army carbine. I loaded that, rolled the window down. When I loaded it he moved about fifteen feet away from the car, showing his teeth and kind of growling like. When I rolled the window down he went fifteen feet further. I shot him about twenty-five feet from the car. The other ones had run off when I rolled the window down. After I got home and opened him up I saw a piece of thread, so I know he was the one who done it."

Ginny and Gordon Mott have raised coyote litters for the University of Maine, and they went up to North Amity to talk to Hazen Hall. Both husband and wife believed Hazen Hall's story. Mrs. Mott says:

"The coyote did rip his pants. And part of it is a gut feeling. We spent almost four hours talking to him and the story didn't change. Whether the coyotes came out to attack him is another question. It sounds to me that if the man did not run, the coyotes would have gone off because coyotes are like dogs. If you run, the dog will chase. Once the man was up on the hood of the car, the coyotes started backing up. There's always the possibility that the man came across the coyotes on a fresh kill, or a young coyote may have misinterpreted the situation. Or it may have been a dumb coyote. . . . I talked to some other people who had worked with him [Hazen Hall]. I just happened to come across them, and they had worked with him in the woods. They said he was credible. There was no reason to disbelieve the story, although they thought he may have embellished the story a bit."

Virginia's husband Gordon says:

"Hazen is a very solid citizen. Having spent four hours with him and the family and heard the story told several different times, and the details come together each time, I feel he did have that experience. No question . . . when you think of the details—he was walking away from the car with a chain saw and they approached him. And they continued to approach him.

His first reaction was not to run but to start the chain saw. . . . They approached close enough so he threw the tool at them, then turned and ran. I would guess at that point a rather heedless pup of the year, eager to prove to mother that he had learned her lessons well, elected to bring the game down but not very aggressively. Hazen was very terrified."

By word of mouth the North Amity incident will travel the woods country, the coyote getting bigger, more fearsome as the story is retold. However, the coyote was a pup of the year, about four months old, and weighed only eighteen pounds and still had his baby teeth. His stomach was full of chokecherries and blueberries but no meat.

Some people do not believe that coyotes attacked Hazen Hall. I myself do not know for certain what happened, can only report what Hall and others said, and I can report what happened about three months after the coyote incident. November 15, 1981, Hazen Hall allegedly shot his wife to death. He hid in the woods, emerging at 3:00 A.M. of the third night when police arrested him.

There are an estimated two or three thousand coyotes in Vermont and a similar number in New Hampshire, about one thousand in Massachusetts, about seven to ten thousand in Maine. Connecticut's wildlife spokesman would not estimate how many coyotes live in that state, nor where they might be concentrated. ("People accuse the critter of being lots of places, but people can't always tell.") The population is stabilizing in all of those states, some biologists say, but no one knows for certain. There is one certainty about the New England coyote: It will not disappear. If the price of coyote fur increases and trapping of coyotes increases, it will do little to the population because as many as 90 percent of the trapped animals will be young of the year. Their parents remain untrapped and will breed again. If a poisoning campaign were begun, the size of the litter would increase. However, the coyote is not indestructible. It could be eradicated by year-round trapping and poisoning and by burning down the forest to the duff of the forest floor. Then there would be no coyotes for a few years, but there would be no other animals, either.

I have begun to watch my cat hunt in the backyard, see how she stalks and lies in wait rather than try to run down a blue jay; and I notice how neighborhood dogs go through my yard, their noses always to the ground as if smelling their way rather than watching where they walk. Now I see tracks everywhere. In Bethel, Vermont, one winter's day I saw hound tracks in new snow, spent too much effort thinking about those tracks and missed the outline of the driveway enough so my car slipped off and down into deep snow where I was stuck. I see lots of deer tracks in a place in Maine I call Summer Island, where I finished writing this book, and one day while walking to the post office I saw what looked like tracks of an enormous hooved animal. I puzzled over those tracks until I saw two holstein cows in the field behind the post office.

I never did see a live coyote in the wild and chose not to seek out captive coyotes, for it would be like watching Atlantic salmon in a fish hatchery, not quite valid. I did see bald eagles, bear, fisher, beaver, deer, moose and the track of the coyote, but I saw no sign of the lion.

Lions are rare, if they exist at all, but coyotes are not rare, only elusive. The coyote is a resourceful animal and will not be pushed out of New England as was the lion. Resourcefulness is an admirable quality. The coyote is admirable also for its loyalty, father and mother to each other and the parents to the pups. It is a mistake to ascribe human motives to an animal, but it seems reasonable to admire qualities in an animal that we admire in ourselves.

I saw the track of the coyote in Coos County, New Hampshire, and saw his scat in Washington County, Maine. I will see the coyote soon enough, probably by chance, when the wind is

## The Coyote and the Wolf (Cousins or Brothers?)

blowing so he does not smell me or hear me and his attention is diverted because he is stalking his prey on silent feet.

# Bibliography

Beckoff, M., ed. 1978. *The coyote: Biology, behavior and ecology.* New York: Academic Press.

Cardoza, J. E. 1976. *The black bear in Massachusetts.* Westboro, Mass.: Mass. Division of Fisheries and Wildlife.

Dobie, J. F. 1947. *The voice of the coyote.* Boston: Little, Brown and Co.

Finnerty, E. W. 1976. *Trappers, traps and trapping.* South Brunswick, N.J.: A. S. Barnes.

Fox, M. W., ed. 1975. *The wild canids.* New York: Van Nostrand Reinhold Co.

Godin, A. J. 1977. *Wild mammals of New England.* Baltimore and London: The Johns Hopkins University Press.

Lopez, B. H. *Of wolves and men.* New York: Charles Scribner's Sons.

Milne, L. J. and M. 1960. *The balance of nature.* New York: Alfred Knopf.

Seton, E. T. 1958. *Animal tracks and hunter signs.* Garden City, N.Y.: Doubleday and Company.

Silver, H. 1957. *A history of New Hampshire game and furbearers.* Concord, N.H.: N.H. Fish and Game Dept.

Van Wormer, J. 1964. *The world of the coyote.* Philadelphia: J. B. Lippincott Co.

Willey, C. H. *The Vermont black bear.* Montpelier, Vt.: Vt. Fish and Game Dept.

Young, S. P. and Goldman, E. A. 1944. *The wolves of North America.* Washington, D.C.: American Wildlife Institute.

Zimen, E. 1978. *The wolf: A species in danger.* New York: Delacorte Press.